TRUMPER

The Illustrated Biography

May the pen not stain the
greatest of games.

TRUMPER
The Illustrated Biography

The greatest batsman of cricket's
Golden Age
ASHLEY MALLETT

MACMILLAN

ISBN 0 333 40906 X

First published in the United Kingdom 1985 by
MACMILLAN LONDON LIMITED
4 Little Essex Street London WC2R 3LF
and Basingstoke

Associated companies in Auckland, Delhi, Dublin, Gaborone,
Hamburg, Harare, Hong Kong, Johannesburg, Kuala Lumpur, Lagos,
Manzini, Melbourne, Mexico City, Nairobi, New York, Singapore
and Tokyo.

Printed and bound in Hong Kong.

CONTENTS

INTRODUCTION

Sir Robert Menzies said in 1968: 'It is not unhealthy to delve into the past, so long as you don't develop eyes in the back of your head.' He was speaking at a dinner to celebrate the 200th Test Match, England v Australia. Appropriately enough that dinner was at Lord's, the Mecca of cricket.

Writing a book on the most charismatic batsman in the world was no easy task. Victor Trumper's personal diary of the 1902 tour of England — Trumper's most successful tour — was the spark that fired my enthusiasm to launch into this work. The diary is a small Collins' book — black with gold lettering on the cover, featuring the all-important year, '1902'. The diary was an exciting find. Flipping through the razor-thin pages one is not immediately struck by the enormity of the find. But when one matches up the Trumper words with official records of each day's play in a host of games on Joe Darling's 1902 Australian tour of England, the jigsaw puzzle falls into shape.

Trumper's early life posed the greatest problem in terms of research. No doubt there are bits and pieces missing, but with the help of the Trumper family and friends, the picture presented is an accurate one. For instance, Victor's parents had nine children, but even the family cannot name all of the Trumper children, as only six survived to adulthood.

By every account Trumper was an exceptional human being. He was generous to a fault and a devoted husband, father and son. He never smoked, drank alcohol, bet or swore. Victor Trumper was seemingly perfect, but he was stubborn when the occasion demanded. He would stand tall and fight if he believed he was being wronged. He took on the Australian Board of Control for International Cricket in its infancy and eventually opted out of the 1912 tour of England along with five other leading Test men. He argued and fought with New South Wales cricket officials and one season played little cricket for his State, partly because of ill-health and partly because he was not given the NSW captaincy when his great friend and mentor Monty Noble retired.

When Victor died in 1915, war news was momentarily put to one side. Placards on newsstands in Britain featured Trumper — GREAT CRICKETER DEAD. Everyone loved him: children adored him and when his funeral procession passed through the streets of Sydney, men wept openly. Some 20,000 people turned out to say their last farewell.

Trumper's deeds on the cricket field have been bettered (in terms of cold hard figures) but it was his style and manner which have been indelibly etched on the memories of those who saw him play. Noble said Trumper opened new horizons for batsmanship. The Great Cricketer W G Grace made cricket an institution. Grace's batting was a triumph for orthodoxy. Trumper brought an exciting flair to batting which was perhaps never thought possible before he bestrode the Test stage.

People flocked to watch him play. His batting had a magnetic quality. Even when playing grade cricket for Paddington or Gordon, the people came in their droves to catch a glimpse of his genius. When he walked on to the Sydney Cricket Ground in an Intercolonial match or Test, the crowd rose as one to acclaim their hero — ample testimony to Trumper's ability.

When Victor Trumper batted he fooled some bowlers all of the time and all bowlers some of the time . . . but all of his many followers loved Trumper's batting all of the time.

1

THE BOY TRUMPER

Victor Trumper left his home at 112 Paddington St., Paddington, at 8 o'clock. He was early. It would take just fifteen minutes to walk across the huge paddock on the eastern side of Moore Park. Finally he made the northern entrance of the arena which was then his Mecca and the stage upon which his famous name is indelibly etched — the Sydney Cricket Ground. He made a quick search in his bag. Yes, all his kit was there: cream shirt, long white trousers (then the veritable love of his life), boots and socks, underwear... He then had an hour's wait for the gates to open. The big match was hours away. Fourteen-year-old Victor searched for pebbles and tested his throwing arm. Even then he had a powerful arm and amazed adults with the distances he could heave a cricket ball. A pebble went like a bullet. He aimed at an old tin, rusting in the tall grass along the wall of the SCG. Bullseye. Satisfied, he delved into his bag. A sandwich. His mother always catered for the super-keen Victor. He had arrived two hours before the Great Cricketer, Dr William Gilbert Grace, would enter the arena with his 1891-92 England team and have a hit-up on the ground, just in front of what is now the M A Noble Stand. A few of Victor's friends arrived and the youngsters played an improvised game of cricket, using the rusty tin as the stumps and one boy produced a worn 'compo' (composition of rubber and cork) ball. Another had an old bat and the asphalt near the SCG entrance was as true a wicket as they needed. Eventually spectators began to arrive. The gates opened and the boys were ushered to a room near the Australian dressingroom in the members' stand.

Victor Trumper as a youth.

Victor and a handful of Sydney youngsters had been invited to bowl and field for Grace's men when they had a 'hit-about' before the New South Wales-Grace's England Eleven game got underway. Grace's team included such stars as Bobby Abel, Surrey and England opening bat; Andrew Stoddart, who three years later captained the England team in Australia; Bobby Peel a left-arm spinner; and brilliant all-rounder, George Lohmann. It was Lord Sheffield who brought the team to Australia, although Grace led them. He was then 43. It was fourteen years since Grace had been to Australia. Victor's chance came on this hot December day (4 December 1891). It was the morning of the first day of the match, which Grace's men eventually won by four wickets. The Englishmen walked onto the field for their leisurely work out. This was the cue for Trumper and his mates to scamper after the Englishmen

The Crown Street Superior Public School cricket team, winners of the Public School Challenge Cup 1890-91. Victor Trumper is reclining with bat in front right.

who, to these keen youngsters, must have seemed veritable giants of cricket. WG was batting and hitting the ball with immense power. One ball cracked a picket, but the boys fielded like demons. Victor shone and the growing crowd gave him warm applause. Head bowed, he blushed. This was no mock display of modesty. Victor was genuinely embarrassed. It was something he learnt to live with, but could never come to terms with: spectator praise and being the centre of attention, yet he was always ready to give warm praise to his fellows. During that pre-match warm-up Victor so impressed The Great Cricketer that Grace invited him to have a bat, facing the bearded Colossus' gentle off-spinners.

Wearing knickerbockers, Victor batted gamely, but on the SCG wicket there were pockets of barren ground and the odd delivery either shot along the ground or reared spitefully, like a cobra about to strike. After having wheeled down a few deliveries, Dr Grace strode towards the youngster. Victor stood in awe of the good doctor: 'You can surely field, m' boy . . . but I'm afraid to say batting is not your forte. You'll never get anywhere as a batsman!' WG's high-pitched voice sounded almost comical to young Victor.

But those fateful words . . . 'you'll never get anywhere as a batsman' . . . boomed loud and clear in Victor's subconscious. Victor was deeply hurt, but he did not show it. He continued to field for the Englishmen. Yet WG's condemnation of his batting prowess cut him to the quick. Many a player has been lambasted by a great player, only to rise to stardom and WG's quick judgement strengthened Victor's resolve to become a great Test match batsman. Less than eight years later Victor played his first Test at Nottingham, England. It was WG Grace's final Test (he was dropped for the next game and never played again at Test level). Neither Trumper nor Grace excelled. Victor was bowled for a duck first innings and Stanley Jackson clean bowled him for 11 in the second. Perhaps Victor needed a psychological boost. Grace's shadow may have clouded his judgement. For it was Grace who told Victor that he would never make a batsman. Grace was soon to find out just how good Trumper had become. After England was bundled out for 206 in the Lord's Second Test in June of 1899, Clem Hill and Victor Trumper took the cream of the English bowling by the scruff of the neck. Hill fell for 135 and Victor remained 135 not out. Australia won by a convincing 10 wickets and at the end of the match, amid the celebrations at Lord's, W G Grace knocked at the door and asked for Victor Trumper. Victor was pleasantly surprised. WG presented him his bat with the inscription: 'From the old champion to the future champion'. That bat is now in the possession of Victor Trumper III, who has it proudly tucked away in his Dubbo, NSW, home.

Victor Thomas Trumper was born on 2 November, 1877. His father, Charles Thomas Trumper, and mother, Louise (Louey) Trumper (nee Coghlan), met in Sydney. Charles Trumper was born in New Zealand and, searching for greener pastures in terms of work, settled in Sydney in the late 1870s. Charles Trumper was a man of medium height, thin with short-cropped hair and a beard and moustache. He was a gentle man who suffered from asthma. A boot clicker by trade, Charles Trumper worked in the Paddington area and finally made sufficient money to open his own business — manufacturing velvet slippers.

Louise Trumper was a jolly and robust woman, who cared greatly for her children and especially Victor, the first born. A loving boy, Victor tended not to worry about the state of his clothes, something which was later a source of great amusement among his cricketing mates when on tours in Australia and abroad. Perhaps only a man of genius cannot be condemned for overlooking the daily humdrum of ensuring that one's clothes are always neat and tidy.

The Trumpers had nine children, but only six survived to adulthood. After Victor came Alice (always known as Nancy), Una, Jackie (a little girl who was born blind and died, aged three), Sidney, May Louise and Charles Ernest Love Trumper (always known as CELT, the formation of the first letter of his Christian and surnames). There were two other

The Great Cricketer, W G Grace, first encountered Trumper in 1891 when a team of Sydney youngsters batted and fielded against Grace's Eleven during a warm-up. WG told Trumper: 'You'll never get anywhere as a batsman.' (*News Ltd*)

Far left: Victor's dad, Charles Thomas Trumper, was born in New Zealand and migrated to Sydney in the late 1867s. (*Tom Nicholas Collection*)

Left: Victor's mum, Louise (Louey) Trumper, bore nine children but only six survived to adulthood.

Victor's sister, Alice (always known by her family as Nancy), tragically died on her twenty-fifth birthday after a family picnic. (*Tom Nicholas*)

Una Trumper was third born after Victor and Alice.

girls, but both died very young, perhaps only a few days after their birth. The Trumpers were neither well to do, nor poor. They lived in Paddington for all of Victor's formative years.

Victor was an agreeable lad, but he had a stubborn trait. In his cricket no one could get through to him. He simply did it his way. Not that Victor would not listen to well-meaning advice; he would listen intently, nod agreeance, or rather thank the person for his trouble and carry on doing his own thing.

Victor's love for cricket appears to have been developed and nutured at Crown Street Superior Public School, just a short walk from his home in Paddington. Monty Noble, five years Victor's senior, went to the school, but would have left when Victor was eleven or twelve. At every possible opportunity the boys would be out in the schoolyard playing cricket. The bats were old and worn, but not quite as primitive as those Don Bradman and his school mates used — bats hewn from the branch of a gum tree. Still, Victor's school was right in the heart of the city. In that way he was lucky. Facilities were generally good. Composition balls, made with cork and rubber, were used on the asphalt wickets. The school has no records of Trumper's scholastic or sporting achievements, but members of the family believe from stories handed down from generation to generation that Victor was an average student with a good head for figures. He was also a brilliant young cricketer.

Victor began going to Crown Street Superior Public School in the early 1880s and he remained a student there until the 1894-5 summer. There were few attractions for teenagers in those days: no motor cars, no surf boards, no television, no moving picture theatres, no radio. Sport was a great attraction for the youth of the 1880s and 1890s and beyond, even to this day. But Test cricket was the ultimate for all the kids of Sydney when Victor was a boy.

Victor was no different to the others in that respect, but he was very different in the manner he wielded the bat. At Crown St. the unwritten law was to bowl the boy holding the bat out and you could bat for as long as you could in the pre-school, play-time, lunch-breaks until another boy dismissed you. Victor was just 10 when he bowled a quick off-break to clean bowl the captain of the school's First Eleven. They took six weeks (many, many sessions) to finally get him out. He played in the First Eleven at Crown St. from that time and in 1890-91 was a member of the school team which won the coveted Public Schools' Challenge Cup.

By the time Victor had reached his teens the word was well and truly out: 'Have you seen Trumper from Crown St. bat?' As Victor grew up, his father, a lover of cricket but a man who had played little of the grand old game, began to notice Victor's obsession. He would stand at the window and watch Victor playing shadow drives for hours on end. Sometimes Victor would throw a composition ball against the wall of the house and then hit it with his bat. But that not only displeased his mother, as the kitchen window was near the spot he chose (the only spot on the brickwork where there was room to move in the backyard), but it also provided no challenge. He was throwing the ball and the wall provided the rebound. It was all too easy. Don Bradman also practised alone, but he had the cricket stump and a golf ball. Throwing the golf ball at a round brick tank stand and trying to hit the ball which rebounded at breakneck speed would have sharpened anyone's reflexes. There Victor would have played the most glorious shots, imagining that he was carving up the England attack or thumping South Australia's answer to W G Grace, George Giffen, for the umpteenth boundary.

Charles Trumper decided to give young Victor more than encouragement: practical help. Every morning for four years father and son would grab their cricket gear (father his work attire and son his school requisites) and rush down to Moore Park. This huge playing area is as near as a Trumper lofted on-drive to the Sydney Cricket Ground. To Victor it was heaven on earth. They began at 6 am and at 8 am Charles went off to work and Victor made the short walk to Crown St. School. Victor's father was a keen cricket follower and watched all the international matches at the SCG, attending most of the Intercolonial games and many club fixtures. While he might not have been a great exponent of the art of batting or bowling, Charles wheeled down his own brand of right-handed deliveries in his quest to help his son. He noted Victor's improvement. 'It was simply surprising to note the rapid headway Victor made as a result of his constant practising,' he told a friend in 1913.

In 1891, the same summer that W G Grace told Victor he would never make a batsman, the Great Cricketer remarked at Lord Sheffield's England v Australia match at the SCG: 'Batsmen are made, not born; bowlers are born, not made.' Charles Trumper noted those words. He firmly believed that Victor had the makings of a great batsman. Yet perhaps Victor Trumper was the exception. Here was a batsman born; a nugget of pure gold. Yet Victor had to be shaped in the atmosphere of top cricket as the nugget is fashioned into a burnished sovereign. Charles Trumper predicted that his son would become a great player. He said in 1913: 'I always prophesised that Victor would some day make his reputation as a cricketer. And time, which pricks so many prophetic bladders, proving my prophecy to be true. After all, it was not a wonderful prophecy, as those who remember Vic in his early boyhood will admit. I recall his first match vividly. He was only a small boy, wearing knickerbockers. It was a Saturday afternoon and he was strolling through Moore Park where a match between the Second Elevens of Carlton and Warwick was about to commence. These were the famous old clubs now unknown, which played such big parts in the history and development of NSW cricket.

'The Carlton second team was short of a man, and as soon as Victor was sighted he was asked to take the missing man's place. This he readily consented to do, and performed so excellently as to open the eyes of all present.'

Victor hit 24 and then destroyed the Warwick side's batting line-up with a return of eight wickets. The similarity with Don Bradman as a boy is uncanny in that The Don also got his chance to play his first senior game at the age of 13 and only because a player failed to turn up. The Don was the Bowral team's scorer. He too was wearing knickerbockers and excelled with the bat that first day.

Charles Trumper said Victor was in no way a precocious cricketer: 'Oh, no. Not in the slightest. At the conclusion of play, Charlie Patrick (well known batsman in Sydney in those days) mischievously took up his bat and dared the youthful players to bowl at him. The boys were not slow to accept the invitation. The first ball served up to Patrick was

Victor's youngest sister May Louise in her Voluntary Aid Detachment uniform during the First World War. (*Tom Nicholas*)

Charles Ernest Love Trumper – always known as CELT – was the youngest of the nine Trumper children. (*Charles Trumper Collection*)

May Nicholas (Victor's sister) cradles baby Tom in 1925. (*Tom Nicholas*).

sent soaring away skywards, but the second, which was bowled by Victor, scattered the stumps in all directions, to the amusement of all, and the surprise of the batsman.'

Victor Trumper was a legend at his school by way of his cricketing deeds and his fame spread throughout Sydney. At the age of 14 Victor was asked to fill in for an absent player. Both teams were made up of adults, but when the opposition team realised that Victor was intending to take part they refused point-blank to play.

Charles Trumper thought that act of veritable cowardice on the part of a team of full-grown men extraordinary. Especially so when Victor was only 14 years old and only a small boy, who appeared two or three years younger. Don Bradman experienced a similar thing when playing for the Bowral school. Other schools refused to play against Bowral if Bradman was in the team. Victor's father also thought it strange that his son never played in junior cricket, other than the inter-school matches while at Crown Street Superior Public School.

'I remember when Victor was 14 he went on a visit to his uncle (Tom Trumper) down at Bulli. While there his uncle took him, in company with a local team, to Mount Kiera, for the purpose of playing the Mount Kiera Eleven. In this match Victor once more covered himself with glory taking nearly all the wickets for about 19 runs.' Victor's father also stressed in 1913 that despite many people taking credit for having taught Victor all he knew about cricket, 'Victor himself will tell you that he alone taught himself to play. It is ridiculous for these people to claim the credit.'

The Trumper home was a happy one. Charles Trumper was an accomplished pianist and Victor also learned to play. He later revelled (as did Don Bradman) in playing for teammates at sing-alongs in the team hotel on England tours. Victor was a happy boy with snowy hair. He had a St. Bernard dog and a pet magpie. Victor's grandmother had the magpie stuffed after it died and for many years it was kept in Una's house at Help St., Chatswood. Victor made his mark at school, literally. One day, during a particularly tedious lesson, he carved 'V. Trumper' on his desk top. That desk has since disappeared. Perhaps some zealous master removed the top and replaced it and had the desk top on show in his room of cricket mementoes, which has since been handed down through the generations.

Ted Gill, sportsmaster at Crown St. from 1941 to 1947 when the secondary school was closed down and students thereafter did their higher education at Cleveland St., remembers seeing the desk top. 'Victor must have used a pocket knife. The name is carved deep into the desk top. I don't know where the desk is now.' Ted Gill played cricket for Paddington and when making the first of his 39 centuries in all cricket, he batted both left and right-handed. Perhaps the Trumper ghost was watching over him as he used his initiative. Gill hit 65 right-handed, then 71 left-handed, finishing with 136 not out. Ted instigated the Victor Trumper Cup, a handsome trophy presented at Crown St. School to the boy who performed the most outstanding feats on the cricket field in any one summer.

In Victor Trumper's time the pocket knife, forerunner to the pen-knife, was something of a status symbol. The boy with the best knife was top dog. They kept them razor sharp and Victor's job on the desk top would not have taken more than an hour or so. Interesting that

Trumper carved only the initial V, rather than Victor on the desk top. He also usually signed V Trumper rather than full out. The Trumper cricketing ability may also have rubbed off on future Crown St. students for in 1947, the last year Crown St. had a senior school, seven Crown St. boys were in the Paddington Under-16 team which won the A W Green Shield in Sydney cricket.

Charles Trumper was a clerk in Sydney until 1892, then he managed Ward's Slipper factory, which manufactured 'Cat's Head' velvet slippers. He later bought the factory. Charles used every available moment at home to play cricket with Victor in the backyard. They had great fun, with the St. Bernard dog and the magpie hindering more than helping their games. But it was all good fun. Charles Trumper never swore. He was a devoted husband and family man and at night played the piano. At every opportunity friends would call at the Trumper home for sing-alongs round the piano. Don Bradman's home life in Bowral featured similar happenings. Victor's mother Louise Coghlan was a third generation Australian of Irish descent. The first Coghlans would have come to Sydney when it was a penal colony. Some of the Trumper relatives had been keen on a family tree, but Louey would say: 'You don't want to look back too far — they might have been sent out!' Louise's father helped build St. Andrew's Cathedral in Sydney.

Victor had a very placid disposition and as Monty Noble said: 'He always had his hand in his pocket.' His sister, Una, nine years younger than Victor said years later that if any of the Trumper children could not get satisfaction when asking for money from their parents, Victor always gave them some. He was generous to a fault with everyone. Victor liked his food and his mother provided wholesome but plain fare. Toad-in-the-Hole with vegetables was a favorite of Victor's. He never touched alcohol or smoked, nor did he ever bet although he learnt to play euchre, perhaps essential during the inevitable card games on the long voyage to England and during train journeys while on tour.

The Trumpers were no different to thousands of families in Australia, although there were very sad moments. Alice, always known as Nancy, died on her 25th birthday. She had accompanied her family on a picnic to celebrate the event and everyone had a marvellous time. The family had been home only an hour when Nancy collapsed and died. It was a traumatic time for everyone and super-sensitive Victor suffered (in silence) more than the others. Una Margaret (born 1886) married George Smith and she subsequently became the mother of a boy who was to become the first Australian-born admiral of the fleet: Sir Victor Alfred Trumper Smith, KBE, CB, DSC, who saw action in the Second World War and Vietnam. He is now retired and lives in Canberra.

Fifth-born Sidney Trumper was a useful cricketer who played in teams, including NSW, with Victor. He died on Australia Day (26 January) 1956 aged 65. It was a sad day for the family for both Sid's death and the fact that on that day Sid and Gladys' only daughter, Truda, was to have married. The wedding was postponed indefinitely. Sid had nominated for the job as assistant manager on Ian Johnson's 1956 tour of England. Sid and Gladys' only son, Norman, was killed in action in the Second World War. Victor's youngest sister, May Louise, was born on 26 October, 1893. She married Herbert (Bert) Nicholas in 1924 and settled in England. They had four children — three boys,

Victor Trumper's nephew, Vice-Admiral Sir Victor Alfred Trumper Smith, was chief of Australian Naval Staff during the Vietnam years.

The Trumper family home, at 112 Paddington Road, Paddington, was recently sold at auction. (*Ronald Caldwell, NSW Cricket Society*)

Tom, Ken and Ron and a daughter, Marie Louise. May died at the age of 63. Charles Ernest Love Trumper (CELT) was born in 1899. He was a useful wicketkeeper and played for Gordon (Victor's last club) for many years. CELT and Sid went to Sydney Grammar School and there was confusion in early stories of Victor Trumper with people linking him with Sydney Grammar. In fact he never attended the college.

Victor began his senior cricket career with the famous Carlton Second Eleven. It was the 1892-93 season and he had just turned 15. Junior cricket was out; it was full steam ahead in the cruel hard world. But Victor revelled in such competition. Victor also was invited to the SCG nets to train and be coached under the expert gaze of Charles Bannerman (who hit the very first Test century) and Tom Garrett, who played in that 1877 Test in Melbourne and had a distinguished career as a NSW and Australian bowler). At Bannerman was as unimpressed as W G Grace had been when he saw Victor bat. 'Too flash,' he would say. But Victor's style would soon finish the old order for ever: a new, refreshing attitude to batting would emerge with Victor Trumper the torchbearer. At that time Victorian and Test wicketkeeper Jack Blackham was chatting with Tom Garrett, then NSW captain. 'Jack, I will show you the most promising boy in the world.' When Blackham ventured down to the SCG nets he said to Garrett: 'My word, Tom, isn't he like Charlie Bannerman.' Garrett agreed that Victor had also reminded him of the style of Bannerman. Victor played two seasons with Carlton then switched to South Sydney for a further two seasons. His first senior team season was 1894-95: the same summer as his 67 in his first international match against Andrew Stoddart's team (see Chapter 3: First International).

In the two seasons with South Sydney Victor did not return great figures. He batted 22 times for an aggregate of 298 runs at an average of 14.90. Victor's first match for South Sydney was played against North Sydney, at North Sydney on 29 September and 6 October (consecutive Saturdays) 1894. South Sydney won the match easily, but Victor scored 4 and 10 (run out) in an inglorious A grade debut.

It must have been on the strength of his brilliant 67 against Stoddart's men that Victor was selected to play for NSW against South Australia from 5-9 January, 1895. SA won outright with George Giffen taking a record haul of 16/186. Victor was run out for 11 and caught by Ernest 'Jonah' Jones off the crafty Giffen for a duck in the second innings. Another failure against Queensland saw Victor out of Intercolonial cricket for two years. In 1896-97 he scored just 149 runs at 21.28 in nine innings. Victor was now with the Paddington club. The move from South Sydney was suggested by Monty Noble, by then a stalwart of Paddington and an admirer of Victor's.

The following summer saw Victor take Sydney by storm. He hit 1021 runs at an average of 204.20 with a highest score of 191 not out. Trumper had arrived. He was back in the State side. Curiously enough his return to the first-class scene saw him hit a stately 55 against Andrew Stoddart's 1897-98 side in Sydney. In the second innings Tom Richardson clean bowled him for a duck. But he carried on and hit a brilliant 292 not out against Tasmania on the SCG and 253 against New Zealand also in Sydney.

But the selectors of that summer (1898-99) were not convinced that Victor was yet ready for Test duty. The Australian team to tour

Far right: A teenage Trumper hits to square leg. (*C B Fry Collection*)

The Crown Street Superior Public School where Trumper once batted for six weeks without losing his wicket. Local schools refused to play Crown Street School when they heard Victor was in the team.

Annie Trumper with young Victor II in the early 1920s. (*Tom Nicholas*).

England in 1899 was picked. No Trumper. Victor was picked for the Rest of Australia team to play in three matches against Joe Darling's team to fit them for the torrid tour ahead. He had scores of 6 and 46 (run out), 46 and 26 and 75 and 0. The 75 in Adelaide was an innings of genius. Victor was a late addition to the side. He agreed to go on tour for half a normal share of the earnings and to help with baggage and laundry.

His friendship with James (J J) Kelly — the Test wicketkeeper, who also played for Paddington and NSW — led Victor to the longest and best partnership of his life. For Kelly was courting the sister of the girl who was destined to become Mrs Victor Trumper. Kelly was born in Melbourne, but moved to Sydney to further his job prospects. He worked at the Sydney Cricket Ground and later at the Sydney Town Hall. Kelly married and when in Melbourne for the second of the Rest of Australia v Australia matches, Kelly and wife introduced Victor to Sarah Ann Briggs at Melbourne station. The Briggs sisters helped James pack for England and Victor helped, little knowing that he would also tour England that very year. The friendship blossomed, especially after Victor was added to the team and they communicated by letter. From that day (9 March, 1899) when Victor first saw Sarah Ann Briggs (always known as Annie) at the station, it was love at first sight. They did not meet again until 22 December, 1899 when NSW played Victoria in Melbourne. But Victor made many visits to Melbourne, with either the Shield team or Test side.

Their marriage took place at St Patrick's Cathedral, Melbourne on 7 June, 1904. Victor was, by then, the world's most brilliant batsman. Sarah Ann Briggs was the daughter of William Alexander Briggs and Ann Guinan. It was a Catholic wedding. Victor took his bride back to Sydney and they lived with his mother and father, Charles and Louey Trumper — first in Paddington and later in Chatswood. There must have been a little uneasiness about Victor's marriage to Annie by some members of the Trumper family (all Protestant), for when Victor returned to live with Charles and Louey, the head of the household said to his children: 'Everybody is entitled to their own opinions, but religion and politics are not to be mentioned in this house.' When Victor died he was buried a Protestant; Annie (who died in 1963) was buried a Catholic.

Victor promised Annie a honeymoon in England. He kept good his promise and they loved it. The day before Victor died he was telling Annie of how he was going to enjoy another trip to England. They planned an England trip in the Australian winter of 1915. Victor died on 28 June, 1915.

Annie and Victor lived with Charles and Louey Trumper in Paddington until the summer of 1908-9. Victor was recovering from scarlet fever, which he contracted in 1907, just before his 30th birthday. His father suffered from lung trouble and used to sleep in a tent in their Paddington backyard. His doctor advised him to move to the north shore. When the decision was finally taken Charles bought a large block of land in Help St., Chatswood. He built a number of cottages on that block, although Victor and his wife always lived in the main house with Victor's parents.

Victor's first child, Annie Louise, was born in 1906, although an

Victor Trumper II glances a ball during a NSW v QLD match in the summer of 1940-41.

exact date is not recorded. She was always known as Nancy, perhaps in memory of Victor's sister, Alice, also known as Nancy and who died on her 25th birthday. Victor's daughter also had a sad life. She was heartbroken when her father died in 1915 and her fiancee, Stan, died just before she was due to marry. In 1902 Cecil Rhodes, according to the family, gave Victor a number of diamonds. However, where those diamonds are today is anyone's guess. Nancy had at least one small one in her engagement ring.

Victor Trumper II was born on 7 October, 1913 — the year of Victor's benefit match. He was not yet two years old when his father died. Victor's son played a number of matches for NSW as a fast bowler and was a stalwart of the Rural Bank in Sydney. He died in 1981. Victor's niece Marie recalls that a beautiful crescent-shaped brooch with sapphires for each letter in his name was presented to him and he gave it to his sister May, Marie's mother. The brooch was given to May with Annie and Victor Trumper's love and May Trumper (Mrs Herbert Nicholas) gave it to her daughter, Marie, on her 21st birthday. It is still a treasured possession. Victor's sister also wore with great pride a gold medallion that Victor won as a member of the 1903-4 winning NSW Sheffield Shield side.

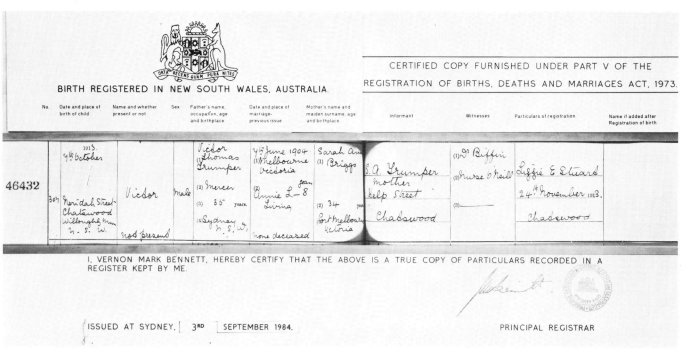

Victor Trumper's son's birth
certificate. Victor II was born
7 October 1913 in Chatswood.
Trumper was 35 and just two short
years away from his untimely death.

2

PENNY WISE

Victor left school at the age of 17 soon after playing against Andrew Stoddart's team, against whom he scored that brilliant 67. He began teaching but soon took up a position in the New South Wales Government Stores Department. He later transferred to the Probate Office where he was under the wing of Tom Garrett, a former Test cricketer who played in Victor's first match for NSW against South Australia in Adelaide. Garrett gave Victor much advice and encouraged him.

By 1898 Victor had begun to make his mark in cricket. He had hit a double century against the Tasmanians and friends urged him to open a sports shop in Sydney. However, Victor refused because his State colleague and teammate of his first match in A grade for South Sydney, Syd Gregory, ran a sports business. Victor did not want to compete with the Test batsman lest it damaged his business. But when Gregory decided to close his sports business, Victor and his friend, NSW and Test wicket-keeper Hanson 'Sammy' Carter, opened a sports shop in partnership. The Trumper and Carter Sports Depot was situated at 108 Market St., Sydney. It boasted the 'highest quality at the lowest prices.'

Vic Trumper the businessman: he and Hanson 'Sammy' Carter (right) went into partnership in a sporting goods store in Market Street, Sydney but Victor was not a good businessman, preferring to heavily discount or give goods away to the local boys. To them, he was a hero.

Hanson Carter was an undertaker by profession. His father, Walter, had a flourishing business in Oxford St. The business is still going today. After a few years Carter's father persuaded him to return to his more sombre profession.

Trumper was not a good businessman. He once grabbed a bat off the seven shilling and sixpence rack after a hectic Saturday morning's trading; hit a glorious century for Paddington that afternoon and on the Monday returned it with the note attached: 'Used bat. Special 3/9d.' A collector would have gladly paid Victor £5 or more, but the champion batsman and careless businessman saw no value in a used bat. Sir William McKell recalled going into the shop with his mates. Sir William was then in his early teens and he had asked for a real cricket ball — a six stitcher. Victor talked the boys out of buying the costlier leather ball and going for a compo ball, because they would be playing on asphalt surfaces. Eventually Victor gave the boys a few balls, a bat, a pair of pads, set of stumps and pair of batting gloves for the cost of the compo ball. No wonder he was revered!

The boys loved Victor. Ragamuffin boys would follow Victor when he played at the SCG and there he would fork out money to these poor urchins (some not quite so poor but willing to accept a handout). He often bought tickets for the boys. Some youngsters took advantage of his generosity. A boy who bought a bat on a Friday would bring the poor broken instrument of his carelessness into Victor's shop on the Monday and without ado Victor would replace it. No questions asked.

Victor teamed up with ex-Test umpire James Giltinan in a cricket depot and mercery business after Hanson Carter returned to his father's undertaking business. Perhaps Carter could see no future in Victor giving away all the profits, but they remained firm friends and Carter often drove a horse-drawn hearse to cricket on a Saturday afternoon. But Victor's soft-heartedness did not help him in the business world. He was continually pestered by cadgers.

It was while he was in partnership with Giltinan that Trumper figured in the formation of the NSW Rugby League. Victor played a number of seasons of rugby union for South Sydney, as full back. But he broke his collarbone twice, which also prevented him playing a number of Sheffield Shield matches for NSW. His nephew, Charlie Trumper, also a kindly soul, told me that every time Victor kicked a ball he had to remove his boot and put his right toe back in place. It appears he had a double-jointed toe, but could not continue the game when the big toe was locked. Victor was concerned that the amateur game (rugby union) had no practical insurance scheme for when a player was injured. Rugby league came into being because a union player — Alec Burdon — was injured during a match with his club, Sydney, during a Northern Rivers trip in 1907. Nursing a broken arm, Burdon lost a great deal of working time having medical treatment. However, Burdon received not a penny compensation from the rugby union establishment.

At that time, Victor had his problems with the Australian Board of Control taking over the control of cricket and he was in the right frame of mind to help the underdog. Victor was one of three men who considered Burdon's treatment from the NSW rugby union a 'very poor show'. These men — Trumper, James Giltinan and Peter Moir — decided to do something about Burdon and the code in general. A meeting took place in Trumper's Market St. store. At that time rugby union was enjoying a peak year. The New Zealand 'All Blacks' v NSW match at the SCG in 1907 attracted a gate of 51,000 people. A H Baskerville was planning to take a New Zealand professional team to England. Among the party was George Smith, who cabled Peter Moir an inquiry as to the prospects of a match in Sydney. Moir discussed the matter with an interested party.

Again Trumper's shop was the venue of the meeting. Moir spoke with Victor, Giltinan, Alec Burdon and Harry Hoyle. Terms were sought for three matches in Sydney, before the side left for England. Baskerville and team manager H J Palmer accepted three dates in August. Giltinan guaranteed £500 for the three games and advised that they would by played on the Agricultural Ground. Trumper and Giltinan outfitted the team and provided the necessary equipment. Victor was the first honorary treasurer of the NSW Rugby League. The NSW Rugby League was formed on 12 August, 1907. During his treasurership, aspersions were cast against Victor because of alleged mismanagement of the league funds. However, there was never any evidence of Trumper having used any league money for his own gain. In 1908 Trumper was one of the auditors for the NSW Referees' Association — a post not likely to have been bestowed upon him if anyone connected with the code did not trust the man implicitly.

Victor also played baseball. He was a member of the 1910 Paddington baseball team, but no records exist of what role he played. It seems likely that Victor could have been a pitcher as he had a powerful arm — having recorded a throw in excess of 115 yards from a standing position and 125 yards with a run-up. Victor used to thrill crowds when a wicket fell during a Test by throwing the ball to Clem Hill on the other side of the ground. Trumper would have been a marvellous outfielder in baseball with such an arm.

There seems little doubt that Noble — a fine baseballer and after his playing days a leading NSW Baseball League administrator — introduced Victor to the game. Although the only record of Trumper playing the game tells us it was in 1910, Victor played for years before.

The Giltinan-Trumper partnership ended and Victor worked for Dudley King and Company, Wynyard Square, Sydney. Soon after Victor's successful benefit match, he wrote to the New South Wales Cricket Associate secretary Mr Bowden suggesting that the association provide Frank Iredale with a benefit match. The letter was dated 20 January, 1914:

'Mr PK Bowden Esq

I would like to place the following information before the NSWCA in reference to Mr Iredale.

He played in the NSW Intercolonial matches from 1890, Test matches in Australia against Stoddart's two teams. Visited England with the 1896 & 1899 Australian XI's. Was a member of the NSWCA for very many years, represented NSW on Aust Board of Control and was also a member of the NSW and Austr selection Committees. Considering these services rendered to cricket both on and off the field I think it would be a fitting act on the part of the NSWCA now at the close of his career to arrange for a testimonial match for his benefit.

Yours faithfully,
Victor Trumper.

By early 1914 Victor's businesses had all failed. He was a commercial traveller selling the King tie. As his business efforts failed, so too did his health. Before his final sports shop business closed (he had taken a Mr Dodge into the shop when Giltinan opted out) a group of newsboys walked in seeking some cricket gear. Victor helped the boys select the gear then, seeing that the boys had only a few shillings, he gave them the lot for nothing. But the newsboys did not forget the generosity of their hero. At Christmas they used all the money they had saved and bought a pair of vases and presented the pair to Victor. To the end of his days those vases were among Victor's most treasured possessions.

Victor wore his bottle green Test cap throughout his career. There was usually pandemonium in the dressingroom when Reg Duff hid Victor's cap. There would be Vic rumaging through his bag in a state of utter despair searching for the cap (his first Test cap) while Duff, Warwick Armstrong and Clem Hill doubled-up laughing. He also was said to have worn the same pair of trousers throughout his Test career. Victor hated the sash which cricketers wore before the turn of the century and had a clothing manufacturer fit his trousers with side levers to enable him to keep his trousers up without the need of a sash or a belt. He not only revolutionised batting, but was perhaps the first cricketer to wear flannels with side straps.

Left: Trumper in his bottle green Test cap and, perhaps, the trousers he was said to have worn throughout his career. Note the open slatted pads and Trumper's grip high on the bat handle.

Right: Victor Trumper early in his business career. (*Tom Nicholas*)

3

FIRST
INTERNATIONAL

Victor was just 17 when he was selected for his first international match — eighteen juniors against Stoddart's touring England Eleven. Victor was suffering from influenza on the morning of the match. His mother pleaded with him not to go to the game. But this was his big chance to impress the State selectors. It was Victor's great determination to play that finally decided his mother to allow him to get out of bed and walk the short distance — about 15 minutes at a leisurely stroll — from his Paddington home to what was the Mecca of cricket to Trumper — the Sydney Cricket Ground. The juniors won the toss and batted. It was Saturday, 21 December 1894. Stoddart's team had just beaten Australia in a Test at the SCG, despite the home team hitting a massive first innings score of 586, with Syd Gregory scoring the first Test double century, finishing with 201. But this day was Victor's day. He came to the crease at the fall of the first wicket.

The Test finished only a day before this game with England pulling off a miracle 10-run victory. Trumper walked in to bat at No 3, after Woods had fallen to an easy catch at point. Archie MacLaren, later to captain England with distinction and to despair every time Victor came in to bat against his men, especially in 1902, accepted the catch off the bowling of Johnny Briggs, a left-arm orthodox spinner with deceptive flight. Victor walked in, hitching up his trousers as he went: the old hands among the crowd may have put this Trumper mannerism down to nervousness, but Victor always hitched his trousers on the way to the crease; likewise after hitting a boundary. He was to hitch his trousers in the centre many, many times during his illustrious career. With opener Hinchy, Trumper scored rapidly, but as the *Sydney Mail* of 29 December 1894 put it: 'Trumper had a narrow escape from being caught at the wickets when he had scored 22, a ball from the lob bowler (Humphreys) coming across from leg, and going away close to Philipson's right hand.'

Stoddart's men had a formidable attack, including Briggs, Bobby Peel, another spinner with good flight and left-hand spin, and Bill Lockwood, a tearaway fast bowler. Tom Richardson, the great England opening bowler, was being rested. During the Test Richardson bowled 66.3 overs for a match return of 6/208.

'At 1 o'clock the score stood at 63, and when it reached 67 Lockwood went on for Humphreys, and Trumper at once cut him to the boundary,

Trumper in his beloved and battered Australian Test cap. Few photographs of Victor as a young man exist. Although this one was taken at Lord's in 1899 on his first England tour, he was always considered to look younger than his age and it is easy to imagine the 17-year-old Trumper, jaw set firm, taking block against the England Eleven four summers earlier. (*S S Ramamurthy Collection*)

Trumper following with a square leg hit out of the ground for 5 off Briggs. At 20 minutes past 1 o'clock Trumper had made 50 runs in as many minutes.

'Peel was given a try with the ball in place of Briggs, Hinchy being caught off him at the wickets after playing a very good innings for 35.

'An adjournment was then made for luncheon, with the score standing at 96, of which Trumper had made 56, including a 5 and seven 4's. Poidevin (later Trumper's NSW teammate, a Davis Cup representative in 1906 and prominent administrator; the Board's London representative for many years, including 1909 and during the 1912 dispute) joined him after luncheon. Trumper brought up 100 with a forward-cut off Peel. They batted on steadily to 113, when Trumper hit out at Peel, but missed him, and was bowled.'

When Trumper departed his score stood at 67; the team total at three for 113. So Victor had hit 67 out of 97 runs in 85 minutes. Stirring stuff for a 17-year-old who had only just played a handful of A grade games for his club, South Sydney. At the end of the first day, Sydney Juniors had scored seven for 327 and on Monday, 23 December, they resumed batting. Monty Noble struck a solid and often brilliant 152 not out when the juniors declared at 9 for 443. Stoddart's team was six for 151 (Noble 2/31 off 15 overs) when the game ended. Only two days were allotted for the game as the Second Test was due to start in Melbourne on 29 December. Andrew Stoddart, who also captained England at rugby, scored only 13 against the Juniors, falling to the wiles of Noble. But in the Test just over a week later he rescued England, hitting 173 in the second innings, defying bowlers such as Charles (C T B) Turner, Hugh Trumble and George Giffen. Ironically, Stoddart died in the same year (1915) as Trumper. However Stoddart took his own life, putting a gun to his head when his hopes and health declined.

While Noble's efforts were the talk of Sydney after the Juniors match, Trumper's valiant 67, against the odds, did not go unnoticed. Straight after the first day's play Victor went home and back to bed. He had promised his mother that he would do so. He stayed there all day Sunday (22 December, 1894) and a good deal of the second and final day's play when the Juniors fielded. Trumper fielded for only an hour or so, then went home to bed. The influenza took nearly a week to shrug off, but his mother was as delighted as Victor that he played and had done so well. As with many Trumper innings, his 67 did not shine like a beacon in the scorebook, but the grace and style of his innings was indelibly etched upon the minds of those people fortunate enough to see that first knock in top company.

SCORECARD
ENGLAND v EIGHTEEN OF SYDNEY JUNIORS
At Sydney, December 21, 23, 1894
EIGHTEEN OF SYDNEY JUNIORS

HD Woods	c MacLaren b Briggs	4
J Hinchy	c Phillipson b Peel	35
VT Trumper	b Peel	67
LOS Poidevin	c Phillipson b Peel	23
E Robinson	c Ward b Humphreys	33
EC Cruickshank	b Brockwell	39
A Atkins	c Brown b Ford	30
LW Pye	st Phillipson b Ford	22
W Hoskings	c Humphreys b Brown	29
MA Noble	not out	152
Sundries		9
	Nine declared for	443

(EJ Hogan, E Reynolds, WE Trickett, M O'Shea, etc–as the *Sydney Mail* so delicately puts it–did not bat).

ENGLAND BOWLING	O	M	R	W
Humphreys	25	5	77	1
Briggs	26	4	89	1
Lockwood	26	9	86	–
Peel	24	6	64	3
Ford	13	4	36	2
Brockwell	7	3	19	1
Stoddart	7	1	22	–
Brown	4	–	32	1
Phillipson	4	1	9	–

ENGLAND
first innings

AC MacLaren	c Hoskings b Reynolds	34
WH Lockwood	c O'Shea b Trickett	23
AE Stoddart	c Cruikshank b Noble	13
W Brockwell	b Robinson	2
JT Brown	c Hinchy b O'Shea	10
A Ward	not out	42
FGJ Ford	b Noble	16
Sundries		11
	Six for	151

(J Briggs, R Peel, H Phillipson, W Humphreys did not bat).

EIGHTEEN OF SYDNEY JUNIORS BOWLING	O	M	R	W
Hogan	12	2	28	–
Noble	15	2	31	2
Reynolds	13	2	30	1
Pye	9	4	8	–
Trickett	14	7	9	1
O'Shea	2.1	–	8	1
Robinson	13	3	26	1

MATCH DRAWN

Trumper preparing for a slashing stroke. On that memorable day in 1894, Victor hit 67 out of 97 runs in 85 minutes against Stoddart's Englishmen. The Sydney Juniors nearly stole the game but ran out of time with England 6 for 151. (*George Beldam Collection*)

4
TRUMPER'S FIRST TOUR

The NSW Eleven, 1899-1900: Back row, from left: Charles Gregory (manager), A W Green, Bill Howell, A McBeth, Albert Hopkins, R Callaway (umpire), Jack Marsh. Middle row: Reg Duff, Frank Iredale, Syd Gregory, Monty Noble, H Donnan. Front row: Victor Trumper, James Kelly, C Saunders (scorer). (*S S Ramamurthy*)

It was during the 1898-9 Australian summer that Victor's genius shone in big cricket. He hit a glorious 292 not out against Tasmania at the Sydney Cricket Ground and suddenly the pundits were speaking of Trumper in glowing terms and that he would make Joe Darling's Thirteen bound for England that winter. In that match against Tasmania Trumper and Frank Iredale blasted 258 for the sixth wicket, with Iredale finishing with 196. The wise critics foresaw a bright future for Victor, but there were still those who considered the innings a flash in the pan; like Halley's Comet, a once in a lifetime show of radiance. Test selectors Syd Gregory, Hugh Trumble and Darling could not agree on the inclusion of Trumper. Monty Noble pressed hard to have his Paddington and New South Wales teammate included, but Trumble

and Darling argued that while the lad had undoubted promise, he had not scored runs in sufficient quantity while they had been at any match in which he batted. That season a Sydney firm struck a shield, called the Pattison Trophy, to be awarded to the player who scored the highest aggregate of runs in all intercolonial matches, including games against New Zealand, which was regarded as a type of colony in those days. Victor needed 250 runs to clinch the trophy in the final intercolonial match, against NZ at the SCG over three days, 24, 25, and 27 February, 1899.

Iredale was streets ahead of Trumper on aggregate before that final match. But on the morning of 24 February, 1899, Victor said confidently to his mother: 'Well, mum, I'm going to get you the best birthday present you ever had in your life...' Victor was true to his word. He thrashed the New Zealand bowling, hitting 253 to bring his six-match aggregate to 674 runs...and clinch the Pattison Trophy.

The 1899 Australian team was duly announced. Thirteen players were chosen, but Trumper's name was conspicuous for its absence. The team was: Joe Darling (SA, capt.), Monty Noble (NSW), Clem Hill (SA), Hugh Trumble (Vic), Charles McLeod (Vic), Jack Worral (Vic), Frank Iredale (NSW), Syd Gregory (NSW), James Kelly (NSW), Frank Laver (Vic), Ernest Jones (SA), Bill Howell (NSW) and Alf Johns (Vic).

Public opinion was on Trumper's side and the young New South Welshman was included in the Rest of Australia Eleven to play Darling's Test men in Sydney, Melbourne and Adelaide before the team left for England. Noble, who had put Trumper's case so forcibly with Gregory, Darling and Trumble for inclusion in the 1899 team, was the man responsible for dismissing the youngster cheaply in two of the three

James Kelly. He and Monty Noble were Paddington teammates with Trumper and more than delighted when Victor made the 1899 touring team. (*S S Ramamurthy*)

Australia in England, 1899. Trumper is in white at top left and certainly looks the 'baby' of the side. Nine of the fourteen men are wearing marvellous handlebar moustaches. Note the man staring through the window at top right. (*S S Ramamurthy*)

Studio portraits of the three tyros from the 1899 team to England. Frank Laver (top), Clem Hill (centre) and Victor Trumper.

trial matches. Noble wrote: 'I was disgusted at being the reluctant instrument of Vic's dismissal on two occasions during the trials...' In the Sydney match, Trumper batted steadily until he had reached 26 and faced up to his comrade Noble. Noble bowled and the ball dipped sharply. Trumper straight drove firmly, but succeeded only in hitting it straight back to the bowler. 'As the ball travelled towards me the thought ran through my mind; "miss it, miss it," Noble wrote, 'It was not an easy catch and I could have very easily dropped it without creating suspicion. But I did not miss it and my disappointment at his dismissal was, I believe, greater than his.' Noble in hindsight had no regrets that he held the catch, as it was not long afterwards that a vice-president of the Melbourne Cricket Club, James McLauchlin came to Sydney. He travelled to Waverley where Victor Trumper's Paddington opposed the local side.

Trumper carved one of his batting masterpieces; compiling 260 not out in better than even time. McLauchlin was so impressed by Trumper's brilliance that he wasted no time returning to Melbourne to sing the praises of the coming champion. In the Melbourne trial Noble again dismissed Trumper cheaply. Again Messrs Darling and Trumble were unmoved by Victor's batting. Then came the final trial match in Adelaide; the last match before the Test team sailed for England. Trumper received plenty of support from the Press as regards his non-inclusion in Darling's team, but he needed an innings of quality on the Adelaide Oval wicket to convince the Test selectors and officials.

The wicket was in poor shape. It had worn badly and Darling's ace spinners, Trumble and Noble, were making the ball turn and jump — truly a big test for a young batsman. They were making a mockery of The Rest's batting line-up. That is, until Trumper came in to bolster the middle-order. Victor played both men with ease. It wasn't an innings of arrogance and brute force; rather one of a super confident man out to show all and sundry that here was a batsman with whom all bowlers should be wary. Trumper let his bat do his talking in a way which made even his most ardent admirers marvel at his skill. Trumper made 76 and as he departed towards the pavilion, Darling sidled up to a thoughtful Hugh Trumble and said: 'He'll do me.' Trumble didn't say a word, just nodded approval. Darling added: 'I don't think that anyone else on either side could have got the runs or played such an innings on that wicket.' Darling and Trumble had formed the majority to leave Trumper out. Now their change of stance brought them first to co-selector Gregory then to tour manager Major Ben Wardill. That night Wardill approached Noble, who had resigned himself to the inevitable conclusion that Trumper would have to wait until 1902 to make his first tour of England.

'Well, Alf, do you want Victor Trumper to go to England?'

Noble was stunned: 'Rather,' he replied, somewhat puzzled.

'Well,' Wardill continued,' you can go and tell him that he has been selected.

Noble sought out Trumper and broke the news to him.

Victor smiled and they shook hands.

News of Trumper's selection was hailed throughout the land. His parents were deliriously happy for him. But there was one overriding condition, which had Victor worried. He was selected on the condition that he accept a half share of the tour profits. It was a severe condition, but Australian touring teams had usually taken only twelve or thirteen men. Any more and each man's profit was substantially reduced. The tourists were prepared to play in every game on an exhaustive England tour, so long as their efforts were amply rewarded. However, touring England under a profit-share scheme was fraught with some risk. Heavy loss, although unlikely, was a possibility, especially if many matches were abandoned in England's fickle summer.

Victor was then 21. He had his future to consider. He wrote to his father for advice. Charles Trumper immediately replied: 'Go on any condition, boy. It will be the makings of you.'

As for the marvellous Pattison Trophy, well, Victor's mother already had it in her keeping. The handsome shield was presented to Trumper by Colonel J C Neild, MLA, Paddington Cricket Club patron, at a function for Monty Noble and James Kelly, then the two Paddington representatives in Darling's 1899 team. Victor Trumper's grandson Victor Trumper III now has the shield in his Dubbo (Western NSW) home. The Paddington club's third representative on the 1899 tour, although rather belated, was Victor Trumper. At 2 o'clock on the afternoon of 23 March, 1899, the tenth Australian Cricket Team boarded the SS *Ormuz* at Larg's Bay, South Australia.

This was the start of Victor's first great cricketing adventure. The journey through the gulf provided pleasant cruising; the seas were calm, protected by Yorke Peninsula and Kangaroo Island. Not so when the *Ormuz* reached open seas in the Great Australian Bight. A day out of Larg's Bay the ocean turned its wrath on the *Ormuz*. Giant waves crashed against the vessel and young Victor nearly drowned in his cabin as the frenzied sea whipped up against the side of the ship and water cascaded through his open porthole. Monty Noble and Frank Laver bunked in the same cabin. Victor dashed out of the water-logged cabin and sought refuge in another part of the ship while Noble and Laver, up to their knees in water, finally managed to close the porthole window.

The Aussies at play on board the S S *Ormuz* on their way to England in 1899. Trumper has his back to the camera at the non-striker's end while a young passenger prepares to defend his off stump. Note the spectators at first slip.

Monty Noble, left, and Frank Laver ride donkeys in Port Said on their way to England. Trumper rode one called 'Lord Kitchener'.

Bill Howell, left, 'king of the off-spinners' and Frank Laver ready for the fancy dress party on board the S S *Ormuz*. (*Charles Trumper*)

The mighty storm broke away the gangway in front of the upper deck and carried away the steps leading to the captain's bridge, dashing both sets of steps between the deck and steerage quarters. One seaman had his ear torn off and another suffered a broken leg. The *Ormuz* dropped anchor off Colombo and Darling's men took no time in getting to land. The team's horse-drawn coach passed the cricket ground and race course, but they could not resist stopping for refreshments at the Galle Face Hotel. Some 70 years later Bill Lawry's Australian team stayed a week at that same hotel. A few days in Ceylon (now Sri Lanka) and the SS *Ormuz* steamed away.

They steamed on up the Suez Canal and Monty Noble was so disgusted with the antics of the Arab men, lining the banks of the canal and whose rude gestures so shocked the women at the rails of the passing vessel, that he took aim at the man he considered the worst offender and hit him smack in the left ear with an apple. The ship stopped at Port Said, sufficient time for the team to listen to the music of an orchestra and ride the donkeys on the wharf. The donkeys were given names such as Lord Kitchener, General Gordon, the Prince of Wales and Captain Darling. Most of Darling's men had a go and Frank Laver, who was an avid photographer, took photographs of the players as they posed on the backs of the donkeys.

Victor sat astride 'Lord Kitchener'. He loved the camaraderie within the team and took part in all the sports, such as quoits and shuffleboard, on board ship. Daily the team practised on board, with nets being set. Often matches were organised between the Australian Eleven and the rest and also between married and single and the first and second classes.

Dances were a nightly event and the fancy dress ball was perhaps the most memorable for the 1899 tourists. Frank Laver, in his book *An Australian Cricketer on Tour* (Chapman and Hall, 1905) wrote that the funniest costumes were 'probably that of Jim Kelly, Victor Trumper and Joe Darling. Kelly and Trumper, with the aid of pillows, increased the dimensions of their chests to an extent that would have caused German officers to turn green with envy. They blackened their faces, and wore high sea-boots and bath-towel turbans. Shouldering old brooms, like trained soldiers, they acted as a sort of bodyguard to the Khalifa (Joe Darling), whose costume would have passed for that of a clown's. Woe betide any person wearing a white suit or bald patch on the crown of his head who chanced to cross their path. Those who happened to come into contact with the broom (previously dipped in

the charcoal chest) that Jim Kelly shouldered, afterwards caused their friends much difficulty in recognising them.'

Team-spirit was at fever pitch by the time Noble, Frank Iredale and Laver re-joined the team in London. This adventurous trio crossed the Continent by train and coach, delving into the history of Rome and France and climbing the Eiffel Tower, before catching a boat to cross the English Channel. It was a relieved manager, Major Wardill, and the the rest of Darling's men who greeted the trio as they waltzed into the specially reserved dining room of the Inns of Court Hotel, London, the 1899 team's 'home-base' for the next five months.

Trumper batted well enough to win a batting spot in the First Test match, played on the beautiful Trent Bridge ground, Nottingham. Trumper's debut also coincided with Wilfred Rhodes' first England cap. That match also marked the end of W G Grace's marvellous career. Trumper walked on to the Test stage for the first time on 1 June, 1899, and was clean bowled by Hearne for a duck! Batting a second time Trumper was bowled by Jackson for 11. The game finished in a draw, but Rhodes fared well taking 4/58 and 3/60. Grace, at the grand old age of 50 years and 320 days, scored 28 and 1 and failed to capture an

The South of England Eleven, captained by the Great Cricketer, W G Grace, played the first match of the Australian 1899 tour. It was at Crystal Palace and ended in a draw. From left, rear: Titchmarsh (umpire), Brockwell, C L Townsend, Gilbert Jessop, J R Mason, Board, Abel, West (manager). Front: C B Fry, Lockwood, W G, K S Ranjitsinhji, Hayward. (*C B Fry*)

Australian wicket in 22 overs. Rhodes went on to take an incredible 4187 first-class wickets in a career which spanned 32 years. His final Test was in the West Indies in 1929-30. The man who played his first Test in the same match in which Trumper made his Test debut, Rhodes rang down the curtain on his career when he bowled against Don Bradman for Yorkshire against the Australians in 1930. Perhaps that is significant, for Bradman took over from Trumper as the world's most charismatic batsman.

After his inglorious Test debut, Trumper did well enough in the county matches to retain his place for the Second Test match, at Lord's. His supporters must have been tremendously disappointed with Victor's debut at Nottingham. A double batting failure; not given a bowl and no catch going his way. But Trumper continued to smile. Success or failure, Victor was always the same.

Australians dream of playing at Lord's. Victor Trumper was no different in that regard to all the others. Lord's was the Mecca of cricket in his day and if you ask any young Australian cricketer today where most would he want to make his Test debut, it would be Lord's.

England skipper Archie MacLaren won the toss and decided to bat. But fast bowler Ernest Jones ran through the England batting like a scythe cutting grass. Jones took 7/88 off 36.1 fiery overs, (Stanley Jackson hit 73 and Gilbert Jessop, in his Test debut, cracked 51) to fire out England for 206. Jessop was dismissed when he went for a big hit off Hugh Trumble only to see Victor sprint around the boundary to make the catch — his first Test catch. Victor joined Clem Hill (65) with the Australian score at 4/189 just before the afternoon tea adjournment. Victor had compiled 15 runs in comfortable fashion when they moved off the ground for tea. During the break, Hill

The England Eleven for the First Test at Nottingham Trent Bridge, Nottingham, 1 June 1899. From left, top: Barlow (umpire), Hayward, Hirst, Gunn, J T Hearne, Storer, Brockwell, Titchmarsh (umpire). Centre: C B Fry, K S Ranjitsinhji, W G Grace, F S Jackson. Front: Wilfred Rhodes and Tyldesley. Brockwell was 12th man.

The First Test at Nottingham in 1899 was W G Grace's final Test and Victor Trumper's first. Here WG leads fellow opener Charles Fry on to the ground. (*C B Fry*)

The Australian team to England in 1899. From left, top: V Trumper, H Trumble, A E Johns, W P Howell, Major Wardill, M A Noble, F Laver, C E McLeod. Front: J J Kelly, C Hill, J Worrall, J J Darling, F A Iredale, E Jones. Sitting in front is Syd Gregory. (*Marylebone Cricket Club Collection*)

The Great Cricketer, W G Grace acknowledged Trumper's batting genius after Vic had hit 135 not out, his maiden Test century, in the Lord's Test of 1899.
(*S S Ramamurthy*)

The famous Lord's ground where Trumper made his first ton. W G Grace later sought him out to exchange bats. WG wrote on his: 'From the past champion to the future champion.'

remarked: 'I'm having a lot of trouble with Townsend's bowling . . . only just keeping him out.'

Charlie Townsend was England's lanky leg-spinner-cum-left-hand batsman. He had yet to take a wicket, but was obviously troubling the nuggety South Australian left-hander.

Trumper replied: 'Oh. Let me have a go at him when we come back.'

'All right,' answered a relieved Hill, unsure whether Victor's gesture was one of utter brashness or supreme confidence. Hill soon found out that Victor's ability knew no bounds. The pair manoeuvered their running between wickets in such a fashion that when Townsend was again invited by MacLaren to have a bowl, it was Victor facing the leg-spinner. Townsend was brimful of confidence. He knew he had Hill in trouble and was keen to exert similar dominance over the young Trumper. His first ball to Trumper and the batsman stepped out and drove it high into the vacant outfield for a boundary. He repeated the stroke two deliveries later. Trumper's strokes astounded not only MacLaren's men, especially Townsend, and the spectators, but also Hill, who knew instinctively that he was batting with a master batsman.

In three overs Trumper's agile footwork and flashing blade plundered 30 runs from the hapless Townsend. His hold was broken. MacLaren was forced to bring back the steady Rhodes and Jessop's medium pace to quell the flow of runs. Trumper and Hill cruised along, picking up runs at will. Hill passed his century and was scoring freely when Townsend was recalled from the outfield for another bowl. Almost immediately Townsend struck gold, having Hill caught at cover by the athletic Charles Fry.

Soon after, Trumper blasted his way gallantly to his maiden Test

century. He was 21 but did not look older than 18. His century was widely acclaimed, but he should have been credited with two centuries, because his 'farming' of the strike against Townsend in protecting Hill, gave his partner a greater chance of hitting the ton. Hill later confessed that had Trumper not knocked Townsend off his length and hit the leg-spinner out of the attack, he would not have scored his century.

Frank Laver and Ernest Jones both fell victim to Townsend's bowling and with only Hugh Trumble (24) giving any semblance of support at the other end, Trumper blazed away to an unconquered 135 in a team total of 421 — a match winning score. Jones (3/76), Noble (2/37) and Laver (3/16) ripped through England a second time, with only MacLaren (88 not out) and Tom Hayward (77) putting up any real resistance. England totalled 240 a second time and Jack Worrall (11) and Joe Darling (17) hit up the required 28 runs to win without loss.

Trumper's brilliant display helped win a famous Test match and stamped him as one of the greats of the future. Immediately after Trumper's innings the Great Cricketer, W G Grace, strode into the Australian dressingroom and asked for Victor. WG shook hands with Trumper and congratulated him on his fine knock. He then asked Trumper to exchange bats. The one he presented to Victor bore the inscription, in WG's own hand: 'From the past champion to the future champion . . .' That bat, along with the Pattison Trophy, takes pride of place in the Dubbo home of Victor Trumper III.

The Second Test match was the only game in the five-match rubber where a result was achieved. In the Fourth Test at Manchester, Victor played a masterly innings on the last day of the match to save Darling's side. Australia had followed on 176 runs in arrears and while Trumper

The famous Manchester ground, Old Trafford, where Trumper saved Australia from certain defeat in the Fourth Test.

Frank Laver, Clem Hill and Victor Trumper (far right) with friend in front of the Queen's Family Hotel during the first tour of England. Note the straw boaters with the Australian coat-of-arms on a green and gold hatband. (*Charles Trumper*)

blasted the England attack, Monty Noble stone-walled. The combination had a demoralising effect on MacLaren's men and the Australians escaped unscathed. Against Sussex at Hove, Trumper savaged the local attack, hitting a career-best 300 not out. Joe Darling hit a fine 70 and a teammate asked Darling what he thought of Trumper's batting.

'What do I think of him?' he said bluntly, 'I thought I could bat!'

Trumper's batting brought more than adulation from teammates and spectators. It also brought him a better financial deal. The players and Major Wardill had an impromptu meeting at Hove and to a man they decided to put Victor on an equal footing with the rest of the squad. He was then officially told that he would have a full share in the profits of the tour.

Brighton, 1899. Daring swimwear from the Antipodeans in Victorian England. Trumper is in the centre, right hand to his head. (*Charles Trumper*)

This hand-painted, colored scroll was presented to Trumper by the Crown Street Superior Public School on 15 November 1899 to honor his successful tour of England.

In 48 innings in England on that 1899 first tour, Trumper hit 1556 runs at an average of 34.57. In the Tests Victor hit 280 runs for an average of 35 in eight completed innings. It was to be his highest Test aggregate and average in any of the four Test tours he made in England. Although he hit 2570 tour runs in 1902, Trumper scored only 247 runs in the Tests at an average of 30.8.

Trumper was the star turn among the younger brigade of Darling's batsmen. When he returned home the Crown Street Superior Public School presented Victor with a magnificent hand-painted scroll, now in the possession of Barrie Trumper, a great nephew living in Sydney. He never forgot the team spirit on board the SS *Ormuz*, where nicknames were found for Syd Gregory (Little Tich), M A Noble (Mary Ann), Frank Laver (Vesuvius), Charlie McLeod (Lightning), Clem Hill (Kruger, because of his resemblance to the Boer leader) and Hugh Trumble (Gertie or Little Eva).

The team song was given a good going over at the team's first smoke night.

'We're Australian cricketers all,
The Major is our father,
And off the cricket field,
We love the ladies, rather.

Toujours, toujours,
Pour Bacchus et les amours,
Yap, yap, yap; tra-la-la-la-la,
Yap, yap, yap; tra-la-la-la-la,
Yap, yap, yap; tra-la-la-la-la —
Pour Bacchus et les amours

Major Benjamin Wardill, manager
of the Australian Test team to
England in both 1899 and 1902.
(*C B Fry*)

5

SUPERSTITION

The great superstition among Australian first-class cricketers today is the number 87 — an unlucky 13 off 100. Whenever the team score or an individual score is 87, the players in the dressingroom shift nervously in their seats. Their hearts pound, fingers cross. Great relief is shown when a run is scored to enable the devil's number to be cheated. Opponents in the field are also aware of that number and let it be known in none-too-uncertain terms. The idea is to catch the batsman off-guard. It is psychological warfare on the Test arena. In England the devil's number is 111 — representing the three stumps. Many cricketers are superstitious. Don Bradman wasn't one of them. He is the most logical of men and considers walking under ladders, cracks in the pavement or the number 87 all coming under the same category — rubbish. However, from the time cricket began players have had their own superstitions.

Some batsmen always buckle on their left or right pad first — to change the sequence courts disaster; some bowlers have been known to discard a once-favourite shirt the day their luck was out or they bowled poorly with a nought for plenty return. Victorian medium-pacer Alan Connolly in the 1960s always wore a piece of the great off-spinner of the Golden Age Hugh Trumble's hat-band in his flannels pocket for good luck.

Celebrated England keeper Alan Knott had the habit of having a hankerchief hanging precariously from his trouser pocket. He also would touch the top of the stumps before each ball when he stood over the stumps to a spinner. Test left-hander Allan Border does not shave during a Test match. Neither did Ian Chappell.

But perhaps the most amazing superstition among great Test cricketers was that of Victor Trumper. Trumper could not relax at the batting crease if he saw a clergyman either on the way to the wicket or in the crowd while he was out in the middle. Teammate Clem Hill wrote of Trumper's superstition years after Trumper had died:

'Trumper could do anything at any time. All the bowling came alike to him, and he was just as likely to get a couple of fours off the first two balls of the day as off the last two.

'In later years, however, Barnes, the great English bowler, worried him. Over and over again Trumper left the dressingroom stating that he would have a go and try to knock Barnes off. He was determined at last

Monty Noble's 1909 side boasted the legendary Victor Trumper. This is how the small boys of London saw Trumper's genius. (*Punch*)

(*By permission of the Proprietors of "Punch"*)

The Batsman: "Tell yer wot. You be England, and I'll be Victor Trumpet!"

From *Punch*, 25th May 1909

to do or die. But instead there was our champion driven further and further back on to his wicket, and made to play a defensive game. I have seen Barnes bowl to Trumper without an outfield.

'With all his greatness, Trumper was a little superstitious. Bowlers held no terrors for him, fiery or sticky wickets did not unnerve him; but he feared if he saw some clergymen while he was going in to bat he would not score.

'Sometimes he did fail to get going after having seen them.

'On one occasion in England he returned to the dressingroom and said, "I knew I would not score with all those clergymen about." '

The reason for Trumper's uneasiness when he saw a man of the cloth may never be known to the modern generation, but it is interesting to note that the man who became the greatest batsman of all time and the man who replaced Trumper as the Australian batting idol, Don Bradman, had no fears in regard to batting. A few years back The Don's Adelaide city office was number 87.

But you can wager that the England captain of 1902, Archie MacLaren, would have paid a King's ransom to know of Trumper's superstition. Perhaps even MacLaren would have donned a white collar to restrict the magnificence of Trumper's superb batsmanship, especially that day in Manchester when Trumper hit 103 not out before lunch. Clem Hill wrote: 'No batsman ever played more for his side. In the Manchester Test he had scored a century before lunch and was promptly dismissed on resumption of play for 104. Trumper was disconsolate:

' "I don't know how it is," he said, "that just when we want runs I can't make them. I never seem to do any good for the side. " '

6

DIARY OF
A CHAMPION

Trumper at age 25 during his
second tour of England in 1902.

The 1902 Australian tour will forever be remembered as Trumper's triumph. Approaching 25 years old, Trumper would excel as had no other Test batsman.

His batting this particularly wet English summer was sensational. In a total of 53 innings Trumper scored a record 2570 runs at an average of 48.49. He hit eleven centuries with a top score of 128.

Trumper also became the first batsman in Test history to score a century before lunch on the first day of a Test match. He scored 104 before Wilfred Rhodes had him caught at the wicket by Lilley. Australia managed just 299 and England, with the Hon. F S Jackson playing nobly for 128, replied with 262. Australia was routed for 86 when batting a second time but when Jack Saunders, the Victorian paceman, knocked Fred Tate's middle stump askew, the Australians found they had won a famous Test match by just three runs.

Trumper's century before lunch was equalled by Charlie Macartney, who had toured with Trumper in 1909, at Leeds in 1926. Macartney was dropped off the fourth ball he faced before lasting his way to 112 not out in 116 minutes. At Leeds in 1930, Don Bradman became the other Australian to also achieve the coveted century before lunch on the first day of a Test match. Trumper in 1902 was out for 104, Macartney in 1926 lost his wicket at 151 and Bradman, the greatest and most ruthless run-getter the game has known, went on to score 334, 309 of those runs on the first day, 11 July, 1930.

The cricket world had to wait until 30 November, 1976, to see the feat achieved by another cricketer. This time it was Pakistani batsman Majid Khan. Majid set the National Stadium, Karachi, alight with his brilliant display, scoring 108 in 113 minutes against New Zealand. So Majid joined a select band of Australians in Trumper, Macartney and Bradman — perhaps the best three Australian batsmen to walk the Test stage — with his extraordinary display.

An amazing feature of Trumper's 1902 England season was that in his eleven centuries his highest score was 128. Trumper's attitude appeared to be that one hundred was enough. He had a reputation for throwing his wicket away once he had scored the coveted century. Rarely did he go on and hit a double or triple century.

But Trumper's batting on the 1902 tour captured the imagination of the public. They marvelled at his genius on the treacherous, sticky

The Australian Cricket Team, 1902.

Captain:
Mr. J. Darling.

Vice-Captain:
Mr. H. Trumble.

Mr. S. E. Gregory.   Mr. R. A. Duff.
Mr. C. Hill.   Mr. A. J. Hopkins.
Mr. M. A. Noble.   Mr. E. Jones.
Mr. V. Trumper.   Mr. J. J. Kelly.
Mr. W. W. Armstrong   Mr. J. V. Saunders.
Mr. W. P. Howell.   Mr. H. Carter.

Manager:
Major Wardill.

Date	Match.	Where played.	Result.
	Eleventh Australian Fixtures. *ENGLAND, 1902.*		
	MAY.		
5	v. London County	Crystal Palace...	...
8	v. Notts	Nottingham	...
12	v. Surrey	Oval ...	...
15	v. Essex	Leyton ...	...
19	v. Leicestershire	Leicester	...
22	v. Oxford University	Oxford ...	..
26	v. M.C.C. and Ground ...	Lord's ...	
29	No 1. England v. Australia	Birmingham	...
	JUNE.		
2	v. Yorkshire	Leeds ..	...
5	v. Lancashire	Manchester	...
9	v. Cambridge University .	Cambridge	...
12	No 2. England v. Australia	Lord's ...	...
16	v. South of England	Eastbourne	...
19	v. Derbyshire	Derby ...	...
23	v. Yorkshire	Bradford	...
	JULY.		
3	No. 3. England v. Australia	Sheffield ..	...
7	v. Warwickshire	Birmingham	...
10	v. Worcestershire	Worcester	...
14	v. Gloucestershire	Bristol ...	...
17	v. Somerset	Taunton ..	..
21	v. Surrey	Oval ...	...
24	No. 4. England v Australia	Manchester	...
28	v. Essex	Leyton ...	...
31	v. Sussex	Brighton	...
	AUGUST.		
4	v. Glamorganshire & Wilts.	Cardiff ...	...
7	v. Hampshire	Southampton	...
11	No. 5. England v. Australia	Oval ...	...
14	v. M.C.C. and Ground ...	Lord's ...	..
18	v. Gloucestershire	Cheltenham	...
21	v. Kent	Canterbury	...
25	v. Middlesex	Lord's ...	...
28	v. Lancashire	Liverpool	...
	SEPTEMBER.		
1	v. St Helens & District XI.	St. Helens	..
4	v. Mr. C. I. Thornton's XI.	Scarborough	...
8	v. South of England	Hastings	...

This is Trumper's personal fixtures card for the 1902 tour of England. Vic cracked 11 marvellous centuries during the tour, including his famous Test 100 before lunch in the Fourth Test at Manchester.

wickets. Where colleagues and opponents alike floundered, Trumper reigned supreme. He was hailed as a master on a wet wicket. And how he revelled in the big wet of 1902. Many of the thirty-eight first class fixtures were rain affected.

The Australians won twenty-two games, lost two (including the exciting Fifth Test at the Oval by one wicket) and fourteen matches were drawn.

Perhaps one of the reasons batsmen rarely scored double centuries in Test matches was because Tests in England were played over three days. Runs had to be scored at a lively rate to ensure a result and that suited Trumper to a tee, for he based his batting on all-out attack. He loved to get on to the front foot and on the wickets of England, with their lower bounce, Trumper was in his element.

During my research into the Trumper story, I came across a tiny Collins diary. The diary, with its gold edged pages, was Victor Trumper's diary — the one he carried with him on the 1902 tour. As a cricket writer the Trumper diary meant as much to me as stumbling across the Lost City of Atlantis would to an archaeologist. It provides us with a fascinating link with the 1902 tour. The diary is not one in the

Trumper memorabilia: Trumper's
personal 1902 diary, a signed cricket
ball, a gold watch presented to
Trumper by Lord Sheffield and a
signed photograph

Australia's 1902 captain Joe
Darling. (*S S Ramamurthy*)

mould of a ship captain's log, but the sort of small notebook a young
cricketer might keep to note coming events, travel arrangements,
shows, Test and county game dates and the like. Perhaps Trumper
wanted to record events chronologically for later reference, perhaps
with the idea of writing a book. Yet Trumper was very much a self-
effacing man. He hated publicity for publicity's sake and if he disliked
anyone, it was the man who boasted about his achievements. The
contents of this diary have not seen the public light of day for some 83
years. Perhaps it was high time we delved deeper into the mystery of
Victor Trumper.

Under the captaincy of South Australian Joe Darling, the eleventh
Australian Test tour of England arrived aboard the SS *Omrah*, docking
at Tilbury on Saturday, 26 April 1902.

The team: Joe Darling (SA) capt, Hugh Trumble (Victoria), Syd
Gregory (NSW), Monty Noble (NSW) Clem Hill (SA) Ernie Jones (SA)
James Kelly (NSW) Victor Trumper (NSW) Albert Hopkins (NSW) Reg
Duff (NSW) Jack Saunders (Victoria) Warwick Armstrong (Victoria)
Bill Howell (NSW) and Hanson Carter (NSW)

It was a closely-knit side, containing a number of marvellous characters including the irrepressible Ernie Jones, the one-time stevedore, miner and dust-cart driver from Broken Hill. The South Australian fast bowler was not as quick in 1902 as he was in 1896 when he demolished an 1896 England XI at Sheffield Park.

Jonah, as Jones was eternally known, blasted through the cream of the England batting team, that day dismissing WG Grace, the Hon. F S Jackson, K S Ranjitsinhji (who later that summer scored 62 and 154 not out in his debut Test at Old Trafford), Charles Fry and Arthur Shrewsbury for just 84 runs. Up until 1896 'The Champion', W G Grace, always led a strong side against the visiting Australians at this Sheffield Park venue in Sussex, under the patronage of Lord Sheffield.

On that day Jonah bowled a brute of a rising ball which bounded through WG's beard and soared over wicketkeeper James Kelly's head for four byes.

'What's this, what's this,' squeaked an obviously annoyed and stunned W G Grace.

Harry Trott, Jonah's skipper, sidled up to his spirited fast bowler and said: 'Steady, Jonah.'

Jonah sported a smile as broad as WG's girth and walked down the wicket towards the good doctor:

'Sorry, Doc . . . she slipped!'

Then there was Clem Hill, making his third tour of England. A pugnacious, tough little left-hander, like the Allan Border of today, he had plenty of skill and grit. He was a formidable opponent and marvellous team man.

In Monty Noble and Hugh Trumble the Australians had great back-up strength of medium-paced swerve and cut, plus Trumble's tantalising off-spin. Reggie Duff was the complete opener, with shots

The Australian team, 1902: From left, rear: J J Kelly, J V Saunders, H Trumble, W W Armstrong, M A Noble, W P Howell, B J Wardill (manager). Middle: C Hill, R A Duff, J Darling, V T Trumper, E Jones. Front: A J Hopkins, H Carter, S E Gregory.

Former Broken Hill miner Ernie 'Jonah' Jones was a formidable fast bowler. (*S S Ramamurthy*)

Jack Saunders, the left-arm medium-pacer who could also bowl spinners, finished the 1902 tour with 127 wickets at 17.07. (*S S Ramamurthy*)

Clem Hill was a tough, little left-hander making his third tour of England. (*S S Ramamurthy*)

all round the wicket, sound in both technique and temperament.

Jack Saunders was a useful left-arm medium-fast bowler who could also slow his pace and bowl orthodox spinners. He began to emerge as a force as the tour went on and finished the tour with 127 wickets at 17.07, second only to Trumble, who captured 140 wickets at 14.27. Warwick Armstrong, leg-spinner and hard-hitting right-handed batsman, did well on his first tour. He scored 1087 runs at 26.51 and picked up 81 wickets at 17.40. He was tall and slender, weighing only ten stone; a far cry from the massive twenty-one stone he carried as captain of the 1921 Australian team to England.

James Kelly again kept in all the Tests. Kelly was a good, sound keeper. He had a marvellous sense of humor and delighted in smoking his briar and telling his teammates humorous stories of past tours. They nicknamed him affectionately as 'Mother'.

Kelly's deputy was Hanson Carter. Carter went about his work with a minimum of fuss. He was the last Australian keeper to wear the open slatted pads in Test matches, but he had to wait until the 1907-8 summer in Australia to make his Test debut. He toured England in 1902, 1909 and 1921, having missed selection (voluntarily) in 1912, because he — along with Trumper, Cotter, Armstrong, Ransford and Hill — declined the invitation to tour. (See The 1912 Dispute.) Carter was known as Sammy or Sep. The son of an undertaker, Carter took over his father's business and often travelled to Sydney grade matches in a hearse. Carter was the first wicketkeeper to squat on his haunches. He would stand a metre back from the stumps to all but the fastest bowling and had to be quick to move forward to effect a stumping chance.

Skipper Joe Darling was a tough customer who had the respect of all the players. A left-handed bat, Darling hit 1113 runs at an average of 24.19, with a top score of 128.

Then there came Syd Gregory, a batsman of purpose and poise; Albert Hopkins, an all-rounder; and back-up medium-pacer, Bill Howell. Howell mainly cut the ball back from the off and was devastating on a responsive wicket.

Let us move through the historic 1902 as Victor Trumper saw it, through his diary.

Victor Trumper opened his mail from Australia. He received a present from his mother of a pen and pencil set. He used his diary for the first time:

Saturday, 26 April: 'Team arrived at Tilbury. Just received present. I am using pencil received from My Sweetheart. 7.40pm. Went to Palace Theatre.'

Sunday, 27 April: 'Met Protheral. Walked in Hyde Park.
Bitterly cold day. Stayed in all night.'

Monday, 28 April: 'Practice. Felt horrible. Went to Pavilion. Received letter from mother first.'

Tuesday, 29 April: 'Practised all day. Went to Empire (theatre) for the first time this trip. Not too good of a show.'

Wednesday, 30 April: 'Saw Mr Fallas, Peace bat maker's representative. Practice all day.'

In the memoranda section of the diary Mr Fallas' address is noted as 34 Leadenhall Street, London.

Thursday, 1 May: 'Practice — all day. Went to Ben Hur at night — Drury Lane.'

Friday, 2 May: 'Practice in the morning. Went to Hippodrome at night. Best show we'd seen.'

Saturday, 3 May: 'Raining. Musuem in the morning . . . Chinese Honeymoon . . . afternoon.'

Sunday, 4 May: 'Went to Hyde Park in morning. Afternoon . . . zoo.'

Next day the Australians played their first game at Crystal Palace.

They were pitted against London County, led by WG Grace, who was then 52 years old. Australia was dismissed for 117 after rain had delayed the start until 3pm. Trumper was run out for 9, with South African spinner Charles Llewellyn claiming 5/52, including having clean bowled

Warwick Armstrong (later known as 'The Big Ship' and weighing in at 21 stone when he led the Aussies to England in 1921), had a marvellous 1902 tour scoring more than 1000 runs at 26.51 and taking 81 wickets at 17.40. (*S S Ramamurthy*)

Syd Gregory, the accomplished NSW middle-order batsman. (*S S Ramamurthy*)

Although Bill Howell was a medium-pacer who could cut the ball back from the off, he was also a solid bat in the Aussie tail. (*S S Ramamurthy*)

Clem Hill for a duck. This is how Victor saw the day's proceedings:

'Graft started. Miserably cold and we'd made a bad start against CP (a reference to the venue Crystal Palace). Score 9. Run Out.'

London County replied with 235 with Len Braund hitting a fine 104. WG Grace was clean-bowled by Monty Noble for 1. Neither event features in Trumper's diary. Australia batted a second time and were 7/213 at stumps, Joe Darling top scoring with 92 before Grace deceived him in flight. Trumper scored 64 before he was stumped off the bowling of leg-spinning all-rounder Braund.

Tuesday, 6 May: 'Few flakes of snow fell. CP batted well. Made a start — 64.'

The scheduled third and final day was abandoned because of rain.

Wednesday, 7 May: 'Rained all day . . . it saved us from a licking. Caught train . . . Nottingham, 6.45. Arrived 9.30.'

Next day the Australians turned out against Nottingham at Trent Bridge. Notts batted first and scored 287, with George Gunn top scoring with 80. Bill Howell took the bowling honours with a fine 4/74 off 35.3 overs and Trumper collected 3/59 off his 21 overs of medium-paced swingers.

Thursday, 8 May: 'Chased leather all day. Cold again. Got 3 wickets. Nottingham made 287. Hard fight tomorrow.'

Friday, 9 May: 'Turned out A1. Made over 400. Gave them 186 to get. Won innings and four runs.'

Trumper inserted the innings victory on Friday's page when, in fact, the win did not eventuate until the next day. Joe Darling played superbly, scoring 128; Hopkins hit 80, Kelly 66 and Ernie Jones blasted 38 to enable the Australians to score 474.

Trumper wrote next day Saturday, 10 May: 'Self 47, Paddy (possibly nickname for Joe Darling) 120. Clum (name for Warwick Armstrong) 8 for 47.'

Sunday, 11 May: 'Stayed Nottingham. Looked around. Spent rather a miserable day.'

Monday, 12 May: 'Surrey . . . raining. Played strongly . . . 47 n.o. S. (Surrey) dinner.'

Trumper flayed the bowling on a waterlogged pitch, after losing Reggie Duff, his opening partner. Duff was bowled by Richardson for 8. Clem Hill joined Trumper and the pair hit merrily. In 16 minutes they plundered 37 runs and after an hour the scoreboard read Australia 1/87. Then the rains came.

Tuesday, 13 May: 'Surrey match. Made 101 . . . first century. Went Middlesex Mr Hall. Been Pro (perhaps an ex-player) Taken P of W (perhaps taken prisoner of war during the Boer War). Congratulated me on score.'

Clem Hill was run out for 33, but Trumper carried on merrily to hit a superb 101. While it was inevitable that Trumper would make his century, as soon as he reached 101 the very nature of this kind and generous soul stood out: he hit a bad ball from Hayward into the hands of Hayes and trooped off the field.

Bad weather helped the Australians storm through the Surrey batting, after Australia had amassed 296 for 5 declared. Bill Howell, John Saunders and Monty Noble starred, dismissing Surrey for 96 and 122 and giving Australia a win by an innings and 78 runs. Howell picked up 11/56 for the match.

This is how Trumper saw the day's play:

Wednesday, 14 May: 'Wet wicket ... won easily. Saw Dolly Grey ... very pretty.'

Next match was against Essex at Leyton. Trumper took 5/33 in the Essex first innings of 178.

Thursday, 15 May: 'Essex match. Nothing but rain. Got a few wickets. Wrote letters.'

Friday, 16 May: 'Batted ... made 9. More rain ... miserable.'

On the following day Australia scored 8 declared for 249, with Clem Hill top-scoring with 104 and Reg Duff showing a welcome return to form with 47. Trumper was bowled Young 9.

Saturday, 17 May: 'Still raining ... Clem got first hundred. Draw thro' rain. Had box at Palace.'

Sunday, 18 May: 'Saw two Lodges. Went to Leicester ... raining.'

As the Australians entrained for Leicester on this Whitsun weekend, far away in South Africa the Boer leaders were arriving in Pretoria preparing to sue for peace with Lord Kitchener and Lord Milner.

Leicestershire batted first on a reasonable wicket and collapsed to the pace of Jones (6/26) and swerve of Noble (4/21). They could muster only 51. Trumper was bowled by King for 20. But rain had the final say.

Monday, 19 May: 'Started match. They batted badly on wicket. We started. Duff and Hill blobs (Reggie Duff and Clem Hill both dismissed without scoring). More rain, finished early.'

Tuesday, 20 May: 'Jonah saved side, made 40. We led by 75. They batted well ... raining again.'

Thanks to lusty hitting by Jonah, Australia managed to reach 126, 75 runs on. Leicester batted better in their second try, scoring 143. Noble took 8/48. Australia hit up the winning runs for the loss of three wickets, including that of Trumper who was bowled Odell 14.

Wednesday, 21 May: 'Made 14 ... bad play to get out ... wanted 68 to win. Won easily, left for London ... FINE all day.'

Thursday, 22 May: 'Arrived Oxford ... No play. Raining went Nureham Park ... Mr A Harcourt ... dinner 8.30 to 11.15. Bed 1 o'clock.'

(Mr Harcourt, a yachting enthusiast, first met Victor at Cowes in 1899. Victor, Frank Laver and Alf Johns were with Harcourt when Queen Victoria passed them in her carriage. She slowed to acknowledge their presence.)

Play began on the second day. Oxford University were bundled out for 77. Noble (5/38) and Armstrong (4/9) were the destroyers before a grand innings from Trumper, who hit a superb 121, stole the limelight. Australia finished the day with 2/213, Hill not out 53.

Friday, 23 May: 'Came in launch from N. Park to match. They made 70-odd. Made 121 self. Saw Banking Races ... fine sight. Back to N.P. in launch. Fine all day.'

Next day Hill was stumped for 64 and Australia closed at 6 for 314.

But the Varsity men were no match for Saunders (7/67) and the Australians won by an innings and 54 runs.

Saturday, 24 May: 'Fine day ... won by an innings. Saw Banking races ... very pretty.'

Sunday, 25 May: 'Went over Nureham Park ... left for train.'

Next day it was back to London where the Australians were to face the might of the Marylebone Cricket Club under the command of the

Two pages from the priceless
Trumper diary of 1902.
(*S S Ramamurthy*)

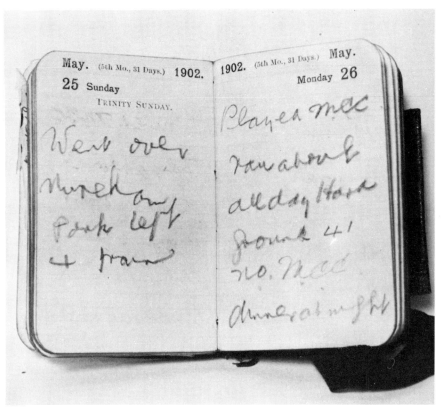

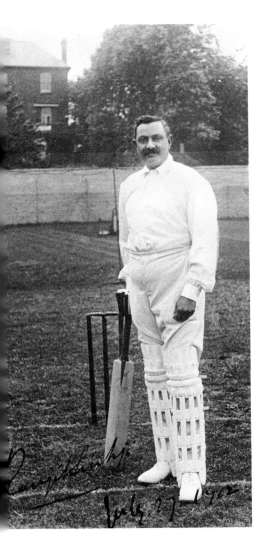

Prince K S Ranjitsinhji (Ranji)
autographed this photo for Clem
Hill during the Lord's Test of 1902.
(*S S Ramamurthy*)

Old Man of cricket, W G Grace. It was in such an MCC side that WG
played in 1878 when Fred Spofforth (the 'Demon') helped Australia
dismiss the MCC team for 33 and 19 and the Australians won by 9
wickets. That was the match when England first began to take these
Colonials seriously. Now here was WG, as large as life, about to take on
Joe Darling's New Breed. Grace had some useful 'Assistants' in C B Fry,
Ranjitsinhji (Sussex); Lionel Palairet and Len Braund (Somerset);
Pelham Warner, J T Hearne and Australian Albert Trott (Middlesex)
and Frank Mitchell of Yorkshire. Darling's team would be tested.

Monday, 26 May: 'Played MCC ... ran about all day. Hard
ground ... 41 not out. MCC dinner at night.'

MCC batted first scoring 240, with Ranjitsinhji hitting a masterly 67
and Bill Howell having WG caught by Syd Gregory for 29. Howell was
the best of the bowlers with 4/54 off 25.3 overs. Ranji was hesitant
early in his knock, perhaps unsettled when a fire-ball from Jonah hit a
sparrow in flight. The bird lay mid-pitch and there were cries of 'kill it,
kill it' from a section of the crowd as the players gathered about the
stricken bird. As a crest-fallen Jonah approached the bird it, to the
delight of all and sundry, hopped up and sprang into the air. Ranji
regained composure and batted superbly from that moment forth, until
Gregory caught him. Trumper hit an unconquered 41 after losing Duff
(16) and the Australians went to dinner at 1/74. Next day Trumper
flayed the bowling, hitting an incomparable 105, before Jack Hearne
bowled him with a prodigious off-break.

Tuesday, 27 May: 'Continued innings made 105. Side made 270.
Poor score. They did not do so well. Very tired. Stayed in and packed
up.'

Australia was all out for 271, then MCC declared at 8/280, with tailenders Mitchell (55 not out) and Hearne (35 not out) denying Darling's men a comfortable win.

Australia was 3/217 at stumps on the last day and the match ended in a draw. Trumper hit 86 before Albert Trott bowled him.

Wednesday, 28 May: 'Last men ran us about. Mitchell made 44, 3 hrs and gave 4 chances. I made 86 . . . wanted double century (meaning he wanted a second century for the match). Left for Birmingham.'

There was joy in the Australian camp after their good showing against MCC and Trumper's form with both bat and ball had him in good humor. He picked up 2/23 in the MCC second innings, including the prize wicket of WG: Trumper deceived the good doctor with a faster ball and clean bowled him. Grace had compiled a slow 23.

The tantalising off-spinners of Hugh Trumble were to confound the Englishmen throughout the 1902 tour. He took 140 wickets at 14.27 on a succession of sticky wickets.

Despite Hugh Trumble being sidelined with a damaged right hand and Jack Saunders out of the running with suspected tonsilitis, Jim Kelly was pronounced fit to take his place behind the stumps. Already Hanson Carter, the reserve stumper, was out of the reckoning having sustained a cut eye in the MCC game, so Australia did not have to call upon Reg Duff to keep.

While Australia was confident of a good showing in this First Test match, the England selectors had picked an extremely strong batting line-up, considered the best ever picked for England. All eleven men had, at some stage of their careers, scored a first-class century.

Archie MacLaren was elected England skipper for all five Tests. The

Yorkshire and Test all-rounder F S Jackson hit a stout 53 in the First Test. This photo was taken by George Beldam, the first cricket photographer to take live action shots. (*George Beldam*)

team: MacLaren (capt) (Lancashire), Hon. F S Jackson (Yorkshire), K S Ranjitsinhji (Sussex), C B Fry (Sussex), G L Jessop (Gloucestershire), A A Lilley (Warwickshire), J T Tyldesley (Lancashire), L Braund (Somerset), G Hirst (Yorkshire), W Rhodes (Yorkshire), W Lockwood (Surrey).

MacLaren won the toss and did not hesitate to go in first on a beautiful hard and fast wicket.

After losing 3/35, Tyldesley batted superbly to restore the England batting. Tyldesley hit a marvellous 138 in 264 minutes, with 20 fours and one five, against an attack including Monty Noble, Jonah, Trumper, Armstrong, Hopkins and Howell. Jackson assisted him with a stout 53 and when the ninth England wicket fell at 295, few would have countenanced the stirring last wicket stand by Lockwood (52 n.o.) and Rhodes (38 n.o.) taking the score to 9 for 376 before MacLaren called a halt to the slaughter.

Overnight rain and continuing drizzle early on the second day had delayed MacLaren's declaration.

This is how Trumper viewed that first day's play:

Thursday, 29 May: 'England won toss. As usual ran about all day . . . very tired. Wrote letters home.'

Trumper and Duff opened for Australia and they walked out to a drying pitch under leaden skies.

In just 23 overs Australia was all out for an incredible 36. George Hirst, bowling fast and accurate, and his Yorkshire compatriot Wilfred Rhodes, bowling his left-arm orthodox spin with deadly accuracy, decimated the Australian batting but for a few proud blows by Trumper, who scored 18. The next best offering came from Hopkins with 5. Rhodes collected 7/17 off 11 overs and Hirst, from a like number of overs, gathered 3/15.

Friday, 30 May: 'Finished innings. Raining . . . wet wickets. A[a] made 36 . . . batted badly. 2nd innings made 8 n.o. Total score for no wickets. Theatre flag ½ mast.'

Australia had begun its second innings and Trumper's 8 not out was the team total when rain intervened.

Indeed, next day rain again had the last say, depriving England of almost certain victory. Australia had lost 2/46, the wickets of Trumper (15) and Duff (14) after a very late start.

Saturday, 31 May: 'Still raining leave for ground 1 o'clock. Started match 5.15pm simply to get the crowd in a good humour. Match a draw. Saved us from a good hiding.'

English disappointment in missing a Test win against the old enemy was short-lived for news came through that the Boers had finally surrendered to British forces in Pretoria. The Boer War was over.

Bells tolled throughout the land. There was great joy among the people and they celebrated accordingly. The Australians caught the train for Headingly to meet Yorkshire, the toughest of all the counties. A record first day attendance of 33,705 people was to greet them.

Sunday, 1 June: 'Left for Leeds. Raining again. News peace declared. Plenty of row in town celebrating it.'

Joe Darling won the toss on a rain affected wicket and with Trumper top-scoring with 38, Australia mustered a poor 131.

Hirst, Rhodes and Jackson shared the spoils for Yorkshire, but Bill

Howell (6/53) and Monty Noble (4/30) bowled superbly in the wet to dismiss Yorkshire for 107.

Monday, 2 June: 'Joe (Darling) won toss . . . went in . . . made 38 . . . wicket bad. Saw Music Hall. Good show.'

Next day Australia was bundled out for a paltry 23 on a treacherous wicket, with Rhodes bagging 5/9 off seven overs and Jackson 5/12 off seven overs. Yorkshire lost five wickets in hitting off the necessary 50 runs for an easy victory.

Tuesday, 3 June: 'Wicket still bad. Side made 23. Yorkshire won. 1st hiding. Saw Mummy and The Humming Bird . . . not bad. Met Mrs Clarke from Hall.'

Wednesday, 4 June: 'More rain. Left for Manchester. Wrote Australian mail and stayed in.'

The side duly arrived at Old Trafford. Darling won the toss and batted. It was just as well, as Trumper had injured his bowling hand. Monty Noble had influenza and was ordered to bed by the tour doctor Rowley Pope. Further, Bill Howell had just received the news of his mother's death and two days later he learnt of his father's passing. This cast added gloom over the party beset by injury and the sodden summer. The Australians decided to get some batting practice. Trumper hit a splendid 70, Armstrong an unconquered 87 and Jim Kelly hit a solid 75. But the innings was spread over three days, the innings being played in fits and starts because of the rain. It was all very depressing.

Thursday, 5 June: 'Noble in bed. Influenza. Fine. Won toss . . . batted made 70. 8 for 356. Jim good score (meaning Jim Kelly) Saw Music Hall. Hackensmidt. JD (Joe Darling) in bed. Influenza.'

Friday, 6 June: 'Nobel and Darling in bed. Went to ground . . . No play. Saw Queens Theatre show . . . rotten. HT (Hugh Trumble) came up.'

Saturday, 7 June: 'Darling up. Not too clever. Match abandoned. Did not go to ground. 12.30 left for London. MAN (Monty Noble) came wrapped up.'

Sunday, 8 June: 'Raining . . . dodged about and done nothing.'

Influenza and injury took its toll and Darling's team was reduced to just nine fit men. It was decided to give Hugh Trumble a chance to try out his injured bowling hand and ask Dr Rowley Pope, the tour doctor, who had assisted H J H Scott's 1886 touring team while he was still a medical student at Edinburgh, to make up the eleven.

Cambridge University's 1902 team was weak in batting, especially in this match against Australia with their star bat, Sam Day, unavailable.

Cambridge batted first and mustered just 108. Trumper excelled with the ball, taking 5/19 off 8.3 overs. At the close of the first day Trumper had an unconquered 27 to his credit. Next day Trumper slaughtered the Varsity attack scoring 128 and helping Australia to 337. Batting a second time Cambridge collapsed for 46, with Albert Hopkins getting a sensational 7/10 off eight overs. Jonah crashed through the top order to pick up 3/30 and the Australians won by an innings and 183 runs.

Monday, 9 June: 'Left for Cambridge. Fine . . . rained at ground. They won toss. Got 5 for 19 and not out 27. Nothing to be done in town at night. JD (Joe Darling) and MAN went to Brighton.'

Tuesday, 10 June: 'Made 128. Total now 851. Abel 18 runs ahead. (The Surrey veteran bat Bobby Abel was 18 runs ahead of Trumper in

South Australian and Test fast bowler Ernie Jones knocked a sparrow senseless with one of his 'fire-balls' during the first game against the MCC.

The great Charles Fry from Sussex was forced to bat on a shocking wicket in the Lord's Test. He was out without scoring but rain saved England. (*C B Fry*)

Trumper's diary entries for 14 and 15 June, 1902. (*S S Ramamurthy*)

the race to the first 1000 runs of the 1902 season). Race for first 1000 runs of season. Match finished. Hopkins 7 for 10. Hattrick. Turned in early.'

Wednesday, 11 June: 'Saw backs of Colleges. Very pretty. Left for London.'

The Lord's Test was ruined by rain. It was, perhaps, just as well the gods decided upon torrential rain as the Australians were sorely depleted. Bowlers Bill Howell and Hugh Trumble were both far too ill with influenza to be considered for selection. Skipper Joe Darling and Monty Noble were also suffering from flu, but they were prepared to turn out and Jack Saunders, still not recovered from a bout of tonsilitis, had also developed eye trouble. Archie MacLaren won the toss and decided to bat. That decision was, in itself, a sensation as the pitch was in a deplorable state. No play was possible before lunch. Perhaps MacLaren thought England might have the best use of what he must have envisaged to be a nightmare wicket, once the sun finally found its way through the heavy cloud cover and turned a sodden track into a treacherous 'sticky.' Albert Hopkins gave the Australians heart by bagging the wickets of Fry and Ranji.

Both great players failed to score. Fry was well held by Clem Hill at slip and Ranjitsinhji was clean bowled. Then, between showers and stoppages, MacLaren and F S Jackson, both blue-blood amateurs, took the score to 102 for the loss of two wickets. Just one and three quarter hours' play was possible on the first day.

Thursday, 12 June: 'Test match . . . raining hard . . . Mac (MacLaren) won toss, batted. Two for none (meaning the wickets of Fry and Ranji) . . . had four chances dropped off me . . . wrote letters.'

Friday, 13 June: 'Rain, no play. Saw Gay Lord Queux . . . passable.'

Saturday, 14 June: 'No play. Rain. Saw Opera, Covent Garden. L'elisir d'amor, The Elixer of Love . . . good. HC (Hanson Carter) with me.'

A bitterly disappointing Test. Australia did not have the opportunity to bat. Trumper bowled eight fruitless overs for 33 runs and lamented the poor fielding of his comrades Next day the team left Birmingham for Eastbourne where they were to combat an England XI on the attractive Saffrons ground. After arriving at their hotel Trumper and Hugh Trumble were driven to the local golf course for a relaxing round.

Sunday, 15 June: 'Left for Eastbourne. Had lunch there. Very pretty indeed. Drove to links with Mr Gambier, caddy for HT.'

Next day the Australians batted first on a brute of a pitch. It was slow paced and very wet. The Derbyshire fast bowler, Bill Bestwick revelled in the conditions, taking 4/30 off 14 overs. He claimed the prized wicket of Trumper when he uprooted Victor's leg stump with a lightning fast yorker. Trumper scored 31 in a team total of 154 and the Englishmen were struggling at stumps, having lost their five top batsmen for just 29 runs. Bobby Abel was still there on 27.

Monday, 16 June: 'Played . . . made 31. Yorked . . . horrible. Bad wicket. Abel 27 not out.'

Hugh Trumble routed the England XI, taking 8/58 off 20.3 overs and the Englishmen were all out for 138. Batting a second time the Australians could manage only 185, with Trumper splitting his right index finger when the ball jammed his gloveless right hand against the handle of the bat. It was a ball of great pace from George Thompson which struck Trumper the cruel blow. Worse was to come. Trumper was bowled for the second time in the match. This time it was Thompson who delivered the death rattle and Trumper departed for 7.

Tuesday, 17 June: 'Abel made 32, one ahead. (Abel was then one run ahead of Trumper in their race to be the first batsman to score 1000 runs for the summer). Rained hard after lunch. No more play. Crawford played well. (he scored 57 in the Englishmen's first innings). Made 7. Bowled . . . H.O.W.'

The reference H.O.W. could refer to disbelief, either how Victor could have missed the ball or initials for having Hit On Wicket. Perhaps that is it, Trumper played the ball on to his stumps.

Next day Ernie Jones fielded for the injured Trumper, still nursing a split right index finger.

The weather played havoc with the wicket on the final day, with Hugh Trumble again bowling superbly. Trumble added 6/26 to his first innings 8/58 and Bill Howell gave him invaluable support with 2/20 to rout the Englishmen for 70.

Wednesday, 18 June: 'Won match. Jonah fielded for me. Left for Derby via London. Arrived 12.30 am.'

Against Derbyshire the Australians opened Albert Hopkins with Trumper. Trumper went with his score at 10, but Hopkins played a valiant innings of 68 in the total of 218. Derby had been dismissed for 152, with Saunders and Howell grabbing four wickets apiece.

Thursday, 19 June: 'Fine. Wicket slow. Made 10, caught behind. Hoppy (Hopkins) batted well. Trumble in form. Saw Trip to Blackpool . . . horrible show.'

Next day Saunders (6/40) and Trumble (3/36) slaughtered Derby, dismissing the team for 78, leaving the Australians just 13 runs for victory. The last pair, Howell and Saunders, were given the chance to open for their country, but both went cheaply and it was left to Reg Duff and Hanson Carter to finish the job, after a rain-marred second day.

Friday, 20 June: 'Rained all day . . . played cards. Storer's benefit concert at night (reference to Derby wicketkeeper Bill Storer's benefit night). Passable show.'

Saturday, 21 June: 'Won match easily. Roamed over town.'

Sunday, 22 June: 'Went to Sir Peter Walker's. Had lunch there. Went to Bradford. Arrived 9.45.'

This return match against Yorkshire was something of a grudge game. The tourists sought revenge after having been humbled at Headingley. Yet the Yorkshire side was weakened by the absence of Lord Hawke and the Hon. F S Jackson, both of whom had already gone to London for the scheduled coronation of King Edward VII the following Thursday, 26 June. Again the weather intervened and the pitch promised to become a spinner's paradise, a battle between Australia's Hugh Trumble and Yorkshire's Wilfred Rhodes. Again Hopkins opened with Trumper, but both batsmen failed and were back in the pavilion with the score at three. Trumper fell to Rhodes and George Hirst clean bowled Hopkins for a duck.

Monday, 23 June: 'Yorkshire. Wet wicket. Made 3. JD (Darling) and C Hill saved side. (Darling hit 40 and Hill 34). They (Yorkshire) done badly. Went to Music Hall. Rotten.'

Victor's poor form with the bat also seemingly affected his grammar when he put pen to his diary that night!

Diary entries for 18 and 19 June. Trumper's entry for the 18th mentions that 'Jonah' fielded for Vic. In fact, Trumper had split the index finger on his right hand during the match against an England Eleven at Eastbourne. (*S S Ramamurthy*)

The Australians managed just 106, but that was enough to lead on the first innings. Trumble (6/17) and Saunders (4/58) skittled the Yorkshiremen for 77. Australia fared little better a second time. Rhodes again dismissed Trumper and Darling's men fell for 87.

Tuesday, 24 June: 'Led by 29 on first innings. Made 7 second innings (actually it was 9). W (wicket) still bad. SEG played well. (Syd Gregory scored a face-saving 42 not out).

Next day Trumble again turned up trumps taking 6/27 and Yorkshire folded for 72, giving the Australians a 44 run win.

Wednesday, 25 June: 'Won match by 44 runs. SEG 40 not out. Golf links. Had a fine day. Home again 10.30.'

During the course of the Yorkshire game Buckingham Palace announced that the King's Coronation (set for Thursday, 26 June, 1902) would be postponed. Five Royal doctors stated that His Majesty was suffering from appendicitus and immediate surgery was necessary. The Australians were to have gone to London to watch the Coronation, but instead another match against an England XI was hastily arranged to be played at Bradford, starting on what was to have been Coronation Day. Well, the King's misfortune turned out to be a marvellous batting day for the Prince of Australian batsmanship, Victor Trumper. The Australians batted first and Trumper dazzled the crowd with a brilliant 113. That century came after a string of failures. He passed the 1000 run mark and this fifth tour century equalled the record for an Australian batsman on a tour of England.

The previous record was held by skipper Joe Darling, who scored five centuries on the 1899 tour. Reg Duff joined Trumper after Australia had lost 4/35, and their partnership ended when Trumper was bowled for 113 and the score stood at 280.

Thursday, 26 June: 'Played XI (An England XI). Made 113. Got 1000 and this fifth century equals record, JD (Darling) last trip. RAD (Duff) 180. Good boy. Wrote letters, finished 11pm.'

There was also a notation on the page '4 for 30, 5 for 280', referring to when Duff joined him and when Trumper was out at 280.

The England XI replied with 240 and Trumper's comment:
'They batted...passably.'

Batting a second time the England XI managed 203, with Noble (3/67), Saunders (4/66) and Jones (2/20) sharing the spoils. A seven wicket victory to Australia.

Saturday, 28 June: 'Won match. Joe (Darling) pair of specs (two ducks for the match). Left for Scotland. Arrived Glasgow 11.30.'

Trumper was rested for the one-day match against 'An Eleven of Scotland' at Edinburgh. However, Victor was not idle with his time. He took every opportunity to meet the people and to have a look at the countryside.

Sunday, 29 June: 'Mr Tod's place. Beautiful horse and grounds. Ride in motor car 27 miles.'

Monday, 30 June: 'Ride 42 miles to Edinburgh. Having a spell. Met Frank and Percy Wall and George Raffau. Back to Glasgow.'

Tuesday, 1 July: 'Up again to match. Good day. Very pleased. Back to Glasgow. Bonfires . . . real good.'

The match against an Eleven of Scotland was played in a very light-hearted manner. Australia scored 305 and dismissed Scotland for 109 and 91.

Trumper's combined rail and ship ticket for the trip from London to Glasgow. (*Tom Nicholas*)

The great England all-rounder Gilbert 'The Croucher' Jessop in 1902. (*C B Fry*)

There was much mirth in the Aussie camp as 'Mother' Kelly turned over his arm, picking up two wickets, while 'Kruger' Hill picked up 3/30 off 9 overs. Reg Duff bowled his off-breaks to good effect, taking 3/17 off eight overs and even Sammy Carter removed his pads to bowl one over, albeit an expensive one, having seven runs taken from it.

It was light relief and the Australians travelled to Sheffield for the Third Test at dismal Bramall Lane in high spirits. The great England all-rounder Gilbert Jessop often criticised the smokestack atmosphere of Sheffield. The pitch was often fiery, but the main problem being the poor light, as much a legacy of the hundreds of smoking chimney stacks which abounded in this industrial city as of the usually inclement weather. This third Test was the only Test match ever afforded Bramall Lane, although the ground was a first-class venue right up until 1973. Perhaps the English authorities took note of Jessop's thoughts on Sheffield. He wrote at the time: 'If there is one ground in England less suitable for matches of so great an importance than Sheffield, then I am yet to know of it.'

Wednesday, 2 July: 'Stayed in Edinburgh and left for Sheffield at 10.30. Arrived 5 o'clock. Telegram from Pro leaving for Egypt.'

Thursday, 3 July: 'Match started. Made 1. Our chaps made 190 odd. Abel and Archie (MacLaren) batted well.'

Joe Darling had won the toss and batted. Trumper was bowled by Braund for 1 and thanks to a fine 47 by Monty Noble, Australia managed to reach a moderate 194. The Englishmen began well with a good opening stand by Bobby Abel (38) and Archie Maclaren (31) in an opening stand of 61. However, Jack Saunders (5/50) and Noble (5/51) turned the tables on the Englishmen and England was all out for 145.

Friday, 4 July: 'England 49 behind. Wickets rolled on the quiet. Made 62 in 47 minutes. Clem 100. England, Jessop 50 not out, bowled fast.'

Trumper's 50 came in 40 minutes and he set the stage for some glorious batting by Clem Hill, who is the only man to score a Test century at Bramall Lane. Now the venue is the home of Sheffield United Football Club, Hill is likely to forever hold that record. Hill

The gold watch presented to
Trumper by Lord Sheffield in 1902.
(*S S Ramamurthy*)

Diary pages for 4 and 5 June, 1902.
The entry for Saturday (5 June) is
unusual. Non-drinking Trumper
wrote: 'Hurrah . . . won match . . .
glorious . . . all drunk.'
(*S S Ramamurthy*)

scored 119 and with Trumper (62), Hopkins (40 not out), Gregory (29) and Armstrong (26), Australia scored 289. The Trumper-Hill partnership realised 60 runs and with the score at 80 Trumper departed, brilliantly caught by wicketkeeper Dick Lilley as he launched himself high and to his left to complete a miraculous catch. Trumper had attempted to pull fine a short ball from Jackson.

The crowd roared its delight at the Lilley catch, but many were sorry to see Trumper depart. On a treacherous wicket which gave the great Sydney Barnes, George Hirst, Len Braund and Wilfred Rhodes more than enough help, Trumper's artistry had held the crowd spellbound. MacLaren later said Trumper's innings was a display of brilliant and aggressive batsmanship the like of which had rarely been seen in England or elsewhere. When Lilley brought off the catch, Trumper rushed to the England keeper, shook his hand and walked briskly to the pavilion.

Next day Hugh Trumble (4/49) and Monty Noble (6/52) destroyed the cream of England. Archie MacLaren hit a sound 63 and Gilbert Jessop reached 55, but the rest fell without a whimper, like ripe corn to the sweep of a scythe. The Australians won by a massive 143 runs.

Trumper, non-smoker, non-drinker, summed up:

Saturday, 5 July: 'Hurras. Won match. Glorious. All drunk . . . Left for Birmingham. Arrived 12pm.'

The Australians, naturally feeling pleased with themselves, left for Birmingham rather the worse for wear on Sunday morning. They were invited to stay at Warwick Castle the day before their match against Warwickshire. The invitation came from none other than the Earl and Countess of Warwick.

Sunday, 6 July: 'Warwick Castle. Met Maree Corelli . . . Great day.'

Warwickshire batted first and Armstrong spun a web of mystery round the county side, taking 6/13 and the locals were all out for 124. Trumper batted ably for 45 and the Australians easily overhauled Warwickshire on the first day.

Monday, 7 July: 'Warwickshire won toss. Soon out Clum (Armstrong) went through them. Made 45.'

Clem Hill (18), Joe Darling (37) and Syd Gregory (83) batted solidly and the Australians reached 316. But the men of Edgbaston were made of stern stuff. They batted better a second time and, helped by the weather, salvaged a draw.

Tuesday, 8 July: 'Good going . . . Clem (Hill), Joe (Darling) and Sid (Gregory) done well. Going easy for win.'

Wednesday, 9 July: 'Rain . . . match abandoned. Left for Worcester.'

Again the selectors decided to rest Trumper from a county match.

Thursday, 10 July: 'Pleasant little city. Left out. Another spell. Wrote letters and had a sleep.'

Friday, 11 July: 'Visited Royal W (Worcester) China works and Cathedral. Very fine and good pleasant day. Drove to Malvern . . . beautiful drive.'

While Trumper toured about Worcestershire, the Australians whipped the county team, winning by 174 runs.

Saturday, 12 July: 'Won easily and left for Bristol. Arrived at 11.45 about.'

That day was a day of great excitement in London, for the nation

A section of the crowd at the Australia v. Worcester game on 10 July, 1902. Although Trumper did not bat, Australia won by 174 runs.

welcomed home Lord Kitchener and General French, heroes of the Boer War, as they drove from Paddington to London on their return from South Africa.

Sunday, 13 July: 'Drove to Portishead, 10 miles. Very dusty. Had dinner there.'

The Australians were about to tackle Gloucestershire, minus skipper WG Grace, who since 1900 was the county captain. Grace was busy hammering the 123rd century of his career for London County against MCC at Crystal Palace on this hot and dry Monday, while his Gloucester charges fell to some good bowling by Howell (2/28), Armstrong (4/51) and Jones (3/56) for an inglorious 155. Trumper and Duff thrashed the Gloucester attack that afternoon, compiling 111 without loss in one hour! Trumper was 83 not out. Next day Trumper fell for 92, Duff for 62, but Clem Hill (123), Monty Noble (100) and Albert Hopkins (105 not out) made merry and the Australians called a halt to the slaughter when Darling declared the innings closed at 5/545.

This is how Trumper saw those first two days.

Monday, 14 July: 'Fine wicket. They batted horribly. Made 155. We 0 for 111 in hour. Self 83.'

Tuesday, 15 July: 'Missed bus . . . made 92. Alf, Clem and Hoppy centuries. Total 545.'

Humor from Trumper: He certainly did 'miss the bus' as he puts it. After having banged up 83 in an hour he was caught by the 'Croucher' Gilbert Jessop for 92 on the second day.

The Australians mopped up the Gloucester batsmen a second time, with Reg Duff and Clem each picking up a wicket and rubbing salt into Gloucestershire's open wound. Gloucestershire fell for 168, giving Australia an innings and 222 runs victory.

After a day's play the tourists always dined together. This, they believed as do the moderns, fostered comradeship and team spirit. Often they would be invited to the home of a notable citizen of a county, or trip off to a lavish dinner party. Left to their own devices they would venture to a music hall or local theatre. Victor Trumper loved the theatre. He also loved music and would provide backing by

Trumper the musician: Victor (left) and Clem Hill at the piano during the tour of England. (*Jack Pollard Collection*)

way of the piano in the smoking-room of the team hotel for the fine baritone voice of Monty Noble. Yet Victor, while he could easily relax in the company of his team mates, still had to be encouraged to partake in any activity which had the slightest bit to do with self-esteem.

A night of song and then it was off to play Somerset in the land of cider and quaint English accents.

Wednesday, 16 July: 'Won easily. Jessop failed. Left for Taunton.'

The Somerset captain Lionel Palairet won the toss and batted, Somerset scoring 274 and the Australians were 2/128 at stumps, Trumper falling to a thunderbolt from George Gill for 5.

Thursday, 17 July: 'Fine wicket. Very fast . . . warm. Palairet batted. Well set, 273 . . . 2 for 128.'

Reg Duff set the beautiful little ground in Dene Park alight with the majesty of his batting. Duff cracked a superb 183 in the Australians' total of 348. At stumps Somerset were 5/159, with Palairet following his first innings 44 with a well-made 90 before he missed a straight quick one from Jonah.

Friday, 18 July (W G Grace's 54th birthday): RAD 183 . . . 348 . . . 5 for 159. No theatres . . . or anything else.'

This was a caustic comment about the lack of theatres or places to visit. Coincidentally he was also not having much luck with the bat, scoring only 5.

Somerset batted on to score 315 in their second innings, Jones finishing with 4/104 off 25.2 overs and Hopkins chiming in with 3/46. The Australians batted briefly a second time (before rain intervened) and at the close of play was 1/16, Trumper being trapped lbw to the paceman Gill, again scoring only 5 runs.

Saturday, 19 July: 'Total 315. Self 5 . . . again. 1 for 16. Rain stopped . . .'

Sunday, 20 July: 'Left for London. Arrived 9.30.'

Darling lost his third successive toss and the Australians took the field against Surrey at Kennington Oval. The Australian captain decided to rest his ace bowling card, Hugh Trumble, and Ernest Jones, along with first choice keeper James Kelly. It was believed, in the Australian camp, that Jonah might be an asset at Old Trafford, venue for the vital Fourth Test match, however, Jack Saunders was also in top

form and the Victorian left-hand swing bowler would press Jonah for an opening bowling berth. Veteran Bobby Abel and Tom Hayward set Surrey towards a useful total in a solid opening stand. Hayward fell to Saunders and Abel hit a brilliant 104, before Trumper had him caught at slip by Monty Noble. 'Billy the Plugger' Howell lived up to his nickname and bowled manfully to return a bag of 5/80 off 28 overs; Saunders chipped in with 3/82 from 34 overs and Trumper took the vital wicket of century-maker Abel for a personal cost of 23 runs from his 14 overs.

Monday, 21 July: 'Played Surrey. Wet wicket. Surrey made 8 for 294.'

The following day rain intervened, spoiling all but a few hours of play. Surrey finished with 296 and after just 100 minutes' batting, the Australians had scored 148 for the loss of three wickets. Trumper blasted the Surrey attack, scoring a whirlwind 85 and Reg Duff was again in the runs with a solid 57.

Tuesday, 22 July: 'Rained nearly all day. Made 296. 3 for 148 in 1 hr 20 minutes. Self 85.'

The Australians batted on to a total of 313, with Clem Hill hitting a solid 90. Then Surrey collapsed against a sensational spell of bowling by Jack Saunders, who took 6/9 off 9.1 overs. This performance put Saunders on the short-list to open the Test attack with Trumble at Old Trafford. Surrey was all out for 111. Australia needed just 94 runs to win.

Wednesday, 23 July: 'Total was 313. Hill 90. Surrey 111 all out. 5.30 left for M'Chester (Manchester) Train 70 m per hour' (miles per hour). The Fourth Test match at Old Trafford has gone down in the annals of the grand old game as one of the most absorbing contests between England and Australia.

The Oval, Kennington, south London was the sight for the game against Surrey just prior to the famous Fourth Test. The gasometers are still there.

Gilbert Jessop, 'The Croucher' was strangely omitted from the England side for the Manchester Test. (*George Beldam*)

England skipper Archie MacLaren found himself without the services of the 'Croucher' Gilbert Jessop (he surely wanted Jessop for his fielding alone) and Sydney Barnes. Yorkshire's George Hirst, who only weeks before had, with Wilfred Rhodes, humilated this Australian team, bowling Darling's men out for 43, was inexplicably dropped in favour of Fred Tate. Tate was enjoying a successful summer with Sussex. In fact it finished up being his most successful season, taking some 180 wickets at 15.71. However, all the critics thought the selectors were completely wrong in replacing Hirst in favour of Tate. A medium paced off-spinner, Tate was thought to be included because rain was imminent. So MacLaren, peeved about the loss of Jessop (especially) and Barnes, thought Tate was foisted upon him in place of the pride of Yorkshire, George Hirst.

England's 143-run loss at Sheffield had the Lion licking its wounds and had the selectors shown enough commonsense, the English Lion would have been at its most dangerous. At least Charles Fry, one of the selectors, counted himself out of the running.

The England side lined up thus: Palairet, Abel, Tyldesley, MacLaren (capt), Ranjitsinhji, Hon. F S Jackson, Braund, Lilley, Lockwood, Rhodes, Tate.

A good side, but MacLaren and indeed England would live to regret the non-selection of Jessop and especially Hirst.

Bobby Abel beat his Surrey opening partner Tom Hayward, probably on the strength of his marvellous 104 against Australia only days before this game.

The Australians' problem was not whom to pick, but just who to leave out. A nice dilemma for the selectors. They had ample men for the task at hand. Jonah was finally pipped on the post by the Victorian left-hander Jack Saunders and 'Billy the Plugger' Howell could not find a spot because of Hugh Trumble's ominious 'No Vacancy' sign, indelibly etched on every Australian XI team since his Test career started in 1890.

The Australian XI: Trumper, Duff, Hill, Noble, Gregory, Darling (capt), Hopkins, Armstrong, Kelly, Trumble, Saunders.

While Howell and Jones were the unlucky specialist bowlers for the Old Trafford Test, Albert Hopkins won a place on the strength of his all-round ability. If anything the Australian team appeared a little top-heavy with batsmen, yet among the leading eight batsmen there was Noble and Armstrong, two of the side's front line bowlers.

Darling won the toss and decided to bat. The wicket and outfield had been saturated by rain, however the sun was now needed by England for the wicket to play tricks. MacLaren rushed back to the England dressingroom and said with relish: 'It's all right, boys, they're batting: the sun's coming out; we've only to keep them quiet until lunch . . .'

MacLaren knew full well that on this sodden and sluggish surface, certain fours on a dry day would be reduced to twos at best, maybe only singles. MacLaren told his men that the wicket would almost assuredly be a 'sticky, after lunch'. He must have been the supreme optimist as 1902 was one of the wettest summers on record and England needed the warmth of the sun and not more rain if the wicket was to become a glutinous and treacherous surface for the Australian batsmen. But MacLaren wanted to instil confidence into his men. 'When the sun shines, we'll bowl 'em out as quickly as they come in. If the Australians are only 80 or so at the interval, we've won the match, and the rubber.' Then MacLaren faltered; his eyes narrowed and the first tone of uncertainty came from his lips. 'So, for goodness sake, keep Victor (Trumper) quiet . . . at all costs.'

MacLaren knew as did everyone at the ground that Trumper loomed large as the one man capable of batting like a genius on any surface. Sticky wickets never worried him. In fact, he was to play some of his grandest innings on wet pitches. The Englishmen had great respect for Trumper, as well they might, because he could swing a match in two hours' batting. As MacLaren's men took the field, the crowd heckled the England captain over Tate's inclusion at the expense of Hirst.

As Trumper and Reg Duff walked towards the middle, a small boy pressed his face against the palings. He was watching his first Test match and he watched in awe as Trumper, his hero, strode confidently forward. 'Please, God, let Victor Trumper score a century today for Australia against England — out of a total of 137 all out.' That small boy was none other than Neville Cardus, later to become the world's greatest cricket writer.

The uncovered pitch was too slippery for Lockwood to use as he would not be able to keep his footing. MacLaren opened with Wilfred Rhodes, the left arm orthodox spinner, and medium-pacer F S Jackson. He set his field deep, hoping to save boundaries and stall for time so the sun would dry the bowlers' footmarks and play havoc with the batting surface. MacLaren also instructed his bowlers to pitch short on the off side so Trumper would have to go after the bowling. Rhodes was not keen on the idea. He always prided himself on being able to maintain a good length and direction. Two years previously he had experimented in a similar way when bowling to Jessop. The plan backfired and he suffered a drubbing.

Rhodes to Trumper. The first ball was full length but wide of the off stump and Trumper sprang like a panther. He skipped down the wicket and launched into a cover drive. Next ball was wider and Trumper hit it majestically behind point. Two balls, two fours! Rhodes stood with his hands on hips and glared at his captain. MacLaren altered his field, bringing a man across from the leg side to strengthen the off side cordon. Trumper was quick to seize the initiative. He glided down the wicket and hit the ball on the half volley — against the spin — to the vacant on side area for yet another boundary. In Rhodes' next over Trumper twice jumped down the wicket and lofted him high over the sightscreen behind the bowler's arm and into the practice ground. The crowd erupted. They loved the majesty of Trumper's batting. Those massive hits of Trumper's were counted only as fours, but no matter, Australia was in complete command. Duff was faring almost as well as Trumper at the other end, giving Jackson (known then eternally as 'Jacker') plenty of stick. Duff drove him on the rise and then slashed a ball past point which screamed across the sodden turf like a tracer bullet. It was overcast, but not so dark that Johnny Tyldesley at deep third man could not pick up its flight. Four more. Trumper faced Jackson for the first time after a Duff single to square leg. Jacker dropped short and Trumper lent back with nonchalant ease and almost contemptuously dispatched the ball to the square leg fence. It seemed all too easy for Trumper and Duff. MacLaren was beside himself.

This is how cartoonist Frank Gillett saw the first day's play at Old Trafford, 24 July 1902, when Trumper scored the first Test 100 before lunch. (*David Frith Collection*)

He decided to rest Jackson and call upon Fred Tate, the medium-paced off-tweaker, to bowl his first over in Test match company. After four tidy overs, costing 13 runs, Duff slashed Tate and then Trumper crashed a ball pitched on off stump to the boundary behind square leg. Young Neville Cardus cheered as much as any member of the Australian XI lapping up the batting of the maestro in the middle. The scoreboard ticked over furiously as Duff and Trumper took Tate for 13 runs in his fifth over. Ones and twos came at will as MacLaren persisted with his deep set field. Whenever MacLaren brought in a man short on either side of the wicket to stem the tide of runs, Trumper would help himself to a boundary. Trumper and Duff's 50 partnership came in 30 minutes, then Trumper took a boundary and two from a cut off Len Braund to bring up his 50 in 52 minutes. Australia was 0/92.

Rhodes was brought back. This time MacLaren relented. Wilfred would be able to bowl how he wanted to bowl, pitching the ball up round middle and off stumps, searching for an outside edge as he brought the batsman forward. But still the brilliant Trumper could not he held at bay. He pranced down the wicket and drove, or went right back on his stumps and impudently pulled Rhodes to the leg side. None of the England bowlers had an answer to the genius of Trumper's batting and Duff was proving a more than willing ally.

With the score at 129, MacLaren finally resorted to bringing on his paceman, William Lockwood. Lockwood was decidedly quick and used the off-cutter to good effect. This match was destined to be his best in his twelve Test and 43-wicket career. Lockwood's years as a tear-away fast bowler were behind him, as he was then 32. He had survived being mauled by a shark and had also beaten the ravages of alcohol after his wife and one of his children were tragically killed. The first over saw him concede just one run. Then Trumper took to Rhodes. Duff scored a single off Rhodes' last ball to keep the strike. Lockwood moved in menacingly. Duff, for the first time, looked unsettled as Lockwood cut one back from outside the off stump and rapped him high on the pads. Next ball cut back, but Duff met it with the full face of the bat. Then Duff played again for the break-back. The ball held its own and Duff got the faintest of outside edges and Dick Lilley, who held down England's job behind the stumps from 1896 to 1909, made no mistake.

Australia 1/135. Duff had made 54 and the Australian pair had been at the crease for only 68 minutes! Trumper was unconquered on 80, with Clem Hill, the solid little left-hander, walking confidently to join him. Trumper and Duff had just made the highest opening stand for their country to that time. They had scored at the rate of 103 runs per hour. Certainly MacLaren had lost a good deal of face with his men! He had wanted the Australians to be something in the vicinity of 80 at lunch, yet at 1/135, there was still an hour until lunch. With Hill's introduction to the crease the runs came at a slightly slower pace, due to the change in the field for the right and left-hander after a single was scored. In addition, the sun was starting to make some impression and the drying pitch was beginning to give England's attack a bit of bite. Five minutes before lunch, Trumper pulled and then hooked the big paceman, Lockwood, for two boundaries; the second of which brought the Old Trafford crowd to its feet, among them an overjoyed 12-year-old Neville Cardus. For that second hook heralded Trumper's century. He had been at the crease for just 108 minutes. At least MacLaren warned his men to 'keep Victor quiet'.

A century before lunch on the first day of a Test match.

The crowd went wild. Trumper stood head bowed as the England team joined in the applause. Dick Lilley removed his right glove and shook Trumper's hand: 'Great knock, lad.'

'Thanks very much, Dick, but I've had a bit of luck.'

The innings was a gem. Chanceless. Perhaps Trumper's reply to Lilley was out of sheer nervousness. He appeared to be embarrassed by all the fuss and just wanted to get down to the business of batting. Trumper and Hill went to lunch with Australia 1/173, Trumper 103. As Trumper led the players off the field, Old Trafford members rose to him as one and cheered the young batting phenomenon.

Years later in his autobiography Neville Cardus wrote of Trumper (Collins, p.182): 'He was the most gallant and handsome batsman of them all; he possessed a certain chivalrous manner, a generous courtly poise.

A famous bat: This is the willow given to Captain E W Ballantine by Trumper after he made the 103 runs before lunch at Old Trafford. The bat face has been cut into three and bears the signatures of hundreds of famous cricketers.

Trumper at the Oval in 1902. This is the big-hitting style which thrilled England and the cricketing world during that English summer of 1902.

'But his swift and apparent daring, the audacity of his prancing footwork, were governed by a technique of rare accuracy and range. Victor was no mere batsman of impulsive genius; he hit the ball with the middle of the bat's blade — even when he pulled from the middle stump round to square leg.'

Back in the relative calm of the dressingroom, Victor was swamped by teammates. Backslapping, laughing and joking, the players knew they had just witnessed the greatest innings in Test history.

During lunch, the sun and the chill wind combined to give the drying pitch added life. Trumper, refreshed after a hearty meal, took a single off Lockwood, then faced Rhodes. The ball was now turning quite spitefully. He played each Rhodes delivery with great care. Then off the fifth ball of Rhodes' eleventh over, Trumper stepped across to back cut. The ball spun and Trumper got a thick outside edge, only to see Lilley shoot out his right glove instinctively and the ball stuck. Australia 2/175 and a brilliant innings was brought to the end by a miraculous catch. Trumper was out for 104. He had batted for 115 minutes, with 14 fours. (Two of those fours would have been sixes today as they cleared the sightscreen over bowler Rhodes' head.)

Monty Noble joined Hill and Rhodes soon deceived Noble into hitting back a return catch. Noble out for 2 and Australia 3/179. Syd Gregory joined Hill and he went soon after, again cutting at Rhodes, as did Trumper, and giving a catch to the ever-reliable Lilley — Australia 4/183! Since lunch the Australians had lost Trumper, Noble and Gregory for just 10 runs. MacLaren was starting to breathe more easily.

Skipper Joe Darling joined Hill and immediately he began to attack Rhodes, whose sharp away turn to the right-handers was not so effective to left-handers Hill and Darling. Rhodes had previously worried Darling with his arm ball, the one which goes on straight with the arm. However, Trumper had told Darling how to pick that particular delivery and Darling said stoutly: 'Why, Vic, I'll hit him out of the ground.'

That was no idle boast, for on the fifth ball of Rhodes' 18th over, Darling put one foot down the wicket and smacked Rhodes right out of the ground — for six!

To score a six in those days a player had to hit the ball right out of the ground, not merely over the boundary on the full.

The mammoth, soaring drive went clean out of Old Trafford, landing near the Warwick Rd. railway station. Hill and Darling picked up their ones and twos and Darling was severe on Rhodes again, twice cracking the left-hander over the covers for four. Darling reasoned that offence was the best way to unsettle the left-handed Yorkshireman. Then, in Rhodes' 21st over, Darling again lofted Rhodes out of Old Trafford. The crowd was delirious. Such a batting feast and the bowling had been good, especially as 'mere mortals' were being pitted against the England attack after Trumper left the scene. During the Darling-Rhodes duel, Hill was quietly picking up his runs, and he clipped Rhodes forward of square for 3 to bring up his 50.

MacLaren was worried. The partnership was looking ominous for England. He decided to bring back Lockwood and immediately the big paceman struck. Hill attempted to drive Lockwood on the rise and succeeded only in hitting a gentle catch to Rhodes at mid-off. Australia 5/256; Hill 65. Albert Hopkins joined Darling and didn't last out

Members of the Kent Eleven v. Australia at Canterbury, 21 August 1902.

Lockwood's over. Hopkins got a short one and fended it away on the on side, only to see Palairet move in quickly to accept the catch. Australia 6/256; Hopkins 0. Warwick Armstrong played pluckily with his skipper, who was still having a battle royale with Rhodes. But when the pair had put on an invaluable 32, Armstrong lost his middle stump to a Lockwood yorker. Australia 7/288. Darling was intent on continuing his onslaught upon Rhodes but was running out of partners. Lockwood was bowling like the wind and Darling knew that the end was nigh. James Kelly was with him when Darling attempted another big hit off the tireless Rhodes and the ball ballooned gently to a grateful Archie MacLaren at mid-off. Australia 8/292.

Rhodes smiled. He had bowled manfully, having to withstand the genius of Trumper and the belligerent Darling. Yet his 23 overs had so far brought him 4/99. The fiery Lockwood quickly disposed of Hugh Trumble, caught low down at slip by Fred Tate for 0, and Jack Saunders had his off stump knocked back for 3. Australia all out 299. Lockwood had taken 5/8 in his final spell of 8.1 overs and Rhodes finished with 4/104 off 25 overs. Lockwood's final analysis was 6/48 off 20.1 overs.

The England openers Lionel Palairet and Bobby Abel reached the crease at 5.15pm. They were apprehensive of having to endure three quarters of an hour's batting on what was now a horror batting strip. Hugh Trumble and Jack Saunders were itching to get at the England openers. Immediately, the Australian bowlers troubled the Englishmen. The ball rose disconcertingly from the wicket and on a number of occasions both batsmen popped deliveries in the air close to a fieldsman. Palairet and Abel found Saunders the more difficult of the two bowlers. Trumble was varying his pace and flight well, but Saunders' slanting approach and his habit of hiding his hand behind his back until just prior to delivery confused them. Saunders struck first, having Abel

Surrey and England opener Bobby Abel. He and Trumper fought a discreet race throughout 1902 to be the first to reach 1000 runs. Trumper won and went on to tally 2570 for the tour. (*C B Fry*)

caught by Armstrong at first slip. The ball reared and struck the top edge of Abel's bat and flew straight to the reliable hands of Armstrong. England 1/12. Worse was to follow when Palairet cracked a ball up from Saunders and the ball flew gently into the safe hands of Noble at backward point. England 2/13. Skipper Archie MacLaren joined his compatriot Johnny Tyldesley. The England hopes rose. MacLaren took a single off Saunders then faced Trumble. He played forward to drive a perfect Trumble off-break and the ball found the gap between bat and pad and crashed into MacLaren's middle and off stumps. Disaster. England 3/14. The Australians were overjoyed. The crowd became almost silent, a great contrast to their earlier shouts of joy especially during the 115-minute reign of Trumper. Ranjitsinhji replaced MacLaren and, with the score at 30 and the innings just 35 minutes old, Ranji played back to Trumble and was found to be out, palpably lbw. England 4/30. The Australian bowlers were very much on top, although 14 runs came in just 15 minutes before Tyldesley cut Saunders high over gully and was caught by the ever-alert Hopkins at third-man. Had the ball been placed a yard either side of Hopkins it would have been a boundary. No such luck this time; Tyldesley out for 22 and England 5/44.

England was in tatters. Jackson and Len Braund fought bravely. Stumps were mercifully drawn while they were still there, Jackson (16) and Braund (13), with England five for 70.

Thursday, 24 July: 'Wet wicket. Fourth Test. Won toss, made 299. Self 104, RAD 50. 1st W 135. England 5 for 70. Tate 1st Test. Fire G Peak and Coy.'

The Australians took the field on the second day hoping for an early breakthrough. A fine day followed a clear night; perfect for cricket on the highest plane. The wicket responded gratefully (for the batsmen) to Mother Nature's kinder side and by the time Jackson and Braund resumed batting, the pitch was considerably firmer than it had been the previous evening. Trumble and Saunders bowled strongly. Runs were hard to come by, but the Australians couldn't break the stand. There was no glut of runs in the sensational style of Trumper in that unforgettable century before lunch, but Jackson and Braund were displaying plenty of grit and fed on ones, twos and the occasional boundary. Jackson survived a sharp return chance to Saunders, when Saunders juggled the ball and finally, to the dismay of Darling's side, turfed it. That miss would prove costly. Jackson brought up his 50 in 105 minutes and he still had staunch ally Braund with him. Darling made a double switch in the attack, replacing Trumble with Noble and bringing in the accurate leg-spin of Armstrong for Saunders. Braund immediately took to Armstrong, belting four boundaries off the big Victorian in one hectic over. Armstrong had seven men on the leg side, but Braund hit with the tide and pierced the gaps on every occasion.

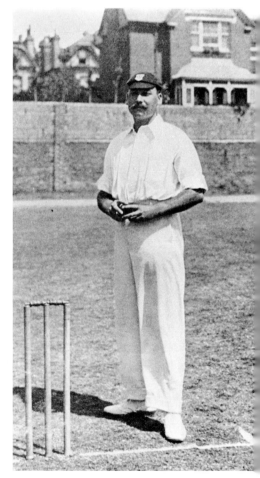

The luckless Fred Tate, English fast bowler and father of Maurice, whose Test career started and ended at Old Trafford when Trumper hit his blazing century before lunch. (*C B Fry*)

That flurry of big hitting brought Braund his well-deserved 50. At 58 he stunned the crowd and partner Stanley Jackson, with a dreadful swipe at Noble. Jackson frowned, walked down the wicket and gave Braund a quiet word, for having perpetrated a stroke which would have brought red faces to the most unorthodox batsman on the village green.

Noble was beginning to frustrate Braund with his guile and deceptive change of pace. It was no surprise when Braund played a Noble delivery onto his wicket just five minutes before lunch. Braund had made 65 and at lunch England was 6 for 186, with Jackson 78 not out. Upon resumption of play, Dick Lilley lurched forward to drive Noble and lost his leg stump. England 7 for 203. Fast bowler Lockwood joined Jackson and, when on 92, Jackson cut Noble like a rocket to Duff at short third man. It was Lockwood's call, but Jackson was slow to respond, despite Duff's misfield. The England pair found themselves stranded in mid-pitch. Lockwood decided to sacrifice his wicket, thus saving Jackson, as Duff recovered and fired the ball fast and low back to Kelly. England had slumped to 8 for 214. The crowd gave Lockwood a resounding cheer as he walked off, acknowledging the paceman's 'supreme sacrifice', in laying down his wicket for that of his fellow batsman.

Rhodes, the dour Yorkshireman, then joined Jackson. A Yorkshire double. Stubbornly the pair kept the scoreboard ticking over, albeit slowly. Jackson then turned Noble gently forward of square leg to bring up his century. Jackson's ton came in 235 minutes, his third Test century and perhaps the most valuable he had scored for England. Rhodes continued to play straight and sensibly, but when Trumble was brought back into the attack he immediately struck gold. Trumble deceived Rhodes with a slower delivery, which Rhodes managed to loft straight back down the pitch and was gratefully accepted by a gleeful Trumble. England 9 for 235.

Test debutant Fred Tate, whose selection over the talented George Hirst displeased many critics, came to the crease with the stern instruction from MacLaren, 'stay with Jacker'. With Tate's arrival,

Jackson threw all caution to the wind and hit out at every ball. Tate somehow survived. When on 123, Jackson slashed Noble to Gregory at backward point. To Noble's horror and the crowd's delight, Gregory dropped the chance and the England pair stole a single. That single brought Jackson to face Trumble. A thundering off-drive brought him another boundary. Trumble tossed the next ball up a little higher and shorter and Jackson hit it high and hard towards the fleet-footed Duff at deep mid-wicket. Duff completed a fine catch and Jackson was out for 128. England had made a great recovery, from being 5 for 70 overnight, the Lion's middle-order and tail wagged vigorously for it to finish with a respectable 262, only 37 runs behind the Australian first innings.

Once again Trumper and Duff bestrode Old Trafford. This session of play was vital for Darling's men. They could not afford to falter, but needed to score at a good rate to give their bowlers time to bowl England out a second time. MacLaren's men had been given a big morale boost by the courageous batting of Jackson and Braund. This pair had turned the match around. MacLaren decided to use his fast man, Lockwood, first up. The approaches, unlike the first day, were now firm and dry.

MacLaren urged Lockwood to give his all; to bowl flat out for a brief but torrid spell. Trumper was the man MacLaren wanted out of the way early. England could ill-afford another Trumper innings of genius. That would demoralise the England attack and make things easy for the rest of the Australians. A mis-hit from a delivery which skipped off this firmer and quicker pitch was what MacLaren hoped for when Trumper faced Lockwood. Len Braund was given first use of the ball. He bowled a superb over to Trumper, making the great man play at every ball. A maiden to Trumper set the pattern. Lockwood was keen to get into the action and perhaps MacLaren giving Braund first use of the new ball had the desired effect to fire the big paceman. Lockwood paced out his run and, with an attacking field of three slips, a gully, and short forward and backward legs, he moved in menacingly from the Warwick Rd. end.

Duff turned the first ball quietly away to square leg for an easy single, bringing the incomparable Trumper on strike. Lockwood to Trumper. The first ball was an outswinger of express pace. Trumper moved back and across and watched the ball climb steeply outside the off stump and thud into Lilley's gloves. Trumper immediately realised that Lockwood posed the greatest threat to the Australian batsmen. The wicket was firm and fast and Lockwood was in a fiery mood. Trumper decided to do what he did best, to attack from the outset. Next ball was another fast delivery, but it pitched just short of a length and Trumper moved rapidly into position and pulled the ball from outside the off stump through the mid-wicket area for a superb boundary.

The crowd cheered the Trumper shot. Young Neville Cardus wondered whether he would be lucky enough to witness another innings of pure genius. Others in the Old Trafford crowd had mixed feelings. They all wanted an England victory, but Trumper's batsmanship bridged loyalties; the most partisan or parochial marvelled at the batting of Trumper. Could Old Trafford see another innings of the quality Trumper dished up on that epic first day?

Perhaps that was too much to ask. The best champagne cannot be bettered and, indeed, the crowd was thunderstruck after Lockwood delivered the very next ball. Delivered at lightning pace, an outswinger, just short of a length but in range for a Trumper cut, the great man moved into position with characteristic speed. He cut, but misjudged the pace and managed only to hit the ball to Braund at second slip, the ball skidding along the ground. No run. No danger to Trumper. But that delivery made Trumper hurry his shot. Was this a sign of things to come?

Braund conceded two runs to Duff next over. Duff had whipped the ball off his pads through the mid-wicket area. Braund was as economical as Lockwood was fast, providing Lockwood with good support.

Once more Trumper faced the pace of Lockwood. A steam train whistle broke the icy atmosphere as Lockwood charged in from the Warwick Rd. end. Three deliveries swept past Trumper, but all three were wide of the mark and Trumper allowed them to pass through to Lilley. MacLaren moved from mid-off to speak with his paceman. Trumper stood and looked about the field. He saw gaps on the off side; a cut would be productive.

Lockwood adjusted his trousers and checked his sprigs. Any excuse for having suddenly become wayward in direction. He steamed in once again to Trumper. The fast rising ball was within range for a Trumper cut, however, it climbed steeply. Again Trumper attempted a cut. He hit it late and the ball flew like a bullet to Braund at second slip. This time Braund latched onto the ball but lost control and the ball spiralled towards first slip. Braund kept his eye on it. The crowd waited and

'Australians on the Pot'; an amusing postcard from the 1902 tour. (*Charles Trumper*)

watched in stunned silence. Braund leapt to his left and brought off the catch. Trumper smiled as if to say; 'well bowled; well caught' and walked briskly from the arena.

The vital breakthrough had been effected; Trumper out for 4, Australia one for 7. MacLaren rushed up to Lockwood and Braund. The Englishmen were obviously delighted. They had just removed the biggest threat to their getting right back on top in this vital Test. Lockwood smiled contentedly. MacLaren had obviously given him great encouragement. As if he needed any boost. After all, Lockwood had just dismissed the most brilliant batsman in the world.

England was very much back in the game. Worse was to follow for Australia. Lockwood had his tail up and he bowled like the wind. It would take some staunch defence to keep the big paceman at bay. Minutes later Duff played an awkward looking backward defensive shot to a Lockwood off-cutter. Duff managed to get a thick inside edge and drag the ball back onto his stumps. Australia 2 for 9. Duff scored just 3 runs. He had looked composed, but the loss of Trumper may have unsettled the moustachioed little opener.

Joe Darling joined an unusually tentative Clem Hill. It was no surprise to see Hill fall to Lockwood, having his off stump uprooted by a ball of blistering pace. The delivery pitched outside Hill's off stump and cut back alarmingly, piercing the gap between bat and pad. Hill went for a duck and Australia was in a precarous position at 3 for 10, just 47 runs ahead of England on a good firm pitch.

Lockwood's inspired spell of great pace had suddenly swung the match England's way. The crowd began to find its voice. England was on the road to victory. Darling was the man of the moment. A tough, uncompromising character, Joe Darling knew what was required. When Duff fell Darling filled the breach, coming in before Monty Noble, who had batted No. 4 in the first innings. Darling thought that if there was to be a collapse, then Noble was the man best suited to halt the slaughter. Noble was listed to come in at the fall of the fourth wicket and Syd Gregory, a batsman of great skill and technically a fine player, retained the No. 5 spot. A man of action, who loved nothing more in cricket than carrying the attack to the bowlers, especially the spinners, Darling rolled up his sleeves for the battle ahead. He knew instinctively that Australia must hit its way out of trouble. Darling and Gregory had added six runs when Darling faced the last ball of a Braund over.

Knowing Darling's penchant for hitting hard and high with the spin, Braund suggested to his skipper that Palairet should move over to deep square leg. Palairet was a specialist deep fielder and was always stationed in that position for Braund's bowling when playing for Somerset. MacLaren looked long and hard at Braund. The temerity of the man. Had Australia not been playing against a country where class was very much in vogue, this Test match may have finished long before it eventually did come to an exciting end. There were the professionals (those individuals who made their living from playing first-class cricket) and the gentlemen (players who played the game at the highest level, but had means and were not dependent on any remuneration from the game). Palairet, after all, was a gentleman.

'Surely you don't expect me to ask Lionel Palairet to run right across Old Trafford for one ball?' MacLaren said to Braund. MacLaren then looked furtively about the field. His eyes focussed on poor old Fred

Tate, the chubby medium-pacer MacLaren did not want in the side but picked in a fit of pique when the selectors (a body of which he was part) wanted Tate if the wicket was likely to be wet. Now, Tate was a useful slip field but his bulk precluded him from running the boundary in anything resembling athletic fashion. Tate was sent into the outfield. Braund was none too happy, but there was just one ball to finish his over; maybe Darling would not go for a big hit. Braund tossed it up and Darling came forward and swung lustily. He did not quite get to the pitch of the ball and hit it high in the direction of deep square leg. Palairet watched in horror from cover.

As fate would have it, Tate completely misjudged the ball. It spiralled towards him and Tate ran forward in a sort of awkward gait. Only a fleet-footed, experienced outfielder such as a Trumper, a Hill or a Palairet could have effected such a catch. As for Fred Tate, well, he needed more than a fair share of luck. The ball completely beat Tate, although in a final, desperate lunge he managed to get his left hand to it, only to see it drop safely. The crowd groaned its agony, MacLaren looked at Palairet and cursed his poor judgement. Palairet shrugged his shoulders. The Australian score had stood at 16 when Darling played that shot. Amazingly it was Tate who finally broke the Darling-Gregory partnership when he trapped Gregory palpably lbw with a good off-cutter, Gregory playing back and across. But Gregory had scored 24 and Australia had reached 64. At stumps Australia was struggling at 8 for 85 and only rain could help turn the game.

Friday, 25 July: 'England 262. Jackson 122. Bowlers done badly. Australia 8 for 85. Things gloomy. Darling 37. Refused admission theatre.'

Thankfully for Australia, Manchester lived up to its dreadful reputation for turning on bad weather. The heavens opened up and the rain came down in torrents, saturating the uncovered wicket at the centre of the famous Old Trafford ground. Hugh Trumble woke. He opened the window and searched the horizon. Rain spattered the window sill. Trumble licked his lips. It took just 15 minutes for England to finish off the Australian innings. All out for 86. Lockwood (5/28) did most of the damage, but he had manful support from Rhodes (3/26) and Tate (2/7). England needed just 124 runs for victory, a task well within their reach.

MacLaren and Palairet were keen to attack. The wicket was still damp although, as the sun remained, it would become increasingly more difficult for the England batsmen. Trumble and Noble opened for Australia, anxious to get Darling a much-needed early breakthrough. There were some close calls, but as well as the Australian pair bowled, the England openers survived. After 50 minutes they had built a total of 36, needing only 88 runs for victory and all ten wickets in hand.

During the luncheon interval, MacLaren breezed up to Darling and said cheekily: 'Ah, Joe, I think we've got you this time.'

Darling smiled and between gritted teeth muttered: 'Oh, have you, we've only to get two or three of you out and the rest will shiver with fright.' Brave words by a skipper whose team was facing almost certain defeat — and a heavy defeat it appeared. But Darling knew he led a champion team. His men would not give up the ghost.

Jack Saunders replaced the hard-working Noble and at 44, Saunders got the vital wicket of Palairet, who lost his off stump to an in-swinging

Presentation time for the winning Australians at the Canterbury game versus Kent in August.

yorker. John Tyldesley joined MacLaren. Tyldesley had a narrow escape almost immediately, cocking a chance in Syd Gregory's direction at forward short leg off Trumble's bowling. Gregory missed the chance as he dived valiantly forward, but that Trumble 'kicker' sounded an ominous warning for England. Certainly Tyldesley decided to hit out, to not be caught by the short field as he fended deliveries away from his body. In 14 minutes he had raced to 16. Meantime MacLaren added eight. Minutes later Tyldesley tapped too often at Saunders outside the off stump and steered the ball straight to Armstrong at slip.

England 2 for 68. While the Englishmen had no cause to panic, Darling's men strove for a miracle. Another couple of quick wickets and Darling's lunch-time remark to MacLaren could still become reality. MacLaren welcomed Ranjitsinhji's occupation of the crease by driving Trumble handsomely to the off for four. The cagey Trumble had set his trap. Next ball he tossed higher and shorter and deceived MacLaren in flight. The England skipper hit with the spin but straight down Duff's throat at deep mid-on. Trumble's first victim of the innings brought the Australians together. England had lost 3 for 72, still no need to worry on their part, but the Aussies thought they had a glimmer of hope.

Trumble was bowling around the wicket. His off-spinners were turning prodigiously and he believed he had a better chance of gaining an lbw decision by 'straightening' a delivery to a right-hander from around the wicket. The veteran Surrey opener, Bobby Abel, joined Ranji and immediately assumed the role of 'senior partner'. Abel made some telling blows, twice belting Trumble for four, one massive hit over mid-on just beat Clem Hill's outstretched left hand before crashing into the crowd. Alas only four in those days.

Meantime, Ranji was all at sea. Darling sensed the Indian Prince's discomfort. He crowded Ranji with two short legs — one forward, one backward — when Trumble was operating. After two raucous and unsuccessful appeals for lbw, the umpire finally upheld Trumble's third demand for blood. Ranji out for a scratchy 4 and England was 4 for 92.

Abel soon departed, attempting to drive Trumble and being clean bowled between a huge gap he had left between bat and pad. It was the sort of delivery England's Jim Laker bowled so beautifully on a treacherous turner on this very ground some 54 years later. England 5 for 97; Abel's contribution being an invaluable 21. Another few overs of Abel in that mood would have sewn it up for England.

Braund and Jackson took the score along to 107 — almost there! Then Jackson received a rare gift. It came in the form of a Trumble full-toss. No-one was more surprised than Jackson. His eyes lit up and he slammed the full pitcher hard and to the right of Gregory at cover point. Trumble prayed that the boundary be averted. Miraculously Gregory flung himself to his right and the ball stuck in his outstretched hand. It was as if Providcence had decided to help; England 6 for 107 and the Australians were united with the one thought: 'We can win it, now.' Those back in the England dressingroom gnashed their teeth. Stomachs became tight balls of tension. Few could have countenanced any problem getting the runs as they ate their cold salmon at lunch, now doubt was written on every worried frown. Jackson's wicket was a big bonus for the Australians. As one they had converged on Syd Gregory. He had muffed a relatively easy catch earlier in the day at short leg. Now he had brought off a brilliant capture.

Trumble was bowling like a man possessed. The wicket was still taking a great deal of spin, but Trumble mixed up his deliveries skilfully. He beat Braund with a straight one, then spun one between bat and pad. As Braund lunged forward the ball cleared the top of middle and leg stumps, but Braund had lifted his toe. Kelly had the bails off in a flash and the umpire raised his finger in unison with the frantic appeal. England 7 for 109.

England's fast bowling hero Lockwood hit out in frustration at Trumble. Here was a man who had set up an England win as match figures of 11/76 would testify. Then he had to endure the good start by MacLaren and Palairet, only to watch Trumble cast an 'evil' spell over the cream of English batsmanship. That frustrated lunge by Lockwood saw him out, clean bowled Trumble. England 8 for 109.

The tension was tremendous. Keeper Lilley and Wilfred Rhodes were in to somehow see England home. Rhodes began the more confident of the two. He met most deliveries with the full face of the bat and showed it wasn't all defence by cracking Saunders high over mid-on for four. With just eight runs for an England win, Lilley hit Trumble with the spin over the square leg umpire's head. The ball was struck with immense power and was heading for rope at deep square leg. The crowd cheered what appeared a certain boundary. But they and Lilley had not figured on the athletic figure of Clem Hill. Immediately the ball was hit, Hill took off at breakneck speed. He ran some 30 metres from his position at deep backward square leg, determined to cut off the boundary. Hill dived at the ball which was about to career over the fence, only to find the red sphere had stuck. Two brilliant catches in the day, but this one infinitely better. After a series of somersaults, a deliriously delighted Hill held the ball aloft for all to behold. Old Trafford gaped in stunned silence. It was if the Empire had collapsed. Then the crowd cheered, as well they might. It was the catch of the century; who knows, maybe the greatest catch in Test match history. England 9 for 116 and very much on the ropes.

Fred Tate, the hope of the side, joined Rhodes. Many spectators bemoaned Tate's clumsy effort in dropping Darling the day before. Were England to lose, they would lay the blame squarely in Tate's lap. For had Tate caught Darling, England would surely be now toasting victory. It was just after 4pm. Then the skies opened. Play stopped for a nerve-wracking forty minutes. MacLaren paced the England dressingroom, Darling sat and watched the heavens. He was worried that Trumble might not be able to grip the wet ball. He knew Saunders must finish it, if only Trumble could keep Rhodes quiet. The tension sapped at the players' reserves of nervous energy. They were all physically and mentally at the point of exhaustion. Play resumed at 4.45pm. Rhodes faced Trumble. Tight bowling and eager fielding won that strategic battle against Rhodes. Now it was up to Jack Saunders to dismiss Tate. Saunders took his time. The ball was wet. Every time Rhodes had played a Trumble delivery the players rushed to field the ball; desperate not to expose the ball to any more wet grass than necessary.

Saunders used sawdust and a rag to wipe the ball, standing with legs astride, taking note of Darling's field placement. His instruction was to bowl straight. If the Australians were nervous, spare a thought for poor Fred Tate. He knew that few people wanted him in the England Eleven. He was castigated in the press and suffered brutally at the hands of the crowd, many of whom regarded Tate to be no more than a poor man's George Hirst and one wag said: 'Aye, an' a very poor 'un at that.' Saunders to Tate. A quick delivery on Tate's middle and leg stumps was almost the perfect ball, but somehow Tate got his bat to it. The ball skidded off Tate's bat and scuttled down to fine leg, through the legs of Duff. The batsmen ran one, two and finally three as Armstrong, who had run from first slip, loomed over the ball. Rhodes was content with three, but the Australian fieldsmen hoped the ball would beat Armstrong to the fence, thus leaving the vulnerable Tate on strike. Armstrong flung himself headlong, but the ball beat him across the boundary. England was four short of victory.

Could Tate do it? Certainly another shot like that one, might restore Tate to favor. Saunders rubbed the ball vigorously with a dry cloth. He moved in and bowled, only to see Tate move forward and present a perfect forward defensive shot. No run. England 9 for 120. Darling moved over to Saunders and gave him an encouraging word. He suggested that Saunders bowl flat out. 'Give it a go, Jack. Bowl quick and straight. That will sort him out.' Saunders moved in and let fly. Tate moved forward again with his bat as ramrod straight as any produced in this epic Test match. He was, however, too late — the ball had crashed into his middle and leg stumps, sending one cartwheeling crazily towards a beaming and dancing James Kelly behind the stumps.

The scenes were incredible. The Australians whooped and hugged one another. They had won a famous Test by three runs, having snatched victory from the veritable jaws of defeat.

It took England 80 years to appease that defeat, when Bob Willis' England side beat Greg Chappell's team at Melbourne in December, 1982. Thanks to a memorable last-wicket stand by Allan Border and Jeff Thomson the game came alive when England had it all but won. Then Thomson was caught at slip off Ian Botham's bowling. England won by three runs. Archie MacLaren would have smiled. That Old Trafford Test had everything. Perhaps all-over performances were overshadowed by the genius of Trumper. His brilliant 104 in the Australian first innings will live forever in the history of great Test match knocks.

This was Trumper at the height of his powers, at the very pinnacle of his genius. And Australia could be justly proud of the old war-horse, Hugh Trumble. He took 10/128 off 68 overs. A magnificent toiler, Trumble always went about his work manfully. On the field he played it hard, but off the green sward Trumble was a great practical joker and revelled in telling the new chums of 1902 tales of his previous tours to the Mother Country. Clem Hill's first innings 65, plus that miracle catch to dismiss Lilley, stood out like beacons, as did Joe Darling's fine, aggressive double of 51 and 37, plus some astute captaincy. In addition, Jack Saunders bowled well, especially in the England second innings. It was Saunders who broke the MacLaren-Palairet stand. And it was Saunders who finished off Fred Tate's Test career, with the ball which won a famous Test by three runs. Saunders finished the match with 7/156 off 53.4 overs.

Stanley Jackson's marvellous first innings 128 and Lockwood's brilliant bursts of genuine pace all paled into relative insignificance with the England defeat. Fred Tate copped it sweet. Tate scored 5 not out and was bowled by Saunders for 4 in the second innings. But then few number elevens are expected to hit many runs. After suffering at the hands of Trumper (0 for 44 off 11 overs) in the Australian first innings, Tate bounced back to grab 2/7 off five tidy overs to help Rhodes and Lockwood rout Australia for 86 in their second dig. But Tate did drop Darling. He was the scapegoat. After the match Tate was in tears. He sobbed: 'I've a little lad at home who'll make up for that.'

And he was right: twenty-two years later Maurice Tate burst onto the scene. Maurice became a great bowler, taking 155 Test wickets in 39 Tests, hitting 1,198 runs at 25.48, including one Test match century. As for Fred Tate, well, that Old Trafford Test was his first and last. Fred, or 'Chubby', Tate, played for Sussex from 1887 to 1905, taking 1,331 wickets at 21.55, hitting 2,891 runs at 10.17 and grabbing 216 catches in all first-class matches. The Australians are thankful to Tate for one 'catch' that was never added to that total.

After a hearty meal and some jovial camaraderie, Victor Trumper and Monty Noble went to the theatre in Manchester. They were naturally in good spirits. When Victor returned to his hotel, he wrote in his diary:

Saturday, 26 July: 'Won by three runs. Australia 86, England 120. MacL (MacLaren) 35. Theatre Knowles . . . glorious time.'

As Trumper and Noble stepped out of the theatre there was a small boy, no older than eight years old selling sheets of music. He stood

An unsourced newspaper clipping of Trumper from the 1902 tour.

under a gas lamp, which struggled to light the cobbled street as the fog and light rain hampered visibility. A hansom cab arrived at Noble's beckoning. Just before he clambered aboard, Trumper asked the driver to wait on. Victor strolled over to the boy, who stood shivering in the lamplight, the rain beating gently on his young face. Without uttering a sound, Victor put out his hand. He gave the boy a coin and took every sheet of music. The boy cried in delight and skipped down the street. Victor got into the cab without uttering another word. To Noble it was as if Trumper had been oblivious to what had transpired. No more was said of it, although Monty Noble never forgot Victor's gesture, that foggy night — the night Australia won a famous Test by three runs.

The celebrations continued well into the night at the Australian's Manchester hotel. Victor went to bed relatively early, although his comrades drank heartily into the small hours. The cold hard light of day found more than a few of Darling's revellers much the worse for wear.

Sunday, 27 July: 'Left for London. Done out of compartment by women. All (Victor's comrades) have sore heads.'

Having been 'done out of compartment by women' would probably raise more than a few eyebrows among the feminists in the modern era. Yet even in 1902, Darling's men, most of whom were suffering withdrawal symptoms from the victory toasts the night before, managed reluctant smiles of virtual defeat when — upon their late arrival at the station — they found their compartment taken over by a group of young ladies from an elite London finishing school. Perhaps they were too 'ill' to argue and the Australians crammed into a series of compartments on the train bound for London.

The epic win at Old Trafford gave Darling's men the Ashes, but few of his men were looking forward to fronting up next day for the encounter with Essex at Leyton. As luck would have it, Darling lost the toss and Essex batted on a dampish wicket. Although it was moist, the wicket played truly enough. The Australian bowlers and fieldsmen struggled to regain their mental toughness. The Manchester Test took a great deal out of them, both mentally and physically. Groans of dismay greeted Darling when he walked into the dressingroom just before the Australians took the field. Darling smiled. The men had done their job well at Old Trafford. It would not hurt his men to relax mentally.

Trumble again did the lion's share of the bowling, sending down 49 immaculate overs of clever off-spin for a return of 3/97, while 'Jonah', who had been pipped for a Test spot by the Victorian left-armer Jack Saunders, bowled enthusiastically and very fast. 'Jonah' was rewarded with 5/50 from 27.1 overs. However, the Australian fielding seemed slapdash in comparison to the sterling efforts at Old Trafford, where Darling's darlings bowled and fielded like demons.

Monday, 28 July: 'Essex ... all dog tired. Lost toss. Fielded all day. Too tired to go out at night. Wrote a couple of letters. Fixed up room.'

Next day the Leyton crowd was held spellbound by an innings of such brilliance that gasps of awe preceded every thrilling stroke. In 90 minutes Trumper cut, drove, hooked and pulled the Essex attack in a magical and masterly display of batting. Trumper employed every conceivable shot in the text book, along with a few that only he could play with effortless ease. The Essex players appeared as delighted with Trumper's display as the admiring crowd. A handsome Trumper off-drive off Walter Mead brought resounding applause from the Essex

Eleven. Eventually Trumper lost his off stump to a perfectly pitched Mead leg-cutter; pitching leg and hitting off. A wag in the crowd suggested that the Mead delivery was unplayable. Another spectator was more to the point: 'If Trumper couldn't play it, that ball was unplayable.'

Tuesday, 29 July: 'Selected J Searle's bat before breakfast. Went to Oxford. Good Show. Made 109, Fielded again 5 to 6. Side over 100 to lead.'

Essex continued on next day to score 3 for 184 before they declared — an overall lead of 297. When the Australians began their second innings they needed 298 runs to win in 170 minutes. Trumper again flayed the Essex attack, but not before he had meandered almost nonchalantly to his first 50, without really cutting loose, as was his custom. After reaching the half-century, Trumper blitzed Essex to such an extent that he was out (lbw to medium-pacer Bill Reeves at 5.40pm for 119 — his second brilliant century of the match. Apart from Clem Hill (59) none of the other Australian batsmen showed anything near their true form. Even Trumper was critical of his own 119, when he wrote in his diary that evening:

Wednesday, 30 July: 'Essex declared. Scratching made 119 2nd innings. 1st time done by an Australian (referring to his feat in scoring a century in each innings of a match in England). Got out 20 to 6. Draw . . . left for Brighton. Arrived 11pm.'

Remarkably, Trumper referred to his innings as 'scratching'. That gives us an insight into the way he saw how he should bat. It was not enough to score runs; the manner in which those runs were accumulated must have been paramount to him. The Australians were 6 for 253 at stumps, just 45 runs short of their target.

On Trumper's first tour of England (1899), Sussex was the county team which suffered most from the young maestro's bat. He hit a

County games against the Australians had a festive atmosphere with marquees, tea and buns, straw boaters and ladies' picture hats. The sign at bottom left reads: 'This tent reserved exclusively for Zingari and their friends by invitation.'

magnificent 300 not out in that match, also played at Hove. It had a quality about it which prompted captain Joe Darling to say: 'I thought I could bat until I saw Victor play today.' That innings proved to be Trumper's highest first-class score. Now three years later, Trumper returned to Hove. Sussex included Albert Relf, a clever swing bowler, who later toured Australia under Pelham Warner in 1903-4. In addition there was 'Chubby' Fred Tate, who was still suffering a mental hangover from taunts over his performance at Old Trafford in his first and what was to prove his last Test match.

The Australians were pleased that Darling won the toss and had no hesitation to bat on what appeared to be a firm, true pitch. Trumper and Duff scored briskly. They helped themselves to a boundary each off Tate and the 50 partnership came in just 29 minutes, before Trumper dragged a wide ball onto his stumps. Relf had struck a mighty blow for Sussex. The likes of Tate and Charles Fry were elated. They had played in the previous tour match where Trumper had reigned supreme with that marvellous triple century. Monty Noble and Warwick Armstrong came together to rescue Darling's men after the side had slumped to 5/152. By stumps Australia was 5/352.

Thursday, 31 July: 'Won toss, wicket funny. Made 21. MAN (Noble), and WWA (Armstrong) making score. Had a great loaf all day. Saw more of Burgless Minstrels.'

If Trumper managed a long, lazy day in the dressingroom that first day, more was to follow. Noble and Armstrong thrashed Sussex, hitting an Australian sixth wicket partnership of 428 with Noble stumped for 284 and Armstrong unconquered on 172. Darling called a halt to the slaughter at 5/580. Relf was the best of Sussex bowlers with 4/142 off 54 overs and poor old Fred Tate suffered again, having 136 runs taken from his 41 fruitless overs. The Sussex batsmen struggled and the side was 2/71 at stumps, having lost Fry, caught by Kelly behind off 'Jonah' for 39. Ranjitsinhji, although still there, was struggling to find touch.

Friday, 1 August: 'Batted well. 4.15 (Time Darling declared) MAN out 284, WWA not 172. Side 550. They. Fry out 30. Went to Music Hall. Still have record.'

Those final three words entered in his diary seem incongruous for a man universally known to be thoroughly modest and self-effacing. For one can do no more than to interpret the line to mean that despite Noble and Armstrong's mammoth scores and both having had fine tours with the bat (and ball), Victor Thomas Trumper still holds the record for the most number of Test centuries by an Australian on a tour of England and the record aggregate number of runs.

Sussex was dismissed for 185, with Ernest Jones getting 3/71 off 33 overs and Jack Saunders chiming in with 4/22 off 12.1 overs. A second time Sussex scored 1/130 and the game petered out into a draw. Darling's bowlers merely went through their paces. Armstrong didn't bowl, Trumble bowled only five overs and the likes of Duff and Hill had a turn at the crease.

Saturday, 2 August: 'Fielded all day. Sussex 170 odd. Ranji 19. Followed on. Fry out. Draw. Side left for London. Standing down. JD (Darling) also. Went to pier, heard band.'

So while the rest of the team went on to play Glamorgan and Wiltshire at Cardiff, Trumper and Darling took advantage of their game off by staying in Brighton. They would rejoin the team at

The master gives himself plenty of room as he prepares to drive a ball. In 1902, over the fence was only worth four runs. To score six, a batsman had to hit the ball right out of the ground. Trumper obliged on a number of occasions.

Southampton for the two-day match again Hampshire. The team itinerary was altered slightly to cater for the Coronation of King Edward VII, scheduled to take place on the eve of the Fifth Test, August 9. The Australians were eagerly looking forward to that Royal event, as the touring party were to have special seats to watch the Coronation at Westminster Abbey. Cutting one day off each of the remaining two games before the final Test would enable Darling's men time to see the Coronation.

Sunday, 3 August: 'Went down to pier and heard band on promenade. Windy and cold.'

Monday, 4 August: 'Monday, pier. Heard band, Devil's Dyke in afternoon. On pier at night.'

Tuesday, 5 August: 'Swim. Heard band. Bus ride to Chalk Cliffs of Old England. Band 11.30, 3.30. 7.45.'

Meanwhile the Australians, under the captaincy of Hugh Trumble, were giving Glamorgan and Wiltshire a drubbing, winning comfortably by six wickets, thanks to Armstrong's 7/36 off 19.4 overs in the home side's second innings.

The Australians, minus Trumper and Darling, spent a free-day at Cardiff before boarding the train for Southampton, where their two comrades would already be settled into the team hotel.

Wednesday, 6 August: 'Left for Southampton. Arrived 5.10. Saw King's train leaving Portsmouth. Good hotel. New and smells of paint. Team arrived 9pm. Letters at G. (those posted to the team hotel at Glamorgan) sent for.'

Hampshire relied heavily on a contingent of army officers stationed at Southampton. Due to the Boer War, Hampshire was bereft of some of its biggest talent. Captain Ted Wynyard, Captain Greig (in India) and Captains Quinton, Bradford and Barrett were in Cape Town, even though hostilities had then ended between the Boers and Britain. Coincidentally, a South African, Charles Llewellyn, was the side's best all-rounder. A left-handed batsman who hit the ball crisply and with considerable power, Llewellyn was also a left-arm orthodox spinner of genuine class. He was later to play for South Africa in many Tests, including the First Test between Australia and South Africa on 11, 12 and 13 October, 1902 at the Old Wanderers ground, Johannesburg.

Players take the field in the match versus Hampshire at Southhampton in August, 1902. Australia won easily.

That match was played on matting and Trumper clean bowled Llewellyn for 90 in South Africa's first innings of 454. Llewellyn also picked up 6/92 off 22 overs, including the wicket of Trumper (for 63),

Syd Gregory, Hopkins, Kelly, Trumble and Jones. In addition to the talented Llewellyn, Hampshire boasted the talents of Major R Poore, who had just returned from the Boer War and had not yet fully recovered from a broken arm. Major Poore was highly thought of by those Australians, including Trumper, who had seen him in 1899. In just 16 innings in that summer, he hit 1399 runs at an average of 116.58, including seven centuries, with a highest score of 304 against Somerset.

Hampshire won the toss and batted, but the men of Southampton soon fell to a brilliant spell of bowling by Noble, who took 6/33 off 12 overs. He deceived Major Poore in flight and had him caught and bowled for 14, then had Llewellyn caught by Hopkins in the covers for 2. Hampshire managed only 130. Llewellyn got rid of both Australian openers, having Trumper caught at mid-off for 18 (out of 46 in 35 minutes), after he snared Duff at slip when the nuggety little opener had scored 13 (out of 21 in 17 minutes). Then to stumps it was Joe Darling, who enjoyed the left-arm spin of Llewellyn, and Noble to the rescue.

Thursday, 7 August: 'They won toss. Wicket funny. We batted also, Made 18, one 6. Horribly out of form. JD (Darling) slapping and not out with MAN.'

Trumper took 46 minutes over his 18 and, despite a prodigious six off Llewellyn on the South African's first ball of his fourth over, Trumper was clearly out of touch.

Next day the Australian pair continued on their merry way with Darling hoisting Llewellyn five times right out of the small Southampton ground for six. Darling finally holed out to the South African at deep mid-wicket for 116 and Noble went for 113. Hampshire batted a second time and was routed by Trumble (6/52), with Major Poore's unconquered 62 standing out like a beacon. Australia won comfortably by an innings and 79 runs.

Friday, 8 August: 'JD (Darling) 100 odd. MAN same — stuffed hand. Won by innings. Major Poore not out 60...bad innings. Left for London.'

The tourists were keen to get to London as tomorrow was the big event — the Coronation of King Edward VII.

One of very few action shots from the 1902 tour, this photo was taken at Southhampton ground during the match versus Hampshire. Because of the slow shutter speed, the moving fieldsman is blurred.

The coronation of Edward VII, 15 August 1902, as seen by the *Illustrated London News* artist. Trumper and the other members of the team would have had much the same view from their special seats in Westminster Abbey. (*News Ltd*)

Britain was to rejoice this day as never before. Despite the sorrow of Queen Victoria's passing, today was the Coronation, the crowning of her son, Edward VII. The Boer War was over and while the Coronation had to be postponed some seven weeks because of Edward's attack and subsequent operation for acute appendicitis, everything was in readiness.

Edward began the new reign by asserting his independence. As Prince of Wales he had always signed his name 'Albert Edward', as his mother had made it perfectly clear that she expected him to keep both these names when he ascended the throne. 'It was beloved papa's wish, as well as mine,' Queen Victoria wrote long ago, 'that you, should be called by both when you become King and it would be impossible for you to drop your father's. It would be monstrous, and Albert alone, as you truly and admirably say, would not do, as there can be only one ALBERT!' But Edward was of stern stuff. He told the world that he would be known as King Edward, a name borne by six of his ancestors.

These matters of protocol in the Royal household were of little moment to Joe Darling's Australians. But then this day (9 August) they were to he greatly honored, as special guests to watch the crowning of King Edward at Westminster Abbey. Such a gala occasion. London was ablaze with color. Banners and flags flew from every window. The Coronation, first scheduled some seven weeks previously, was now ready to roll. Darling's men had ringside seats in the Abbey. A marvellous day, eve of the Fifth and final Test match.

Saturday, 9 August: 'Coronation. Baroness Burdett Coutts. Good view of show. Disappointed. Had lunch there. Saw decorations. Not nearly as good as ours.'

Sunday, 10 August: 'Up lake ... went in afternoon, had photo taken at Harwell.'

Kennington Oval was the venue for the Fifth Test. Australia had already won the series, but MacLaren's men were keen to turn the tables on Darling. Stung by the narrow loss at Old Trafford, which effectively meant Australia kept the Ashes, the England selectors reacted in ruthless fashion. They dumped the luckless Fred Tate, the out-of-touch Ranjitsinhji and veteran Surrey opener Bobby Abel. 'The Croucher', Gilbert Jessop, and Yorkshire's George Hirst were restored to favor and Surrey's Tom Hayward replaced his opening colleague, Abel. The Australians retained their Old Trafford winning line-up.

Darling won the toss and batted on a sluggish but nevertheless true pitch. A biting wind swept across the Oval as MacLaren's men took the field, followed by Australia's champion opening pair, Trumper and Duff. Lockwood opened from the Vauxhall end to Duff. His fifth delivery was a fast, attempted yorker on leg stump, which Duff turned

The Oval in August 1902, scene of the Fifth and final Test. England won a memorable match but the Aussies had already sealed the series.

neatly off his pads for 3. Trumper greeted his first ball of the game and Lockwood's final delivery of his opening over by straight driving it for 2. Australia was off to a bright start.

MacLaren used the clever left-arm spin of Rhodes from the other end. Duff took a single to mid-wicket first ball and Trumper played out the rest of the over watchfully. Gradually the batsmen got on top, with Trumper in especially fine touch. The runs kept ticking over while Lockwood and Rhodes operated in tandem. Then MacLaren introduced Hirst into the attack and he had immediate success. Duff attempted to hook a short ball slanted down the leg side. He managed only to get a glove to the ball and keeper Dick Lilley threw himself away to his left to bring off an amazing catch. Australia had lost Duff (23) at 47, made in 32 minutes.

Clem Hill joined Trumper and immediately the pair struggled against Rhodes' accuracy and Hirst's persistency. Trumper soon threw off the shackles, but Hill continued to mistime his shots. It came as no surprise when Hirst bowled him neck and crop with a superb in-dipper, breaching the gap between bat and pad and thudding into Hill's middle and leg stumps. Australia 2/63, Hill 11. Darling (3) went almost immediately, edging Hirst to the ever-reliable Lilley and Australia was 3/69.

Trumper was hitting the ball with great authority, although many stinging off and cover drives were cut to ones or no run at all by the brilliant fielding of Jessop in the covers. Jessop was like a panther in that position and he could well have contributed to Trumper's downfall. Trumper (42) attempted to cut a Hirst rising ball just outside the off stump to the left of Jessop, but got a thick inside edge and the ball jagged back and onto his off stump. Australia 4/82, with Trumper's contribution 42 in just 56 minutes.

The Englishmen were overjoyed. Trumper out and the innings in disarray after less than an hour's play was more than MacLaren could have wished on this first morning. The solid, unflappable Monty Noble and Syd Gregory took the score to 107 at lunch. However, after the adjournment Hirst struck again — removing Gregory — to give him all five Australian wickets to fall for 38 runs. More than 20,000 people had, by now, crammed into Kennington Oval. They sensed the English Lion was on the kill. But neither they nor the England team could have envisaged the superb rearguard action of Darling's middle and lower order. The Kangaroo tail would wag long and strongly. Noble (52) formed the backbone of the fightback, but he found gallant allies in Albert Hopkins (40), Jim Kelly (39) and a superb innings from the old warhorse Hugh Trumble, who outdid his more accomplished batsmen with a brilliant 64 not out. Len Braund trapped Jack Saunders lbw for 0, off what was to be the final ball of the day's play with Australia all out 324. Hirst was the England hero, taking 5/77 off 29 overs. Rhodes was economical with 1/46 off 28 overs and Stanley Jackson (2/66) and Braund (2/29) played good supporting roles.

Monday, 11 August: 'Test match. Good crowd. Made 42, batted fairly well. Side shaped well.'

Certainly Australia could have had a bigger total, had it not been for Jessop, who saved an estimated 30-odd runs in the covers. Trumble, during his heroic innings, had baited Jessop and annoyed his partner Hopkins when he started off for what appeared a suicidal run.

'Get back...noooo,' cried Hopkins.

Trumble made a hasty retreat with the words: 'Come on Hoppy, let's take two . . . it's ONLY Jessop!'

Jessop's fielding that day was to have a significant effect on the result of this Test match.

The second day loomed bleak and dreary for England. The rain fell in veritable buckets after midnight and Hugh Trumble awoke with a broad smile. His medium-paced off-breaks would be even more difficult were the sun to turn the sodden Oval strip into a 'sticky'. The game got underway at 11.04am. MacLaren and Palairet were watchful in the gloom against the wiles of Trumble and the quickish Saunders. Both men opened with maidens. At 11.30 the players came off in bad light. Thirty-nine minutes were lost before the Australians again took to the field. Minutes later MacLaren departed, popping up a catch to Armstrong at short leg off Trumble. England 1/31, MacLaren 10.

Trumble was getting plenty of lift and worrying all the England batsmen. Tyldesley immediately found the ball in the middle of the bat. He was confident and began to play his shots. Then at 36, Trumble lured MacLaren forward, found a huge gap between bat and pad, and gleefully watched the big off-break crash into MacLaren's middle and leg stumps. Tyldesley waded into the Australian bowling, being particularly severe on Trumble, while the tentative Tom Hayward struggled for survival. The pair put on 26 in 19 minutes before the uneasy Hayward was clean bowled by Trumble. Only Tyldesley (33) and tailenders Hirst (43) and Lockwood (25) showed any resistence to the Australian attack, headed by the crafty Trumble. Trumble finished with 8/65 off 31 overs with 13 maidens, a marvellous piece of off-spin bowling on a helpful wicket.

The Australians had dismissed England for 184 — a total which

The Fifth Test in progress; England batting. Note the temporary cloth sightscreen.

seemed way beyond the Englishmen's capability when Trumble was bowling to the likes of Braund. Then Hirst and Lockwood saved the follow on before Trumper took a brilliant one-handed catch at deep mid-off to get rid of Lilley for 0. Australia 141 runs ahead, seemingly in an invincible position. Trumper and Duff took to the crease at 3.45pm. Rhodes nearly had Duff caught in the first over. Duff, using his feet, lofted the ball straight to Hirst at mid-off and Rhodes' Yorkshire teammate dropped the easiest of catches. Then came disaster for Darling's men. Trumper (2) pushed a ball wide of Jessop at cover point and set off for a single. But Duff saw Jessop swoop on the ball and yelled 'No, Vic. No!' Too late. Trumper turned, then slipped in his desperate attempt to make good his ground. Meanwhile Jessop had the ball back in Lilley's gloves. Lilley swept off the bails with Trumper tragically yards from his crease. Jessop's marvellous fielding had once more put Darling's men under pressure. But even with Trumper's dismissal the Australian XI held the whip hand. Australia 1/6, with Duff and Hill together. Duff did not last long. He played on to his wicket, giving the fast man Lockwood the first of five second innings wickets. Rhodes again gave grand support, but it was Lockwood who destroyed the Australian innings. At stumps Australia was 8/114, Rhodes finally claiming a wicket in his 19th over, having Saunders brilliantly caught by Tyldesley running full bore at deep long-on to take the ball cleanly with one hand. With two wickets in hand Darling's men led by 255 — still very much in the box seat.

Tuesday, 12 August: 'Wicket worse. Lead of over 100 for 2nd inngs. Run out 2 . . . easy run. Clem 30. WA (Armstrong) not out. HT (Trumble) and JK (Kelly) to go in.'

Trumper was obviously displeased with his opening partner, Reg Duff. He writes: 'Run out 2 . . . easy run.' Trumper obviously thought Duff should have responded to his call for a single when he was sent back by Duff and failed to regain his ground after slipping in mid-pitch and scrambling in vain to beat Jessop's bullet-like return to Lilley.

The night rain pelted down, but the day dawned fine and clear. Perhaps an ominous sign for Darling & Co. Lockwood yorked Armstrong for 21 and had Kelly palpably lbw to finish the Australian innings at 121. Lockwood's return was a handsome 5/45 off 20 overs. Trumble again finished not out (7). He was having a great game, for what proved his last Test in England.

Saunders made early inroads into the strong England line-up, bowling openers MacLaren (2) and Palairet (6), then knocking Tyldesley's off stump out of the ground. Three wickets had fallen for 10 runs, with Tyldesley going for a duck. Worse was to follow with Hayward touching one behind, again off the Victorian left-hander and it was 4/31. The Australians sensed victory; the Kennington Oval crowd was silent and glum. And when Braund was beautifully taken off Trumble for 2, England was in dire trouble at 5/48.

Stanley Jackson was on 31 when the energetic figure of Jessop emerged from the England dressingroom. Surely this pair was England's last hope. Jessop had shown his ability at Sheffield, smacking 55 in the England second innings. He would need to do as well, perhaps better, here for England to have any hope. Jessop began well, cracking the first ball he received from Trumble to Trumper at deep mid-off. An easy single. After scoring 9 runs in 5 balls, Jessop

played his first superb lofted shot. He sprang down the wicket at Trumble (operating around the wicket) and hit him high and hard straight back down the ground. The ball landed in the pavilion awning — four runs! The next ball Jessop swung lustily to the fence, another four. At 22 Jessop rushed down the wicket at Saunders. The ball kept low. He missed it. So too did Kelly and Jessop had a narrow squeak. Then, after a magnificent off-drive which careered over Armstrong's head at cover point for four, Jessop again hit hard and high. This time it went in the direction of Trumper at deep mid-off. Trumper dashed for it and threw himself forward, just getting his right hand to the ball but turfing it. Another 'life'. Any other fieldsman would have been hard pressed to get within yards of the ball.

In the 20 minutes before lunch Jessop hit 29, while Jackson scored a further 8 to be 39 not out. After this pair would come Hirst, Lockwood, Lilley and Rhodes. A group of New South Wales lancers were sitting in front of the Press box. The lancers, in London to attend King Edward VII's Coronation, stayed on for the Fifth Test. One yelled: 'All over by tea. We've got 'em.' They were confident that Jessop would get himself out and that Saunders and Trumble would mop up the rest of the England batting without much ado.

The crowd was now not far short of 20,000. Could London have known 'The Croucher' was at his most belligerent best? The compact Gilbert Jessop walked purposely to the crease. He was flanked by the tall, impressive figure of F S Jackson, complete with knotted kerchief about his neck and upturned moustache.

The sun was out and Jessop warmed quickly to his task. A couple of singles, then Jessop late cut Trumble; the ball sped like a tracer bullet

Players leave the Oval for lunch during the final Test. Gilbert Jessop saved and won the match for England.

passed Syd Gregory at slip. Trumble was being treated with respect, but Jessop hit out lustily when facing Saunders. In a flurry of strokes Jessop reached his 50, out of the 70-run partnership with Jackson in just 43 minutes. Meantime Jackson had a life when he snicked Saunders to Kelly. Kelly fumbled the ball and it fell just short of a diving Hugh Trumble at first slip. Trumble then found the edge of Jackson's bat. A straight forward catch to Armstrong and the big fella turfed it. The Australians were getting rattled. Jessop was in complete control. In Saunders' 19th over, Jessop hit out, scoring four fours in succession then a single. All four boundary hits came from Jessop's fearsome power on the leg side. Saunders had now conceded 75 runs from his 19 overs, and Jessop was going merrily along on 71. Darling immediately took Saunders out of the attack and replaced the Victorian's left-arm pace with Warwick Armstrong's leg-spinners. Armstrong asked for five men on the leg side. Operating each time by pitching his leg-spinners outside the line of the leg stump, Armstrong's leg theory stemmed the torrent of runs. Jessop took a single off the last delivery.

He then took 2 from Trumble's bowling and when Jessop had reached 75 the 100 partnership had been realised in 57 minutes. Armstrong again and Jessop stepped back and hit the leg-tweaker through the off side and later in the over, swung against the spin, but hit the ball in the meat of the bat, over mid-wicket and crashing over the boundary fence. The crowd yelled themselves hoarse. They sensed now that Jessop could bring off a miracle England victory. Then at 157, Jackson was completely deceived in flight by Trumble and hit back a simple return catch which the big, angular, off-spinner gratefully accepted. Jackson had made an invaluable 49, but it was justice that Trumble 'got him' as he had beaten him so many times during his innings.

Trumble's first ball to Hirst so nearly trapped the Yorkshireman. A confident appeal for lbw was turned down. Those watching the action from the pavilion, including Charles Fry, were visibly uncomfortable about the decision. But Trumble only dealt in reality, not in what might have been. He bent down and picked up the ball without the slightest murmur. But it was a very near thing. George Hirst was the least shaken of all. He immediately pulled Armstrong for two fours.

Not to be outdone, Jessop turned his attention to the crafty Trumble. He hit the off-spinner high into the pavilion balcony (four runs only), then took two twos before hitting the final ball of Trumble's 23rd over to the top of the pavilion again. Twelve runs had come from Trumble's over and Jessop had raced to 96. Then Armstrong presented Jessop with a long hop, to which the Glouscester captain said 'thank you very much' and hammered past point for four.

A century in 75 minutes. Jessop had not only given England hope when all hope had flown out of the window at 5/48, but his hurricane ton had given England the upper hand. The Australian bowlers were at Jessop's mercy. There was a tumult of excitement. Hats, umbrellas, scarves and walking sticks were thrown in the air. Jessop reacted by sweeping Armstrong to the fence. Then on Armstrong's final delivery Jessop swept at a ball on leg stump, got a top edge and the ball lobbed gently to Noble at backward square.

Jessop had scored an amazing 104 out of 139 runs in just 77 minutes. His 100 came in 75 minutes, still the record fastest Test century in

England-Australia Tests. All the Australians joined in the applause. They had just witnessed one of the great innings of all time. Jessop had saved the match. His shots defied description. Some were copybook strokes, but most were startling shots that only Jessop could play. He hoisted Saunders over square leg from deliveries pitched wide outside his off stump and hit Trumble against his considerable off-spin through the covers. Although Darling stacked the leg side, Jessop continued to hit boundaries on the on. C B Fry (writing later in *Life Worth Living*), saw it this way: 'Jessop let himself loose like a catapult at the bowling and scattered it to smithereens. If ever an innings ought to have been filmed, that was the one.' Yes, that one on film would be marvellous to look back at, as would Trumper's 104 at Old Trafford.

Even though England required 76 to win with just three wickets to fall, Hirst was playing well and he found staunch support from Dick Lilley. Slowly the score crept along. Then Lilley hammered Trumble wide of cover, only to see Joe Darling dive and take it one handed. England 9/248.

Wilfred Rhodes joined Hirst. The two Yorkshiremen would not let England down.

Rhodes, batting No. 11 now but who in later years would open so nobly with the great Jack Hobbs, met each delivery with the straightest of straight bats. Trumble missed a difficult caught-and-bowled chance off Rhodes and, with just three runs to win, the rain began to fall. Hirst pushed a ball from Trumble down the ground and Rhodes responded well. The scores were level. The crowd went wild. A parson threw off all dignity and dashed (fully clothed off course) on to the centre of the field exclaiming: 'Well done, well done, we can't lose now.' The batsmen

Another view of the Oval during the final Test. This photo was probably taken on the first morning as players are still practising in the nets at the far side of the ground while groundmen appear to be preparing the wicket.

smiled as did the fieldsmen. Trumble was hampered by a wet ball. The England batsmen knew they had the game in their keeping. Rhodes made the winning hit, driving Trumble crisply between Trumper and Duff at mid-off. He ran past the stumps and straight on towards the pavilion. The game was over, England had won another heart-stopping Test by one wicket. Hugh Trumble, who had bowled so manfully (12/173) and batted so bravely (64 not out, 7 not out), was warm in his praise of 'The Croucher': 'The only man living who could beat us, beat us.'

Trumble had toiled all day, taking 4/108 off 33.5 overs. Saunders too, did a lot of the work, 4/105 off 24 overs. Both suffered at the hands of Jessop. But Armstrong had just four overs, albeit expensive ones. Twenty eight runs came from Armstrong's bowling, but his last delivery brought him the wicket of Jessop. Surely Darling could have given him a couple more overs, as there was still 76 runs to get when Jessop went. Curiously enough Noble also had little bowling, just five overs for 11 runs and no wicket. While Jessop was superb, the Australians were in a virtually unbeaten position when they began their second innings some 141 runs ahead. Just how important was Jessop's run out of Trumper, when the great man had scored two runs?

While Victor Trumper was high in his praise of the England victory, his notation in his diary told of the mental strain on the players. They were glad the Test matches were over. It had been a long and arduous tour and still there were games to play. But now the pressure-cooker atmosphere of a tense Test match was over, for the time being.

Wednesday, 13 August: 'Test over. England a glorious game. Deserved to win. Wicket bad. Catches missed. Great excitement. Glad Tests all over . . .'

Trumper summed that Test match up pretty well. Interesting that he makes no mention of Jessop's incredible century.

After that epic final Test it was business as usual next day. This time Darling's men came up against an unusually weak Marylebone Cricket Club Eleven. One player of note was Ranji, who hit a fine 60 out of MCC's 212 all out. Bill Howell relished a return to a hard day's toil, taking 6/105 off 40 overs. Armstrong gave solid support to Howell, picking up 3/53 off 27 overs. Trumper and Duff began well and at stumps Darling's men were 2/80. Trumper was out for 29 (five fours) and Duff 36 (seven fours).

Thursday, 14 August: 'MCC match. Poor team against us. They made 212. Wicket bit bad. Made 29 slogging. 2 for 80.'

Next day the Australians, led by Clem Hill (136), Noble (70) and Syd Gregory (86) thrashed the MCC attack and the team finished with 427. Next day the Australians easily accounted for MCC, with Armstrong taking 6/44 off 21 overs. MCC made 181 and the Australians won by an innings and 34.

This is how Trumper saw those two days:

Friday, 15 August: 'Clem 100. Missed twice. MAN (Noble) batted well. Easy day, fielded for half an hour, Saw Country Girl. Dr Laver had boxes.'

Saturday, 16 August: 'Won by innings. WWA (Armstrong) got wickets. Match over 2.30. Wisdens closed.'

The Australians completed the 1902 tour of England with further wins against Gloucestershire (Armstrong bowled Jessop neck and crop for 13), Middlesex, Eleven Players of England (Trumper hitting 127), South of England and back to Kennington Oval to draw against Players (Trumper hitting 96).

In the Memoranda section at the back of the little diary Trumper has listed advance payments, under the heading 'Stuff Advd'.

A total of £123, with £25 going 'home' on 27/6/01 (a slip: it should be 27 June, 1902), was followed by a list of scores and averages taken every so often. But Trumper lists only 15 innings. Then there is the notation: 'Joe Bates . . . niece, 20 Curzon St, B'ham.' A few names of bat manufacturers are all there is at the back of the book.

And the Trumper sense of humor shines through at the end. His last 'official' entry on the tour, Saturday, 16 August — 'Wisdens closed.' If only the great batsmen knew then that those words would not see the public light of day for more than 83 years.

Australians at play: The two men standing on the limb thumbing their noses at each other are Victor Trumper (left) and keeper James Kelly. Team manager Major Wardill is sitting on the limb at far left.

The Canterbury ground where the Australian played and beat Kent in August 1902. Note the tree inside the boundary.

7

A NIGHT TO REMEMBER

Joe Darling's men began the first of Australia's Test battles with South Africa when the team visited Cape Town and Johannesburg on the way home after the triumphant England tour. While Darling's charges were tired, as Trumper wrote — 'glad Tests over' — the short tour of South Africa was designed to dispel any ill-feeling towards Australians, as Australian soldiers had fought in the Boer War battles at Ladysmith, Spion Kop and Majuba Hill. The Australians were apprehensive about the tour. After all, the visit of Lord Hawke's 1896 England team had coincided with the Jameson Raid. Along the Pretoria-Johannesburg road, Hawke and his men managed to escape arrest by a posse of Boers by handing over a number of signed bats.

Now, only months after peace was declared, Victor Trumper batted in such compelling splendor that even the most hardened soldier acclaimed him as the world champion. Trumper hit a masterly 218 not out against a Transvaal XV (eleven fielded). The Australians scored 392, of which the next highest score was Mr Sundries (38), followed by Reg Duff (36) and Joe Darling (35). The magnificence of that innings forever endeared Victor Trumper to all South African cricket lovers. How his brilliant straight driving might have been used at Mafeking! In the Tests, Trumper hit 63 and 37 (Johannesburg), 18 and 13 (Second Test also at Johannesburg) and 70 and 38 not out (Third Test at Newlands, Cape Town). Trumper was overshadowed by Clem Hill in the Tests. Hill averaged 81.76 in the three-Test rubber. Darling's men left South Africa in mid-November, 1902. They were undefeated, winning two of the three Tests and three of the four first-class matches. Two second-class fixtures were played and both were drawn. Trumper finished the South African visit with 307 runs at an average of 43.85.

Trumper's brilliant tour of England won him a special place in all Australian hearts. A grand night was organised for Trumper, under the direction of his admiring Crown Street School Old Boys' Union. It was indeed a night of splendor. Some 5000 people crammed into the Sydney Town Hall to pay the great batsman homage. That day, Friday, 12 December, 1902, Trumper had taken 3/18 off 13 overs of medium-pace for the Australian XI against thirteen of New South Wales. He scored only 12, being caught and bowled by Tom Howard, who took 6/118 off just 16 overs. Perhaps Victor's nerves were on edge. He would come face to face with a sea of admirers that night.

Public Reception to Victor J. Trumper.

The Council of the Crown Street School Old Boys' Union

Request the pleasure of

Mr & Mrs W. Caban's, company

at a Public Reception (and Presentation), which will be tendered

❀ **VICTOR T. TRUMPER**, ❀

in the Sydney Town Hall, on his return from England, to appreciate the excellent manner in which he has upheld the honor of the School, as well as the State of New South Wales and the Commonwealth of Australia, on the Cricket Field in England during the tour of the Eleventh Australian Eleven.

R.S.V.P. to Hon Secs., 4 Trent Terrace, Percival Road, Stanmore.

Trumper returned to Australia a hero. Public receptions, accolades and awards had been organised even before the team left England for home. This invitation was for the reception and presentation organised by Trumper's old school, Crown Street. Mr and Mrs Caban were Victor's uncle and aunt. (*Tom Nicholas*)

The gold medal awarded to Trumper in 1902-3 when NSW won the coveted Sheffield Shield. The medal is now proudly worn by Ginty Lush, ex-NSW all-rounder and State captain. (*Ginty Lush Collection*)

They came in their droves. Many of the distinguished guests were ex-Crown Street Superior Public School students. They included Monty Noble and politician Mr D Levy, who presented Victor with a set of cutlery and two silver fruit dishes, on behalf of the past and present teachers. The accolades came thick and fast. Sydney Lord Mayor, Alderman Thomas Hughes, said: 'I am proud to say that Victor Trumper not only showed the Englishmen, but the whole world, what Australians are made of; and it was no mean honour to the State of New South Wales to have produced the greatest batsman in the world.' The cheers erupted and drowned the Mayor's voice. 'It is only fitting and proper that we should honour Victor's homecoming, after such a remarkably successful tour.'

It must have seemed an eternity for the quiet, reserved Victor Trumper before it came his turn to rise to his feet to respond. The moment he rose the crowd acclaimed him with loud clapping and cheering. The noise was deafening. Victor blushed. Wave upon wave of ovation flooded the Town Hall. It took nearly five minutes before relative calm was restored in the wake of that veritable storm of praise.

As Victor began in his quiet tone, deathly silence befell the throng: a deafening quiet. Few outside the front row could hear the great batsman speak, but those fortunate to have won a front stall hung on every word. It was no eloquent piece of oratory, but it had his admirers spellbound:

'I am so very lucky to have received such a reception and such presents. My performances have been over-estimated and I did the same as the others in endeavouring to uphold the reputation of Australia on the cricket field.' Trumper then thanked all and sundry for their kindness. He was, according to those who were present on that historic night, visibly moved.

There were many distinguished guests. Apart from the Australian XI, including skipper Joe Darling who made the trip from Adelaide

especially for Victor's night, there was the NSW thirteen, which
included the jovial and personable Aboriginal fast bowler, Jack Marsh.
Just before Trumper rose to speak, the NSW thirteen was introduced
individually to the crowd. Marsh nearly brought the house down when
he stood up to acknowledge the ovation. He bowed to each section of
the hall, waved his arms above his head and had the people in hysterics.
Only Trumper rising to his feet brought louder cheers. Although State
Governor Sir Harry Rawson, Sir Edmund Barton, Madame Melba
(later Dame Nellie) and the Premier, Sir John See, and members of the
ministry were unable to attend (Melba was performing on another stage
and the politicians were detained in Parliament), there were many
others present who were at the very top of their fields. The then Federal
Attorney-General Mr Alfred Deakin, who within a year would become
Prime Minister, holding the 1903-4, 1905-8, and 1909-10 terms of
office, watched proceedings with great interest. No-one laughed longer
or louder at Jack Marsh's antics than Mr Deakin.

Captain of the 1902 team, Joe Darling, responded to repeated calls
for him to give a short speech. Darling said: 'On behalf of the
Australian Eleven I want to thank you in the way you have honoured
our return. No one but those who saw Trumper's performances had any
idea of their worth. They were made on pure bowlers' wickets.'

Darling added that the 'Australian team was subject to a good deal of
criticism, especially the selectors. The selection turned out to be a good
one. We received a fair bit of criticism, especially from one old player in
Victoria, and it is only right for me to say that it was purely a matter of
chagrin on his part because he was not selected.' He may well have been
referring to Alfred Johns, who was a controversial selection on the 1896
and 1899 tours.

There were also calls for the Victorian champion off-spinner, Hugh
Trumble, who on the last of his five England tours took a brilliant bag
of 140 wickets at an average of 14.27. But Trumble had slipped quietly
away. Not one for fanfare, Trumble was at his best in a team situation,
far from the madding crowd. He was a practical joker and later when he
became Melbourne Cricket Club secretary, Trumble delighted friends
with countless stories of the Golden Age of Cricket.

The night was interspersed with recitals and musical scores. The most
amusing item on the program came from Mr W W Walsh in his recital
of *How McDougal Topp'd the Score* (by T E Spencer). It told how
Molongo challenged Piper's Flat to a cricket match. Piper's Flat had
hard work to get a team, so they sent for McDougal of Cooper's Creek.
Though he had never played he was determined to try and started
practising with a paling for a bat. He got Mrs Mac to bowl to him and
he trained his sheepdog, Pincher, to scout and fetch the ball. McDougal
was the last man in and as his side wanted 50 to win, long odds were laid
against them getting the runs. McDougal played a ball back softly to the
bowler —

> '... But McDougal crying "fetch" started running like a hare
> Molongo shouted "victory" he's out as sure as eggs;
> When Pincher started through the crowd and ran through
>   Johnson's legs.
> He seized the ball like lightning, then he ran behind a log;
> And McDougal kept on running, while Molongo chased the dog.
> To make a long story short, McDougal ran the 50 required to win.'

Cover of the official souvenir and program for the Crown Street School public reception for Victor Trumper in December 1902. The original is printed in red and dark blue and carries advertisements for such famous items and companies as Bushell's Tea, Player's Navy Cut tobacco, Singer Sewing Machines, and Joe Davis, hatter and mercer of 116 Pitt St., Sydney.

There was such an imperative encore for this, and, anticipating such, Mr Spencer wrote the following verses, eagerly taken up by a beaming William Walsh:

'On evening just at sundown, I was sitting on a rail,
When up rode big Tim Brady, who had been to fetch the mail;
Taking out a newspaper, he handed it to me,
And pointed to a paragraph, ''Just look at this,'' said he.
''Here's a cove called Victor Trumper, an Australian by birth,
Has been moppin' up the cricket records all around the earth;
Such centuries and aggregates were never known before.
And New South Wales is dotty because Trumper's topped the ''score''.
I says, when I had read it,
''Yes, I think I've heard his name,
Accordin' to the cablegrams he plays a decent game.
In breakin' English records he's been making game for us,
And I think, in spite of Kipling, that a young man might do wuss.
But before he breaks all records, he has got to wait a bit,
For he hasn't broke McDougal's

Trumper's Eleven Centuries.

101—Surrey, at Kennington Oval, May 13.

Trumper, at 185, completed the century, after batting two hours and a half. He scored only another run, and then was secured off Hayward—a smart catch low down in the slips, Hayes in effecting it falling forward. He had been favored by luck in the two unaccepted chances which he offered to Hayward in the slips off Richardson; yet he had played some brilliant all-round cricket, his 101—subscribed out of 187 in two hours and thirty-five minutes—including nine 4's, nine 3's, and ten 2's.—"Sportsman."

121—Oxford University, May 22.

Trumper completed his second century of the tour in an hour and a half out of 168. . . . The second century was completed with only one wicket down in seven minutes under two hours, the last hundred having been obtained in 65 min. Trumper had a further life when one hundred and seventeen, skying a ball from Kelly on the on-side, Whately at mid-on getting it into his hands but letting it drop. Happily for the fieldsman's peace of mind the mistake was not a costly one, as at 213, having only raised his contribution to one hundred and twenty-one, Trumper was well caught at cover-point, after batting a couple of hours for his brilliant innings, which included fifteen 4's, half a dozen 3's, and twelve 2's. The partnership with Hill for the second wicket had yielded 105 in 65 minutes.—"Sportsman."

105—M.C.C. and Ground, at Lords, May 27.

For the third time in the tour Trumper managed to place three figures against his name, reaching the century after a stay of a couple of hours, his proportion being one hundred and one out of 174. Five minutes later, with his contribution raised to one hundred and five and the total to 182, he was bowled middle stump by a good length ball from Hearne. Nothing in the shape of a chance marred his fine, free innings, which included as its principal strokes eleven 4's, a 3, and five 2's.—"Sportsman."

128—Cambridge University, June 9 and 10.

Trumper, with the total 211, completed three figures for the fourth time in the tour, having then been at the wickets two hours and a half. He stayed another thirty minutes, and then, going out to a slow one from Dowson, fell to the vigilance of Winter behind the sticks. He claimed one hundred and twenty-eight out of 252, which three hours cricket had produced—a fine innings but for a possible c and b at the outset, and the chance of Fry at mid-on at the start of yesterday's play, both being off the bowling of E. R. Wilson. Among his strokes were eleven

Above, right and far right top: Three columns from the Crown Street School reception souvenir program describing Trumper's record 11 centuries against England in 1902.

Who scored fifty in a hit!
I aint the least bit jealous — I don't speak because of that —
But we'll let no Bloomin' Trumper's take the cake from
Piper's Flat.
When McDougal piled his record up, and knocked Molongo dead
He didn't play them with his bat, he played them with his head!
If Trumper comes to Piper's Flat, he'll find we're not asleep,
For what we had the head to win, we'll have the head to keep
'He'll meet with every kindness. He shall have a horse to ride.
But if he rides the chestnut mare, he'll have to get inside.
She threw Flash Mat the horse breaker, and damaged his profile.
And the man will make a record that will ride her half a mile
We'll fill him up with gooseberry wine, and cream, and nice fresh
    cream.
And then, if he is fit to go, we'll show him Bowler's bees;
They're very fond of strangers,
And, if Trumper plays at all,
After he's done inspectin' them, he'll never see the ball
He'll find the wicket bumpy and the bowling rather mild
And then we've still got Pincher left, and Pincher aint no child
He understands McDougal
If his master tells him so
He'll get a grip on Trumper's pants, and never let them go
When every man is equal, why, then no man will be best,
And every score that's made will be the same as all the rest;
In the socialistic language there is no such word as strife
And the man that breaks a record will be put in jail for life
Then Trumper's or McDougal's fame will not be fame at all
And perhaps we'll drop our record, just as Pincher dropped the
    ball;
But until then our record shall remain at Piper's Flat,
We've only one, and you may bet your boots, we'll stick to that.
If Trumper is contented with the records he has got
And don't come up to Piper's Flat to try to scoop the lot,
Then Brady and McDougal and the men of Piper's Flat
Will wish "good luck" to Trumper, and they won't forget the hat.
We mean to keep our record, but we all acknowledge worth,
And hail him as the most accomplished cricketer on earth.
Our cheers shall make the gumtrees shake, we'll pledge him in a
    bumper,
While breath holds out we'll roar and shout "Long life to Victor
    Trumper!"

That recital must have moved Trumper for he pasted a cutting of it in his copy of the souvenir program. He also cut out a number of newspaper cuttings with articles on the night of nights in his then young life. Trumper cut out a photograph printed in the *Sydney Mail* days later. It shows the splendor of the occasion. Men and women dressed to the nines, Trumper in tails (with his back to the camera and at the top table) looking out at the admiring crowd. Few cricketers have been feted in such a manner. Certainly, that night for Victor Trumper was the most dazzling for any Australian sportsman who had done the nation proud.

Trumper's Eleven Centuries.—*Continued.*

113—England Eleven, at Bradford, June 26

The batting honors on the Colonial side were carried off by Duff and Trumper, who came together when matters were going very badly with the Cornstalks on Thursday morning—Darling, Noble, Hill, and Hopkins having all been sent back with 35 on the board—and by splendid cricket completely turned the tables on the attacking party. In an hour and fifty minutes they increased the total to the extent of 191 before Trumper was bowled by Knutton round his legs. The outgoing batsman was responsible for half the score of 226 at the time he left, and the only blemish in his display was a sharp chance to Snowden, at point, when he had made 61. Trumper had the satisfaction of reaching his 1000 runs during this innings.—"Sportsman."

104—England (4th Test), Manchester, July 24.

Trumper and Duff put on 135 for the first wicket. Trumper completed his sixth century of the tour after he had been batting rather less than an hour and a quarter, having made his hundred out of 168. The total at the adjournment read 173 for one wicket, Trumper being 103 and Clem Hill 14 not out. A change came over the game on resuming, and at first it seemed likely that a Colonial collapse would be brought about by Rhodes, who shared the attack with Lockwood, bowling from the city end. The Yorkshireman in his first four overs secured three victims for 6 runs. His fifth ball saw the termination of Trumper's career, the great Australian batsman, who at first shaped as if to cut the ball, apparently changing his mind and just directing it into the hands of the wicket-keeper, Lilley, who effected a very neat catch. Only a single apiece had been added to the luncheon figures, Trumper having batted five minutes under two hours for his faultless 104, the chief features of which consisted of fourteen 4's, three 3's, and half a dozen 2's.—"Sportsman."

109—Essex, at Leyton (first innings), July 29.

Apart from one man, the Australians gave a most disappointing display of batting, nobody approaching Trumper in a remote degree in brilliancy of execution and mastery over the attack. This famous batsman played an innings of 109—his seventh of three figures this tour—which in grace of style could hardly be equalled. It was noticeable that he made fewer runs than usual by his favorite method of pulling—relying chiefly upon powerful and well-kept-down drives and clean, hard cuts—and hardly once did he mis-time a ball until beaten by a beautiful break-back from Mead. It is very doubtful if the Australians have ever sent over a batsman with such fertility of resources in scoring off so many good balls. Even Massie, with all his wonderful powers, had not such extraordinary aptitude in making runs by all sorts of strokes—and good ones, too—as this young cricketer from New South Wales. He certainly made the batting of his colleagues look very poor stuff yesterday, and but for his brilliant innings the Australians would have been in a bad way indeed.—' Sporting Life."

Trumper's Eleven Centuries.—*Continued.*

119—Essex (second innings), July 30.

On Tuesday Trumper rattled up 109 in an hour and thirty-five minutes, and yesterday he was not disposed of till he had subscribed 119 out of 237 for five wickets. His runs were not made at the same pace as on the previous day, seeing that they occupied two hours and thirty-five minutes in putting together, but his contribution was again faultless and a treat to witness, by reason of its grace, ease, and brilliance. He started, however, unusually slowly, and occupied nearly 40 minutes in reaching double figures. He was dismissed leg-before. His great and faultless innings of 119 included seventeen 4's (one a grand drive between the pavilion and stand), two 3's, and seven 2's.—"Sportsman."

. . . Trumper, having made a huge drive over the ring between the pavilion and the stand was leg-before at 237. With seventeen 4's, two 3's, and seven 2's as his best hits, Trumper had played really superb cricket for two hours and forty minutes, never giving the slightest approach to a chance. His innings was, as it were, divided into two parts, one marked by great steadiness and considerable restraint, and other by extreme brilliancy.—"Sporting Life."

Speaking of Trumper's couple of hundreds against Essex, Mr. Home Gordon writes in "The Sportsman":—"Vigil and Dante invoked the Muse to help their pens, and some such assistance is needed to do justice to the magnificent batting of Victor Trumper. It seemed to some of us on Monday that the Australians after the test match were, excusably, taking matters a little easy. But the subsequent days showed no relaxation in the fascinating punishing powers of Trumper. Essex were a thorn in the flesh of the colonials in 1899, and if their present attack is not of the star type, it is certainly calculated to inspire respect. But apparently all attack is powerless to trouble Trumper, for, as the balls kept fairly below bail-height, he proceeded to make happy havoc of them and succeeded in piling up a double century as flattering in the quality of its brilliant freedom as it is useful to his average. To convey in phrases the ease with which he played in both innings is impossible, and so admiration can only be expressed in compliments, sincere and deserved."

125—Gloucestershire, at Cheltenham, Aug. 18.

Trumper was caught off Jessop at 223, after making 125 in two hours on a wicket affected by rain. He hit 16 fours and was out sixth.

127—Players, at Harrogate, Sept. 1 and 2.

First 101 runs made in 95 minutes. Darling and Trumper made a fine stand, and gave an attractive display. At 168 Trumper was 101 and Darling 27. It was Trumper's tenth century, and was compiled in 95 minutes. Trumper, when 127, was stumped off Vine. 3—127—205.

120—South of England, at Hastings, Sept. 10.

Trumper's 120 runs were obtained in two hours, and included some splendid hits, one being a 6 and seventeen 4's. He was fourth out at 190.

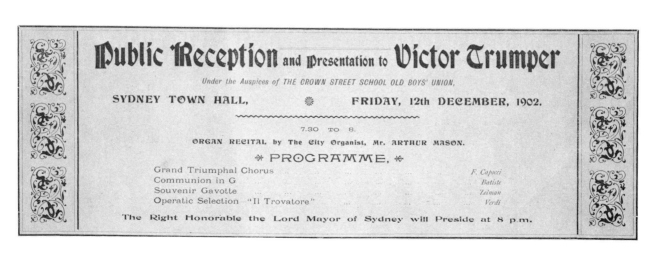

Another page from the souvenir program. An advertisement nearby is for 'Sons & Daughters of Temperance'.

Far left: More accolades for
Victor . . . a hand-lettered scroll
presented to him by the mayor and
residents of Newcastle in October
1903

Above: A night to remember:
Thousands crowded into the Sydney
Town Hall on 12 December 1902
for the public reception to honor
Trumper. Note the two grand
pianos at bottom left.

8
END OF AN ERA

Joe Darling's 12th Australian team to England in 1905 – the last player-run tour. (*Marylebone Cricket Club*)

Joe Darling's 12th Australian team to England in 1905 was the end of an era: it was the last tour to be run by the players. Although the Australian Board of Control for International Cricket was formed that year, it was too early for that august body to take over.

Victor promised Annie a honeymoon in England. He loved England and wanted his bride of less than a year to join him on the tour. South Australian wicketkeeper Philip Newland won a berth as second wicketkeeper, beating Victor's New South Wales teammate and great friend Hanson 'Sammy' Carter. Newland's wife and Clem Hill's wife, along with Annie Trumper, toured with the side.

En route to England, the Australian team travelled via New Zealand, Fiji and Canada. In New Zealand, the Australians took time out to go shooting birds on the Whangunai River. Trumper is at far left behind the man aiming his gun. (*Frank Laver Collection*)

The team visited New Zealand, Fiji and Canada before finally reaching the Mother Country. During the sojourn in Christchurch the team was feted by none other than Arthur Sims, the NZ captain. Sims was later to take a team of Australians back to NZ and hit up a partnership of 433 with Victor against Canterbury at Lancaster Park nearly nine years later.

The Governor, Lord Plunkett, and Lady Plunkett went to the first Australia-NZ match, played in Christchurch from March 10-12, 1905. Trumper hit a brilliant 84; Hill, 118; and Warwick Armstrong, an unconquered 126; with the side scoring 533. NZ replied with 138 and 7/112 — Armstrong picking up 10/52 in the two innings. In the second match, Victor hit a dazzling 172; Hill, 129; and Australia thrashed the New Zealanders to the tune of 9/593. NZ was dismissed on a wet wicket first up for 94, then a second innings total of 141. Bill Howell (4/45), Albert 'Tibby' Cotter (4/46), Charles McLeod (5/56) and Armstrong (6/51) were the chief wreckers.

It was on 16 March, 1905, that a small, slim boy named Clarence Victor Grimmett stole away from school to watch the match. He was wearing his new blue suit and, in his haste to get into the ground for the chance of a lifetime to watch his boyhood hero — Victor Trumper — bat, Clarrie tore his trousers on a piece of barbed wire. The 13-year-old Grimmett marvelled at Trumper's batting. This was the ultimate for him. Trumper drove, cut and pulled with great power.

It was an innings to savour; an innings which Grimmett never forgot. He was to become the greatest leg-spinner in Test history — leaving his native NZ in 1914; packing his swag and bag of bowling tricks for the greener cricketing pastures of Sydney. Years later Clarrie finally made Test cricket. He was then 32. A few years in Sydney, then Melbourne and finally Adelaide, which Johnny Moyes once affectionately dubbed '. . . a haven for unwanted bowlers and the staging post for England.' But before Clarrie left NZ he played a couple of games against Arthur Sims' Australian team.

Clarrie was given a hiding for tearing his trousers on the barbed-wire

A 1905 painting of Trumper in full flight. Note the slatted pads still in use at this stage. (*Marylebone Cricket Club*)

Australians at play in the hot springs of Rotorua, New Zealand, on their way to England. Trumper is at rear with arms held highest. (*Frank Laver*)

fence that day in 1905. His parents did not share his enthusiastic conviction that his torn pants were nothing compared to having the chance of watching Trumper in full cry. The tear meant a few pennies, or more likely more toil for Mrs Grimmett while the Trumper innings was a priceless gem.

Clarrie was 22-years-old when he trundled up to bowl to Trumper in 1914. The venue was Basin Reserve, Wellington. 'No, he (Trumper) didn't knock me out of the firing line. He disappointed me by getting out the next over at the other end. Still, I was delighted to have had even this fleeting chance to send down a few balls to this incomparable batting idol,' Clarrie recalled years later.

Grimmett was a great student of the game; especially leg-spin bowling. 'During the game the Australian manager (Bill McCall) said that all the players in his team would only be too pleased to help the locals, if they wanted any advice,' Grimmett recalled back in the 1970s.

'After much hesitation I at last plucked up courage to ask Arthur Mailey, when he was practising, if he would show me how he bowled the googly (or Bosey, or in modern parlance, the wrong 'un). At that time I could bowl the googly as well as I could bowl my leg-break, but I wanted to find out if his methods were better than mine. Without speaking Mailey ran up and bowled one, and then he turned his back on me and walked away. Strange that we should later be companions in arms in the cricket fight against England (Mailey and Grimmett were the key spinners in Herbie Collins' 1926 Australian team in England).'

Victor Trumper's record in England that summer was nowhere near that of his previous tour. In the Tests he scored a total of just 125 runs in eight innings for an average of 17.8. He had trouble with a bad back, but managed a total of 49 innings on the tour with a top score of 110 and a total return of 1754 runs at 36.54. England medium-pacer Walter Brearley dismissed him on no less than six occasions, three times in the Tests (once in the Leeds Fourth Test and twice at Kennington Oval in the Fifth Test). Trumper was so impressed with Brearley's bowling on that tour and on Trumper's final tour (1909) that Victor presented his bat to Brearley in 1909. That bat was years later given to the Lord's museum where it is now housed, within the protective glass walls of a cabinet. In 1905 Brearley hit Trumper's stumps three times.

Among the tourists was none other than Bill Ferguson, soon to be known universally as 'Fergie', the scorer-cum-baggagemaster whose name will live on perhaps longer than many of the men for whom he scored in Tests from 1905 to 1956. His score sheets were as much a work of art as Trumper's batting or Hugh Trumble's bowling.

Just before the 1905 team left for England, Fergie visited the dentist. He hated dentists, but it was a planned visit. He wanted to win the confidence of Sydney's most famous dentist, M A Noble, the vice-captain to Joe Darling and, more importantly, a selector and thus in a position of much influence when it came to selecting a scorer-baggagemaster.

But the team left for NZ without Fergie. Then Ferguson received a letter from manager Frank Laver. He was offered the job at the rate of pay of £2 a week, plus board and lodging. For that he would score, run messages, look after the luggage and be the general dogsbody. He found that international cricketers expected to be waited on hand and foot (nothing has changed in that area). In 1907-8, the England team left Australia while Fergie was dashing about trying to find spinner Len Braund's camera. He finally found it and at his own expenses parcelled it up and sent it via sea-mail to England. Fergie never received an acknowledgement for that gesture.

In 1905, during Fergie's first tour, he came to know Victor Trumper. Years later Fergie wrote a book on his travels with Test teams and his experiences in scoring in 204 Test matches. But that 1905 tour had a special place in his heart: 'As the tour progressed I became more and more confident of my scoring ability, being complimented on my books by everyone, with the exception of one of the three ladies (Mesdames Trumper, Hill and Newland), Mrs Clem Hill. For reasons best known to herself, Mrs Hill also used to keep the score! At the end of each day's play, she invariably badgered her husband with the complaint that there had been scoring mistakes — just because my books did not agree with the one which she kept for amusement. Clem would look at his wife indulgently and then appeal to me: "For goodness sake Fergie, check the wife's book. She insists you're wrong, but I can't be bothered with it".

'Perhaps there is something to be said for the countries which impose a strict ban on wives travelling with cricketers!

'My favorite batsman was Vic Trumper. Probably the neatest and most elegant bat in the world at the time, Vic was anything but neat when he was in the dressingroom, or at a hotel. He was the despair of his charming wife, and the not-so-charming baggagemaster, because he simply refused to worry about the condition of his clothes or equipment. Any old bat would do for him, whether there was rubber on the handle or not, and I can still see him now, after slaughtering the

England bowler Walter Brearley snared Trumper's wicket many times during the 1909 tour. Trumper presented his bat to Brearley at the end of the tour. (*Marylebone Cricket Club*)

Players' wives watch net practice on board the ship to England in 1905. Mrs Newland (left) is pointing to a laughing Mrs Annie Trumper (right, foreground) while Mrs Clem Hill is seated behind the two women sitting between Mesdames Newland and Trumper.

best bowling in England, taking off his flannels in the dressing-room, rolling them in a ball and cramming them into an already overloaded cricket bag — there to remain until they were worn again next day. Mrs Trumper used to say to me: "Just look at Victor's clothes. Whatever does he do with them?"

'On such occasions I would often fold his clothes neatly and re-pack his bag but, within 24 hours, chaos again reigned supreme.

'The Trumpers were real aces for my money. If Victor caught me packing my bag, he would say: "Don't bother about that, Bill. You have enough work to do without me causing you extra trouble." In my opinion Mrs Trumper was not treated at all well by the other ladies on tour, Mrs Clem Hill and Mrs Philip Newland. Maybe they thought Vic's wife did not measure up to their class socially, yet she was worth the pair of them, as far as I was concerned.'

Strange that Mrs Hill was off-side with Annie Trumper. Clem Hill and Victor were great mates. Whenever in Adelaide, Hill's home town, Victor went to the races with Clem, even though Victor did not bet. They were often seen at the piano together and during Test time in Adelaide, a famous trio — Hill, Trumper and Warwick Armstrong — went together to the races whenever time permitted.

Fergie had to watch the generosity of Victor. In 1905 in London it was commonplace to have gangs of infants following strangers about the streets. For a coin the youngsters turned somersaults and put on gymnastic displays to extract further monetary rewards. Trumper had to be restrained from spending his entire tour payment on any one day. Bill Ferguson kept an eye on Victor in this way.

In Bill's book *Mr Cricket* (Nicholas Kaye, London) Fergie picks his all-time best team. Fergie's side — Monty Noble, Don Bradman, Victor Trumper, Wally Hammond, Jack Hobbs, Len Hutton, Wilfred Rhodes, Clarrie Grimmett, Harold Larwood, Ted McDonald and Bert Oldfield.

He wrote of Trumper: 'Like Bradman, Trumper made his runs instinctively, treating each unpremeditated innings as only a genius can treat such a work of art. Possessing an elegance of style the like of which I have never seen equalled, he could dispatch a ball to the boundary with the merest flick of the wrist and the gentlest, almost imperceptible raising of the left foot. Long after Trumper's stately figure, clad in its comically-creased cricketing attire, had ceased to entertain enthusiasts of the game, I spun tales of his prowess to his successors. Bradman, himself, once taxed me on this when he asked: "If Victor Trumper was everything you claim, why did he not score more runs for Australia?" Here was the essential difference between Bradman and Trumper. Victor was never interested in ruthlessly amassing huge scores: maybe his temperament did not allow him to sustain Bradman-like concentration for hour after hour. As a batsman he had everything, yet Victor Trumper believed in enjoying a good knock, and when he felt he had achieved enough, calling a halt.

'While possessing skill with the bat which, in my opinion equalled that of Sir Donald, Trumper had the human failings which Bradman, the run-collecting machine, would not tolerate. Once Trumper reached his century, he was satisfied: it mattered little if he swung at a full-toss in the next over and watched the ball drop on the bails. Trumper paid little heed to the state of the pitch, or even the quality of the bowling: many a time I have watched, enchanted, as he nonchalently clouted a 50 or 60 while a succession of partners at the other end of the pitch were scratching about, patting the turf and complaining about the shocking conditions.

'What a lesson Victor could have given the Australians who, at Old Trafford in 1956, preferred to blame the pitch, rather than their own puerile batting efforts, for an abysmal failure.

'As a fielder, Trumper again revealed an affinity with Bradman, stationing himself in the long grass. He specialised in the long throw, itself a testimony to the latent strength and power contained in his sunburned limbs.'

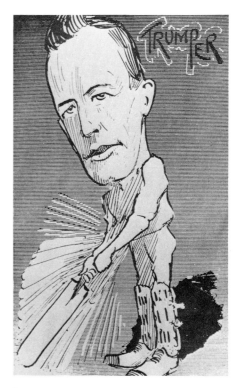

How one cartoonist of the era saw the flashing blade of Victor Trumper. The caption reads: 'Victor Trumper, Australia's batting star of the "Golden Age".'

After the match against Oxford University, the team rushed back to London to accept Madame Melba's invitation to hear her sing in La Traviata at Covent Garden. Melba sang like a veritable nightingale and so enthused Trumper and his colleagues that Darling's men sent Melba a bouquet of flowers arranged in the form of cricket stumps with the word 'Australia' emblazoned across them. It was at Southampton on the 1899 tour (Victor's first England tour) that he, along with Frank Laver and Alf Johns, went to the Cowes Regatta. There the Emperor of Germany's victorious yacht *Meteor*, the Prince of Wales's *Britannia* and a fleet of other distinguished yachts swayed gently at anchor. After strolling down the crowded parade, peeping at many side-shows, the trio went to the Marine Hotel for lunch. There they met a Mr Harcourt (Trumper mentions Harcourt in his 1902 diary). Mr Harcourt took the Test trio under his wing and took them to look over his yacht, the *Heloise*, and for refreshments. They went with Harcourt to the Royal Squadron Yacht Club just in time to see the finish of the race for the Australia Cup. They began a series of introductions to all the distinguished guests. Barons, Earls — starting with the Vice Commodore, the Marquis of Ormonde, and ending with the Club

Opposing captains Joe Darling (left) and W G Grace at Hastings, England, 11 September 1905. (*Frank Laver*)

Commodore, King Edward VII (then Prince of Wales).

On the lawn at the back of the club house Trumper, Laver and Johns were introduced to many heiresses and ladies of title. The ladies were intrigued by the Australian trio and urged Mr Harcourt to introduce them. After strolling among the ladies, laughing and joking, Mr Harcourt asked them to accompany him up the street where he wanted to conduct some business. On their return they happened to come across Queen Victoria. Her Majesty was seated in a carriage, beside the Duchess of York and Princess Victoria of Schleswig-Holstein. Noticing Mr Harcourt as the carriage moved slowly past, Queen Victoria graciously bowed to Mr Harcourt and then the Australians. It was a great moment for the Test trio.

In his book *An Australian Cricketer on Tour* (Chapman and Hall, London, 1905), Frank Laver hits out at the England players who persisted in writing articles for the press. The Australians had a clause in their contract which prohibited them from so doing: 'No member of the team shall correspond for any newspaper by letter or cable or otherwise during the tour. A breach of this renders the culprit liable to a fine of £100.' Such stringent conditions prevailed right up until the World Series Cricket incursion, although the captain or manager of Australian touring teams was allowed to handle media matters. Other players could be quoted in the press, radio or television, only after having sought and been given permission by the manager to do so. These days in Australia, players are given a free hand to a certain extent, although were they to write or say anything to the detriment of the game they would incur the wrath of the Board — and such penalty these days hits the pocket hard.

Trumper did not have a great 1905 tour. In the Tests he scored a sequence of 13 (retired hurt), 0 (absent hurt), 31, 8, 0, 11, 30, 4, 28, but averaged 35.96 in all matches. He injured his back in the first innings of the First Test, at Nottingham, over 29, 30 and 31 May, 1905. Significantly, with Trumper sidelined, England won that match by a massive 213 runs. England won the series 2-0.

Victor and Annie enjoyed their honeymoon trip to England,

The Australians went to Wimbledon and watched American Miss Sutton defeat Miss Douglass of England. Trumper can be clearly seen in the middle foreground. He is the taller of the two young men in straw boaters. (*Frank Laver*)

Trumper ready to drive . . . two goats! Annie Trumper is at left in white dress and dark hair. This photo was taken at Hastings during the 1905 tour.

although Annie could have received better treatment from the other women in the party. But Annie and Victor visited the theatre and Annie helped nurse Victor back to health after the traumatic First Test when he ricked his back. They went to Wimbledon to watch Miss Sutton, the American girl, beat Miss Douglass. Against Kent they found themselves embroiled in a confetti fight — all part of Canterbury Week. The Australian team might have lost the good natured paper fight where male and female were locked in mortal combat, but they won the match by an innings and 35 runs, Victor scoring 59 and Tibby Cotter bowling like the wind to grab 12 wickets for the game.

In 1909 Victor toured England for the last time. By then the Board had full control, yet both he and Warwick Armstrong refused to sign the Board contract. These senior men were appeased. Soon the Board would not be so tolerant. It was the first real act of defiance since the trouble in 1906. Ill-health did not help Victor and again he had a relatively poor time of it in England.

Victor played just one first-class match in the 1908-9 summer and he scored a duck. He played just seven innings for Paddington, his last summer with the club he had adorned since 1896, hitting a total of 604 runs at 86.28 with a top score of 260. Victor's 1909 tour of England saw him hit just 1435 runs at 33.37 in 45 innings. But he toured under his friend and mentor Monty Noble and in the Tests managed a highest score of 73 at Kennington Oval, on 10 August, 1909. In that match Warren Bardsley became the first Test batsman to score a century in each innings of a Test. It was also Frank Woolley's Test debut. Many thought Trumper had turned the corner, or rather was over the hill as a Test batsman. But he returned to Australia and settled in to his new home. His health had improved, but it may have been more the flush of sickness rather than the glow of peak fitness. Yet strength remained for one more glorious assault on the Test stage. Again family and business

The Trumper home in Help Street, Chatswood, Sydney. This is a postcard of the era.

dominated for one more Australian summer. Victor played just one first-class match for NSW v Rest of Australia. He hit 105 and for Gordon, his new club, Victor scored 518 runs at an average of 47.09.

Despite this aggregate and average, few people could have envisaged the batting that was to come the following Australian summer. Percy Sherwell's South Africans were to take the full brunt of Trumper's genius. For Gordon in 1910-11, he scored 482 in nine innings. In 20

A postcard from 1905: 'A handful of Australians.' They proved just that when they retained the Ashes, beating England 2-1.

THE AUSTRALIAN CRICKETERS 1909

W.W.ARMSTRONG

V.TRUMPER

F.LAVER

P.A.MALISTER   A.COTTER

A.J.HOPKINS

W.CARKEEK

R.HARTIGAN

W.J.WHITTY

W.BARDSLEY   S.E.GREGORY

C.C.MACARTNEY

V.RANSFORD

H.CARTER

J.A.O'CONNOR

M.A.NOBLE
captain

DAVIES COPYRIGHT

A HANDFUL OF AUSTRALIANS

first-class knocks (for both NSW and Australia) Trumper hit 1246 runs at an average of 69.22. He flayed the South Africans in the five Tests. His sequence of scores: 27, 34 and 159, 214 not out and 28, 7 and 87, 31 and 74 not out — 661 runs at 94.42. It was the only time in his career at Test level that Victor's aggregate and average approached what everyone became accustomed to expecting Don Bradman to achieve. But it proved that Trumper was no spent force. He played against Pelham Warner's 1911-12 England team in Australia and was selected vice-captain to Clem Hill for the 1912 tour of England. But fate took a hand and neither Trumper nor Hill toured.

It was indeed, with the Big Six (Trumper, Hill, Warwick Armstrong, Hanson Carter, Vernon Ransford and Tibby Cotter) opting out of the 1912 tour, the end of an era; the twilight of the Golden Age of Cricket.

9

THE RELUCTANT CHAMPION

Victor Trumper was a somewhat reluctant champion. It is a strange feature of Trumper's career that he declined so often to take the field for New South Wales. The *Referee* of 17 February, 1915, commented: 'When the career of the wonderful Trumper is written up by historians of the future, his fitful appearances in the eleven of New South Wales from 1904 to 1910 will puzzle them vastly.' It certainly puzzles this writer and in Phil Derriman's *History of the NSW Cricket Association* it is stated that if Trumper had reasons for declining to play so often, those reasons are not recorded in the minutes of the association.

One year the *Sydney Mail* said Trumper had withdrawn from the team to play Victoria in Melbourne because the match was to be played over Christmas and Victor could not afford the time away from his business. On another occasion, when Trumper declined to play against South Australia in Sydney, the *Sydney Mail* recorded: 'Because his family had gone up to the mountains to stay for some days, and it would have been inconvenient for him to have played.' One might surmise that Trumper's frequent absence from NSW sides was because by 1904 he was a world class batsman, veteran of two England tours and that mere Intercolonial matches held little interest for him. However, this cannot be so as Trumper continued to play club cricket for Paddington (later Gordon). It might well have been money. Before 1905 there was no Board and even though the Test men received little in way of expenses to play Intercolonial matches, there was always the chance to tour England and make up for the shortfall, with plenty to spare in most cases.

That Austin Diamond was made NSW captain over Victor in 1909-10 (when Noble retired) was probably because of Trumper's frequent failure to turn out in all matches. Significantly in that 1909-10 summer, Trumper played only one first-class match. He played for NSW against Rest of Australia and hit a brilliant 105 in what was Charles (C T B) Turner's benefit match. The previous summer Trumper did not play any matches for NSW but played in a trial match, the Australian XI v Rest of Australia in Sydney. Trumper scored a duck. But he won a trip to England in 1909, his fourth and final tour of England.

In 1908-9 Trumper had a bumper season for Paddington, scoring 604 runs in seven innings for an average of 86.28. His highest score was 260. The following summer he switched clubs, joining Gordon, with

Chatswood Oval its home base. The main pavilion is now called the Trumper Pavilion. In his first season for Gordon, Victor had 12 innings, scoring 518 runs at an average of 47.09. His highest score was 105. Club matches, too, were held in esteem; far more highly in Trumper's time than today; although administrators realise that club cricket is the grass roots and without such a competition, a strong Test team could never be selected. But in Trumper's time there were fewer State games and a player's club performances came under closer scrutiny then than nowadays. It is also worth noting that Trumper toured England in 1909 yet he played just one game for NSW in 1908-9 and in his one innings, he got a duck. On his return from England he again opted out of big cricket, playing only for his club team, then returned to play against Percy Sherwell's South Africans.

In all first-class cricket that season (1910-11) Trumper had 20 innings, hitting 1246 runs, with a highest score of 214 not out against South Africa at Adelaide Oval, although Australia lost that match.

Trumper set to drive in this posed shot.

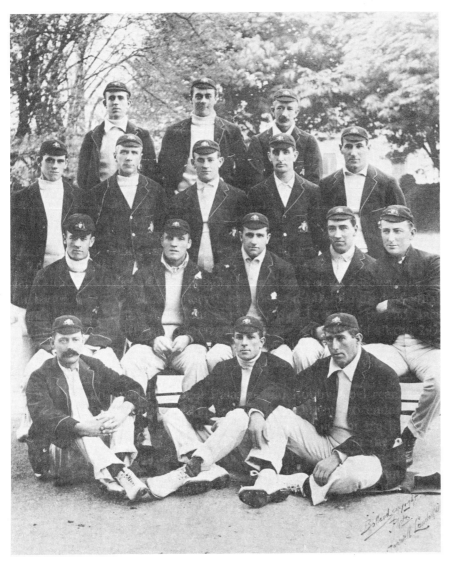

The Australian team of 1909. This photographed was signed by the players and presented to team scorer Bill Ferguson. It reads: 'To Mr Ferguson with the best wishes of the Australian Cricket Team, 1909.'
(*S S Ramamurthy*)

This is the ball that Trumper hit . . .
for 159 runs against Percy
Sherwell's South Africans in the
summer of 1910-11. (*S S
Ramamurthy*)

Here are Trumper's first-class figures in all countries. Note the
seasons in Australia where Trumper played very little cricket for NSW
or, as in two summers, not at all:

VICTOR TRUMPER'S FIRST-CLASS RECORD IN AUSTRALIA

Year	Inns	Not Out	Runs	H/Score	Average
1894-5	4	1	22	11	7.33
1897-8	10	–	192	68	19.20
1898-9	15	1	873	292*	62.35
1899-00	10	–	721	208	72.10
1900-01	7	–	458	230	65.42
1901-02	18	–	486	73	27.00
1902-03	9	–	446	178	49.55
1903-04	21	3	990	185*	55.00
1904-05	4	–	198	81	49.50
1905-06	6	–	250	101	41.66
1906-07	3	–	23	11	7.66
1907-08	19	–	797	166	41.94
1908-09	1	–	0	0	
1909-10	1	–	105	105	105.00
1910-11	20	2	1246	214*	69.22
1911-12	20	3	583	113	34.29
1912-13	13	3	843	201	84.30
1913-14	5	–	107	32	21.40
1914-15	–	–	–	–	–

* = not out

Not included in those figures was the fabulous 67 Victor Trumper scored against Stoddart's 1894-5 England team. Victor scored those runs on Saturday, 22 December, 1894, despite his mother pleading with him to stay in bed. Victor had influenza. He played in that match for the Sydney Juniors — a side of 18 promising Sydney youngsters — alongside old schoolmate Monty Noble, who hit an unconquered 152. Straight after the game Victor went home and straight to bed, where he stayed for the next two days. After a dismal start to his first-class career, just 22 runs in four innings, Victor was banished from the NSW team until the 1897-98 season. His first State match was against South Australia at Adelaide Oval, where he was run out for 11 in the first innings and caught by Ernie 'Jonah' Jones off George Giffen's bowling for a duck in the second. When Vic returned to the side in 1897-8, he averaged only 19.20 in 10 completed innings, but NSW stuck by him. Next summer he hit two double centuries and averaged 62.35, eventually winning a trip to England with Joe Darling's 1899 Australian team.

In England

Year	Inns	Not Out	Runs	H/Score	Average
1899	48	3	1556	300*	34.57
1902	53	–	2570	128	48.49
1905	47	1	1667	110	36.23
1909	45	2	1435	150	33.57

In South Africa

Year	Inns	Not Out	Runs	H/Score	Average
1902	8	1	307	70	43.85

In New Zealand

Year	Inns	Not Out	Runs	H/Score	Average
1905	5	1	436	172	109.00
1914	9	–	628	293	69.77
Career total	401	21	16,939	300*	44.57

* = not out

In all first-class matches Trumper scored 42 centuries. However, the number of centuries Trumper scored varies from book to book. It intrigued me that Monty Noble could have the figure at 41 in his book, *The Game's The Thing*. Noble excludes Trumper's 293 against Canterbury, at Christchurch in 1914. This was Trumper's last great knock. Some researchers have included the 211 Trumper hit against Southland, Invercargil, NZ on 11 March, 1914, but this was a designated one-day match and so it could not be deemed a first-class fixture. And against a Transvaal Fifteen over 15, 16 and 17 October, 1902, Trumper hit a whirlwind 218 not out, but again this was not a first-class match. Irving Rosenwater, one of the world's leading statisticians, confirmed Trumper's first-class run total and number of centuries to be 42.

Trumper's centuries
(first-class matches only)

1898-99

292*	NSW v Tasmania	Sydney
253	NSW v New Zealand	Sydney

1899

300*	Australians v Sussex	Brighton
135*	Australia v England	Lord's
104	Australians v Gloucestershire	Bristol

1899-1900

208	NSW v Queensland	Sydney
165	NSW v South Australia	Adelaide

1900-01

230	NSW v Victoria	Sydney

1902

128	Australians v Cambridge University	Cambridge
127	Australians v The Players	Harrogate
125	Australians v Gloucestershire	Cheltenham
120	Australians v South of England	Hastings
109		
119	Australians v Essex	Lyten
113	Australians v An England Xl	Bradford
105	Australians v MCC	Lord's
104	Australia v England	Manchester
101	Australians v Surrey	Kennington O

1902-03

178	NSW v South Australia	Sydney
130	NSW v Victoria	Sydney

1903-04

185*	Australia v England	Sydney
113	Australia v England	Adelaide

This series of sequential photographs are taken from the only known movie film of Trumper in action. It was taken at Lord's in 1905 and shows Victor clouting a ball through the leg side. Note the blurring of Trumper's bat in the third photo as he rapidly brings it down to meet the speeding ball. (*Cinesound Movietone Library*)

1904-05		
172	Australians v New Zealand	Wellington
1905		
110	Australians v Worcestershire	Worcester
108	Australians v Gloucestershire	Bristol
1905-06		
101	NSW v Victoria	Sydney
1907-08		
166	Australia v England	Sydney
135	NSW v South Australia	Sydney
119	NSW v Victoria	Melbourne
1909		
150	Australians v An England X!	Blackpool
132	Australians v Cambridge University	Cambridge
115	Australians v Derbyshire	Derby
1909-10		
105	NSW v Rest of Australia	Sydney
1910-11		
214*	Australia v South Africa	Adelaide
159	Australia v South Africa	Melbourne
142	NSW v Victoria	Melbourne
1911-12		
113	Australia v England	Sydney
1912-13		
201*	NSW v South Australia	Sydney
138	NSW v Victoria	Sydney
126*	NSW v Rest of Australia	Sydney
1914		
293	Australians v Canterbury	Christchurch

* = not out

Trumper's bat from the 1907-8 season versus England. It has more than 400 signatures of famous cricketers on the bat face and back. (*S S Ramamurthy*)

Trumper in partnerships of more than 200

433 with Arthur Sims   8th wicket Australia v Canterbury   1914
298 with Reg Duff   1st wicket NSW v SA   1902-03
270 with Eric Barbour   8th wicket NSW v Victoria   1912-13
269 with Clem Hill   6th wicket Australians v
                                        New Zealand XI   1904-05
267 with Reg Duff   1st wicket NSW v Victoria   1902-03
258 with Frank Iredale 6th wicket NSW v Tasmania   1898-99

Fastest partnerships
165 in 50 minutes with Herbie Collins NSW v Tasmania   1912-13
269 in 107 minutes with Clem Hill Australians v
                                        New Zealand XI   1904-05
433 in 180 minutes with Arthur Sims Australia v
                                        Canterbury   1914

Century first wicket partnership in each innings of one match
113 and 119* with Reg Duff NSW v Victoria   1903-04
122 and 121 with Warren Bardsley NSW v South Africa   1910-11
* = not out

Bowling

In all first-class matches Trumper took 64 wickets for 2031 runs at an average of 31.73. For NSW, he took 33 wickets for 1154, at 34.96 apiece. Trumper's best performance with the ball was 5/19 against Cambridge University on 9 June, 1902. Trumper took 5/33 off 13 overs against Essex just weeks earlier and between those two grand bowling feats, he clean bowled the great WG Grace in the Australia v MCC & Ground fixture at Lord's; not forgetting his 86 and 105 in the same match. In addition to those 64 first-class wickets, Trumper took 171 catches in his 255 matches.

Test cricket

Opponent	Year	Inns	N.O.	Runs	H.S.	Av.	100's
England	1899	9	1	280	135*	35.00	1
England	1901-02	10	–	219	65	12.90	–
England	1902	8	–	247	104	30.87	1
South Africa	1902	6	1	239	70	47.80	–
England	1903-04	10	1	574	185*	63.77	2
England	1905	8	1	125	31	17.85	–
England	1907-08	10	–	338	166	33.80	1
England	1909	9	1	211	73	26.37	–
South Africa	1910-11	9	2	661	214*	94.42	2
England	1911-12	10	1	269	113	29.88	1
		89	8	3163	214*	39.04	8

* = not out

Record for New South Wales

Matches	Inns	N.O.	Runs	H.S.	Av.	100s
73	123	9	5823	292*	51.07	15

Bowling: 33 wickets for 1154 at 34.96 apiece.

*Trumper captained NSW 24 times in first-class
matches between 1907-08 and 1913-14.

The record is impressive, but certainly suffers greatly in comparison
with Don Bradman's incredible record and with that of many other
batsmen of great ability and even those who might be termed players of
application and fierce desire rather than batsmen of flair and more than
a touch of genius.

There seems little doubt that Trumper was a reluctant champion. In
the *Referee* of 29 December, 1909 it was pointed out that Trumper
would have been given the NSW captaincy on Noble's retirement,
but for Victor's all-too-frequent absences from the State side over many
seasons: 'In the ordinary course of events, V Trumper must have
become captain of NSW in the absence or withdrawal of M A Noble
from first-class cricket. But VT has figured so rarely in inter-State
matches of late years that a few weeks back it was not surprising to find
the position awarded to another player apparently more keenly
interested in the supremacy of the State.'

The *Referee* also brought to notice that Trumper had played in just
four of the NSW team's last 16 Sheffield Shield matches.

'It may astonish you,' the *Referee* said. Trumper was evidently more
surprised than the *Referee*, because he sent a letter of protest to the New
South Wales Cricket Association and copies to the Press, asking for it
to be published 'so as to prevent any misunderstanding in the public
mind regarding my attitude in the cricket field.' The letter, dated
January, was addressed to NSWCA secretary Mr Percy Bowden:

'In reply to your notice of the 4th instant, I must state that I am not
available for the forthcoming match against South Australia. Your
selectors will not be surprised. For the first time in the history of
Australian cricket your association has adopted the English custom
of appointing the captain of their State team, but why not have
followed that custom and appointed a senior player, providing he
could play in a majority of matches.

'Your association not doing so is an injustice to me, and leaves
me only one course to adopt, and that is to withdraw from the eleven.
On my arrival from England the First Eleven was selected to play
against the Second Eleven, and a captain other than myself appointed
by the selection committee. I immediately withdrew from that team,
and a similar action of the committee regarding the team for South
Australia and Victoria necessitated me dropping out of these teams
also. Had the selection of the captain been left to the different teams,
I have no objection whatever to playing under any captain, no matter
even if he be the junior member, and (if necessary) giving him any
advice at my disposal. I would like to state that Mr Diamond is a very

dear friend of mine, and this action I am taking must not be construed as being against him. Under usual cricket conditions I would have been pleased to have made the trip to South Australia and Victoria in accordance with my promise to some of the leading cricket people in South Australia, but, owing to your committee's new action in appointing the captain I could not possibly do so. I greatly regret that the treatment of your association leaves me no other course but to retire from the team to meet South Australia.'

Trumper wrote that Diamond was a 'dear friend of mine' and that may well have been so, but certainly Victor was upset that Diamond won the captaincy over him. He stated that had the players picked the captain he would have been satisfied. Certainly Trumper would have been pleased, for it seems certain that Trumper would have been the players' first choice. Trumper was peeved that the selection committee was empowered to select the NSW skipper.

Perhaps Trumper's frustration was a hangover from when the Board wrested the initiative away from the players touring England and now another once-exclusive players' right was being taken away. However, Trumper's stand finally won the day. At the beginning of the 1910-11 summer, Victor was made NSW captain. He did not have immediate success and the *Referee* of 7 December, 1910, wrote a rather premature piece, hitting Trumper's captaincy: 'As captain, V Trumper was not seen to advantage. He started badly, and never seemed to be able to get a grip on things in the way that M A Noble used to.'

Cricket correspondents of the day wrote that Trumper did not appear to find it easy to impose his will on his fellow players. He would, for instance, often signal quietly to a fieldsman when he wanted a fielding position changed only to find the fieldsman not watching his captain. However, Trumper had the last laugh. He led NSW to victory in the Sheffield Shield competition and the NSWCA presented him with a dressing case and lady's silver set worth twenty guineas in recognition of his fine captaincy.

As if to knock the *Referee* for a towering six, an English cricket magazine commented: 'At first he was not happy guiding the reins as could have been desired. But he quickly got a grip of the side, and his leadership in the match with Victoria was as skilful as anything one has seen in interstate cricket for many a day.'

10

MONEY, MONEY, MONEY

In December 1899 Victor Trumper had his first run in with officialdom over that most evil of evils . . . money. Victor had requested ten shillings as match expenses, but the New South Wales Cricket Association shelved his request on recommendation.

One of the delegates in 1899 was one William Percy McElhone who was later to emerge as the strong man of Australian cricket and chairman of the Australian Board of Control for International Cricket during the 1912 dispute. It was the first occasion when Trumper and McElhone found themselves at loggerheads. Yet following his brilliant 1902 tour of England, Trumper received a handsome sum of 100 guineas from the NSWCA in recognition of his deeds. The amount would have taken a low-grade public servant a good part of 12 months to earn. Philip Derriman, in the history of the NSWCA, writes: 'The cheque was handed him by the association's president George Reid, a former premier of NSW, who later became the Prime Minister of Australia. Reid told him: "Whilst thus offering to you our heartfelt admiration of the consummate skill and rare capacity you have evinced in the arena of contest, we take this opportunity to express our appreciation of your manful bearing, genial personality and all those many qualities of heart and mind which have endeared you to all with whom you have been brought into contact".'

The 1899 incident apart, Victor's first conflict with NSW cricket officials came in 1906. He was one of ten NSW players suspended by the association for signing an agreement to play for the Melbourne Cricket Club if the club brought out an English team in 1906-7. The history of this flare-up appears in the chapter: Before the Storm. The Board had been formed less than a year before and its very survival seemed to be at stake. The dispute was settled a few months later and the suspensions were lifted, but the bitterness remained. At the beginning of the 1906-7 season Trumper and a few other NSW players declined to play for their State in a couple of matches. Trumper denied this had anything whatsoever to do with the dispute he had had with the NSWCA, but most newspapers of the day did not believe Trumper and hauled him over the coals.

Throughout the dispute the Sydney press generally sided with the NSWCA and against the players. When Trumper withdrew from an early game against Western Australia, with the excuse that he believed

The cover of the official souvenir booklet of Trumper's Eleven to Queensland in 1906.

ABOUT TRUMPER'S TEAM
QUEENSLAND TOUR, 1906.

The Captain of the Eleven.

VICTOR THOMAS TRUMPER is by common consent Australia's Champion batsman, and beyond a doubt his records entitle him to that distinction. Born at Sydney on November 2nd, 1877, he began scoring his hundreds at Crown Street Superior Public School, where he was educated. His first experience of Senior Cricket in Sydney was with a club known as the Sydney Cricket Club, composed chiefly of promoted Junior players, among them M. A. Noble, S. E. Gregory, and A. L. Newell. On the introduction of the local system, Trumper was connected first with South Sydney, and afterwards with Paddington, for whom his performances have been unparalleled. His highest score is 335 against Redfern, made in January, 1903. On that occasion he and D. A. Gee (172) made 423 together for the first wicket in 135 minutes. During the summer of 1897-8 his batting average for Paddington was as follows:—8 innings, 3 not out, 191* highest score, 1421 runs, 204.20 average. His scores were—82, 123, 125, 85, 120*, 191*, 133, and 162*. Trumper has always been a marvellously rapid scorer in club cricket, and has quite an extensive following in Sydney. The Champion's introduction to great matches occurred in December, 1894, when he scored 67 for Eighteen Sydney Colts v. Stoddart's English Eleven. Almost immediately he appeared in Sheffield Shield Matches—at the age of 17—but it was not until 1898-9 that he began his succession of brilliant run-getting efforts in important matches. His greatest scores in chronological order have been 292* v. Tasmania, in December, 1898; 253 v. New Zealand in February, 1899; 300* v. Sussex, in July, 1899; 208 v. Queensland, in November, 1899; 230 v. Victoria, in February, 1901; and 218* v. Fifteen of Transvaal, in October, 1902. He visited England with Australian Elevens in 1899, 1902, and 1905, each tour being a pronounced success. In 1899 he scored 135* in his first Test Match, since when he has made three other such scores in the greatest of all cricket contests. In 1902, which, it will be remembered, was an exceedingly wet season, he established Australian records by scoring 2570 runs without once being dismissed without scoring, and by obtaining two separate hundreds v. Essex. Last year he was handicapped a good deal by an injury to his back, but still he was far from being a passenger. Victor Trumper can bowl as well as bat, and used to send down a few very fast overs. His best performance with the ball in first-class matches was his taking of 5 wickets for 19 runs v. Cambridge, in 1902. Fine fielding at third man and in the outfield add still further to his greatness. There are very few first-class cricketers indeed who can throw a greater distance. The Champion stands 5 feet 10½ inches high, and weighs about 12 stone.

Page one from the souvenir booklet. (*S S Ramamurthy*)

the NSW team unrepresentative, the *Bulletin* attacked him in a savage editorial: 'Trumper's decision not to go to Perth is good news for West Australian spectators. Whatever Trumper may have been in the past and may be again, he is at the present time not worth going across the street to see. This is the gentleman who objected to accompany the team to Westralia because he considered it weak and unrepresentative! Certainly it is a lot stronger since he kindly eliminated himself and made way for that sterling batsman Hopkins. In the light of his recent performances on the field, Trumper's other performances are amusing, and if he only had some glimmering of humour he would go away into a corner and smile at himself.'

That autumn Trumper took a side to Queensland, the first time a star outfit had gone to that area. The team arrived in Charters Towers on 25 April, 1906. The team was mobbed at Charters Towers railway station and with deft footwork Victor escaped the mob armed with cigarette cards of their heroes and keen to hug a real 'live Australian Test cricketer'. Trumper's men had already played in Townsville and wondered what they had struck when they got off the train. Albert 'Tibby' Cotter was besieged outside the station, while Trumper and the others clambered aboard a coach bound for Winterbottom's Hotel.

'We have had some rough times,' Cotter laughed, 'but this is the savagest place we have struck yet.' Cotter's immense strength (he was built like Jeff Thomson) enabled him to break ranks and join Trumper's coach as it started off. But until midnight, hundreds of cricket lovers crowded about the team hotel to get a glimpse of their favorites. Next day there was a mayoral reception for Trumper's team and Victor replied to a warm reception. He thanked the welcoming committee and said: 'Our reception at your railway station last night was rough but hearty (laughter). During our sojourn we hope to show you something to recompense you all for your trouble (applause). The Mayor has spoken of obedience to the captain. I have heard rumors that my team are going to leave me out (laughter). We look forward to a good game. If we lose I hope to find bowlers — which Australia wants badly.'

Then Mr J Carroll, Queenton Shire chairman, proposed a toast to the Mayor, Alderman Clark. During his address, Mr Clark said: 'I told Captain Trumper that I am the oldest cricketer present, having played the game 30 years. I told Captain Trumper that I had once played a game when the temperature reached 110 degrees (F), but he went one better and said he had played in Melbourne with the glass registering 120 degrees F. I was settled.'

Trumper's team comprised Albert Hopkins, Robert Hickson, S J Redgrave, Albert 'Tibby' Cotter, Andrew Newell, Ernest Bubb, James Barnes, Thomas Foster, William McIntyre (wicketkeeper) and Charles Gorry. It was wholly arranged by the players and all profits went to the players. The NSWCA had nothing to do with the promotion or the organisation of Trumper's 1906 Queensland tour. At the same time, the tour did not endear him to the NSW authorities. Already a black mark was against his name for daring to sign with the Melbourne Cricket Club in the hope that the club would bring an England touring team to Australia the following summer. Victor had always liked the idea of the players controlling the purse-strings. A financial flop and the players paid dearly; a bonanza and the players shared the spoils.

Trumper conducted many interviews with local pressmen throughout the tour. In one such interview he called for a North Queensland Cricket Association to be formed, so cricket could be brought to the fore in that area. 'Southern cricketers have never been in touch with North Queensland,' he said. 'I believe there are some good cricketers here and I hope my team will discover them. This team I lead is a pioneering team bringing cricket to a new frontier.'

Despite Trumper's enthusiasm, his side was the only such tour undertaken until Alan Kippax, a NSW and Test colleague of Don Bradman, took a side there in 1931. Kippax was also thought to have been one player who resembled the style of Victor Trumper with the bat. Another was Archie Jackson, who toured England in 1930 but died at the age of 23 in 1933. One of his pall-bearers was Don Bradman.

Trumper told the correspondent that there was insufficient interest in cricket at the club level in North Queensland. 'The youth after he leaves school loses all interest and drifts away from the game,' he said. In NSW the city was divided into electorates for Parliamentary purposes and each electorate had its own cricket team and cricket ground situated in the electorate. 'Before one can play in one of those electorates, a six-months' residential qualification is necessary,' Trumper said.

'This means that any person living in an electorate when he visits his electorate to see the play knows that every member of that cricket team is a member of the electorate. Hence we obtain a local following and the matches in Sydney are splendidly patronised. The wickets must be of turf. Any member of the club is always within a short distance of the ground. And consequently it is no trouble for him to get to the ground for practice.'

Trumper said the electorate system had been in play for 10 to 12 years in Sydney and had revived the interest in cricket. 'We have had a crowd of 10,000 people watching a Saturday afternoon electoral match in Sydney.'

How are the games played?

Trumper: 'The match has to be decided on two Saturdays, but this means that the side winning the toss takes the wicket and scores as fast as possible so as to be able to declare the innings closed on the following Saturday and give themselves sufficient time to win the match. We lose no time. We get three points for an outright win and two points for a win on the first innings. This has made the best of us fast scorers. We take the risk. But the more risks we take the more alert we get and it has made it very interesting for the spectators.'

'The stonewaller gets a bad time. In fact his days are numbered in Sydney. If it is possible to do without him in Sydney he is done without. He may be picked, but only to make up a team.'

Asked how Australia was off for bowlers, Trumper said the standard of bowling by 1906 had not improved at the same rate as the batting.

'We have a number of really good bowlers, but for exceptional bowlers for the next Test matches we are sadly lacking. Perhaps North Queensland will be good enough to give us one or two. A bowler is born — he is like a poet — he cannot be made. A natural bowler who runs up and bowls the ball — the ball doing what it likes — swerving and breaking without the bowler knowing what he is doing is the bowler that is wanted.'

'The batsman cannot find out what the bowler is trying to do because

VICTOR TRUMPER

What W. G. Grace was to England, so is Trumper to Australia. He shines among the cricketers of the day—with all the lustre of a star of the first magnitude. He is like no one, and no one is like him. As he stands to receive the ball he is not exactly a stylist, for there is an ungainly bending of his right knee; but the moment he gets into position to make his stroke, he becomes the most brilliant and fascinating batsman I have ever seen. It is somewhat disconcerting to your best bowler to find three fours knocked off the first over of the match, each four in all probability a different stroke, and each one rushing to the boundary as with the speed of thought. There is not a stroke in the game that he does not play to perfection, and he is extraordinarily quick on his feet, often jumping out to hit, and as often jumping out, and then, finding the ball too short to drive, getting quickly back and cutting it. He is the idol of the Australian crowd, and to hear him talk one would imagine he had never made a run in his life.—P. F. WARNER.

Another page from the booklet shows a signed photo of Trumper and words of high praise from Pelham Warner.
(*S S Ramamurthy*)

In a recent interview with C. B. FRY,
VICTOR TRUMPER said:
" The Australian boy learns his CRICKET by means of a piece of wood fashioned into the shape of a BAT with a hatchet, and a TIN CAN for a WICKET, but as soon as he is able to procure THE BEST, he will have it."
Everybody knows this statement to be true.

EVE IN THE GARDEN of EDEN

Not Dressed in Fig Leaves,
Nor Surrounded by Fruit Trees or Serpents.

SELLS ONLY THE BEST MAKES OF

CRICKET & LAWN TENNIS MATERIAL,

FOOTBALL, LACROSSE, BASEBALL,

And every other Ball(y) game under the sun.

PRICES LOWER AND QUALITY MUCH HIGHER THAN ANYONE ELSE.

REPAIRS

Club Secretaries and Players are advised that Repairs to all descriptions of Broken Bats will be effected by a first-class workman. One trial is asked for, when satisfaction is guaranteed to follow.

OLD BATS MADE EQUAL TO NEW.

New blades selected and fitted to old handles at lowest prices.

TENNIS REPAIRS A SPECIALTY.

R. W. EVE, 160 Queen Street,
BRISBANE.

An advertisement from the souvenir booklet. (*S S Ramamurthy*)

Three advertisements of various games played by Trumper's Eleven during the 1906 tour of Queensland.

the bowler does not seem to know what he is doing himself.'

Our correspondent was non-plussed. He quizzed Trumper: 'That sounds like a contradiction in terms?'

'I will give you an instance. In the beginning of 1899, Young, the Essex bowler was in the British Navy. The county bought him out of the Navy and, in his first county match, which was against the Australian Eleven, Young bowled wonderfully well. Essex defeated us by an innings. The ball swerved and came off the pitch at a great rate. He represented England in about three Test matches that summer. After 1899, Young tried to learn to bowl, with the result that he has not played for England since.'

(Harding Young was a strongly-built left-handed bowler with a deceptive curving flight. In that match against Trumper and the Australians, Young took 11 wickets for 74 for the game. He also took 4/30 against Australia in the Leeds Test. He played only two Tests for a return of 14 wickets at 21.83 apiece).

The interview continued: Are there natural bowlers? 'Yes, there are many natural bowlers. McBeth of Sydney was one of them. There may be many who have never even handled a ball. Let some of them try.'

Do you advise catching a cricketer when he is young? 'Yes, certainly when he is very young. School cricket must be encouraged and silver medals, which cost only a few shillings each, are great incentives to school teams to win their competitions. In Sydney the great public schools have always had a competition, but in the superior public schools, only since the formation of the Public Schools Amateur Athletic Association. The boys receive a half holiday on Friday to play their matches.'

Where did you first learn your cricket? 'At school, Crown Street Superior Public School, Surry Hills — right in the heart of the city — playing on uncovered asphalt wickets with a composition ball. The fastest and as true a wicket as one could wish to have. I played in the school competition every Friday. I used to get very fair scores. I was very fortunate. I got amongst the Second Carltons under the captaincy of Charles Bannerman at a very early age, and learned a good bit about the game both from Charlie and Alec Bannerman.'

In a jovial mood, Trumper allows a ball to pass for the photographer. On the tour of Queensland, he allowed few such balls to pass untouched and, in fact, became the first man to hit a ball out of the Brisbane Cricket Ground.

Do you like cricket? 'Well, I like it after a spell, but having had three seasons straight off, and this trip on top of it, I am beginning to feel a little stale and I will welcome the winter spell. In the off seasons I used to play football, but now I play baseball.'

Trumper's team was feted everywhere they travelled during this historic Queensland tour. The Southerners were astonished by the amount of thick and lush grassland; the standard of accommodation, shops and business houses and especially the warehouses in most of the larger towns, which were far superior to that which they had expected.

Victor displayed his great talents to best advantage against the Mount Morgan Eighteen, when he hit a brilliant 179; against Maryborough Fifteen, when he slammed 128 (his century coming in 45 minutes) and against a Brisbane Eleven when he revealed his artistry in a scintillating innings of 207 not out. In the Brisbane XI was none other than G S

Grouch, the man who six years later won the job to manage the 1912 Australian team to England. Grouch scored only 2, falling to a catch by McIntyre off the bowling of Tibby Cotter. This was the second match against a Brisbane XI, the first was all over in one day, Brisbane going for 16 and 68 (Grouch, bowled Albert Hopkins 2 and lbw Hopkins 2) and Trumper's team hitting 68 and 1/31 (Trumper 30 and 16 not out).

Trumper came in with the score at 93. He batted at No. 4. Brisbane's first innings realised only 87 and Trumper had scored only 13 when he drove a ball firmly to Atkins at mid-off, but the chance went begging, a most expensive miss, as events proved. Soon after, Trumper snicked a ball high over first slip, but he soon settled down to dominate as only he could dominate an innings. At 93 Trumper drove low and hard to Mr G S Grouch at cover. Grouch missed the chance and the spectators must have been pleased that Grouch muffed that one. Trumper played all the strokes one could attribute to the text book, plus many of his own making.

Until that steamy May day in 1906, no batsman had hit a ball right out of the Brisbane Cricket Ground. The first match was played there in June, 1897, and Trumper, in May, 1906, became the first man to achieve the feat by running out to a ball from M McCaffrey. As one correspondent put it: 'It was a hit, a palpable hit. A few balls previously he almost succeeded in performing the feat, the ball pitching on the top of the fence.' Trumper's massive hit soared out of the ground and landed in Stanley St. A mighty blow. Trumper's 207 not out was compiled in 123 minutes.

The tour was a resounding success. The team visited Townsville, Charters Towers, Bundaberg, Rockhampton, Maryborough, Gympie and, of course, Brisbane. The magic of Trumper's batting lured packed houses wherever the team played and the tour was a success, although there are no official records of just how much each man on Trumper's team collected. All the towns and cities afforded Trumper's team a smoke concert. They were feted and Trumper's men rewarded that hospitality with some brilliant cricket.

Trumper led the batting figures with 1044 runs from 17 innings at an average of 104.40. He hit three centuries, including the 207 not out against Brisbane. Thomas Foster scored 706 runs at 54.30 in 14 innings and S J Redgrave compiled 478 runs at 43.45, with one century. Tibby Cotter headed the bowling averages with 63 wickets for 490 runs (a best effort of 9/30). Albert Hopkins returned 50 wickets for 452 (best 8/30) and Andrew Newell took the most wickets — 64 for 612 with a best performance of 11/103.

Trumper's team included three current Test players — Trumper, Cotter and Hopkins — and Newell, who was a fine medium-paced off-spinner whose best performance in Sheffield Shield cricket was 8/56 against Victoria in 1897-8.

There was just one sour note on the tour. Money raised its ugly head before the Trumper match at Gympie. Five local players objected to having been asked to pay for admittance to the Smoke Concert for Trumper's team the night before the game was due to start. The committee stood firm and the five players stood down from the match. The players had threatened to stand down from the game if the Gympie committee did not allow them free admission to the Smoke Concert. The local press described it as a 'storm in a tea-cup'. The match went as planned and the Smoke Concert was well received. Trumper's team hit 360 (Bubb 75, Hickson 80) and Gympie XV scored 144 (Albert Hopkins took 5/19).

Roger Hartigan, who captained the Brisbane teams at the 'Gabba against Trumper's men, was destined to have his name etched in Test cricket history. Batting No. 8 in his first Test — against England at Adelaide (Third Test) — Hartigan hit a first innings 48, then a magnificent 116. He became the fourth Australian to hit a century on his Test debut. However, Hartigan's chances were limited on the Test stage. Living in Brisbane did not help him, for Queensland was isolated from the mainstream of Australian cricket before it won Sheffield Shield status in 1926-7. He was on the Board for 35 years and worked tirelessly to get Queensland a Test match, it finally came in 1928 — both Don Bradman's and Queensland's first Test.

Trumper returned to Sydney for the winter and a spot of baseball. The Englishmen were not to come to Australia in 1906-7 as there was not time for the Board to arrange the tour and the Marylebone Cricket Club was worried that the Board was not fully representative of Australian cricket. By 20 April, 1907, South Australia joined with the Board and Tasmania followed suit on 9 August.

In the 1906-7 season Trumper played only three innings, scoring a modest 23 runs at an average of 7.66. It was his worst summer at the first-class level. He withdrew from a number of matches because he had considered the NSW team 'unrepresentative'. Also, illness struck in the form of scarlet fever, business was similarly ailing and, after three successive seasons (1904-5, the 1905 England tour, then 1905-6, plus the Queensland tour in April and May of 1906) Victor needed a rest.

Although the suspensions were lifted in 1906, the players who signed with the Melbourne Cricket Club were disqualified from holding any office in the NSWCA. Trumper was interviewed in early 1907 and he was quoted in the *Star* on 7 February, 1907, as saying that he would not allow the NSWCA disqualification to prevent him from playing for NSW:

'Yes, I will play on. We (the 10 players) think our duty to the game and to the public is greater than that to the NSWCA.' Asked if he would move to have the disqualification lifted, as he had earlier applied to have the suspension lifted, he said: 'Not again. Once bitten twice shy. For one I won't crawl to them, especially as their object seems to be to heap every indignity upon us. I revel in cricket, but it is too much to put up with the continued insults from a body which is largely influenced by men who represent nobody but themselves.'

Phil Derriman writes in the NSWCA history that 'this is, perhaps, the strongest language Trumper was ever quoted as using. Trumper kept his word and did not move to have the disqualification lifted, but a few months later the association decided to lift them of its own accord.'

11

BEFORE THE STORM

The formation of the Australian Board of Control for International Cricket put many top cricketers' noses out of joint. Before the Board was formed in 1905, tours of England were principally arranged and financed by the leading players. The players often gambled their own money to make England tours and, after hotel and travelling expenses were deducted, they divided up the profits.

It was an arrangement which suited the players admirably, although there were misgivings among the destitute club teams, especially those in Sydney and Melbourne. With each England tour rumors ran riot of how well the players were doing in financial terms. It became increasingly apparent that there was a need for a controlling body at national level to enable profits to be handed back to the clubs through the various State cricket associations. The players were scooping the cream for themselves and the clubs struggled for their very survival.

The Australasian Cricket Council was formed in 1892. It comprised four representatives from the New South Wales, Victorian and South Australian cricket associations. Its aims were to regulate and control international tours, to arrange intercolonial matches and to amend and interpret the Laws of Cricket. New Zealand was not represented although, at one stage, it was hoped to have NZ representation. The Council was disbanded in 1898. It had organised the 1893 Australian tour of England and the 1896 tour.

However, the leading players were seething. As George Giffen wrote in *With Bat and Ball*: 'The captains of seven of the first eight Australian teams to tour England were chosen by the players. The exception was in 1886 when the Melbourne Cricket Club made the appointment of H J H Scott as captain and Ben Wardill as manager — appointments with which the players agreed.' Giffen wrote that in 1896 the Council wanted total control.

'The Council resolved in 1896 (ninth team) to take the reins into its hands,' wrote Giffen.

'In common with many other cricketers, I cannot see what the Council has to do with the matter. If it financed the tours, the position would be entirely different, but it did not take on its shoulders one iota of financial responsibility, as in former years the players had to bear the whole responsibility.' The Council lacked finance and had hoped to raise funds from the first few England tours to enable it to do so, however, the players pointed out to the States that a Council that could not finance tours could not control them and the Council was disbanded. The major lasting contribution to Australian cricket by the Council — which was really the forerunner to the Board — was the instigation of the Sheffield Shield for competition between the States. A gift of £150 by Lord Sheffield in 1891 had made it possible for a Shield to be made and that trophy is the most prestigious in one of the toughest domestic competitions in world cricket.

The Melbourne Cricket Club had been the most powerful governing body in Australia. It had planned many of the early England tours and teams visiting Australia, helping with itineraries and dividing tour profits with the leading Test men. In 1899 and 1902 Ben Wardill was again the manager and the Melbourne Cricket Club was back in power. Yet the leading Australian players were happy with the MCC's backing. They looked upon the Melbourne club as a friend and together they would reap the rewards of successful tours both in England and on home soil.

So it is little wonder, after further rumors of big player profits from England tours, that discussions started about forming a controlling body to wrest control from the players and place it firmly in the grasp of a Board of Control. A meeting was held in Sydney in January, 1905. A draft constitution was discussed by representatives of the NSW, Queensland, Victorian and SA associations. SA strongly urged some form of player representation on the new Board.

Players were incensed. The captain of the Test side, Joe Darling, held a meeting in Adelaide. He and many of the top Test men were concerned that a proposed tour of Australia by England in 1906-7 would be in jeopardy. The Board of Control was about to hold its inaugural meeting when it was learnt that Darling and others had signed allegiance to the Melbourne Cricket Club, agreeing to play against England in 1906-7 if, indeed, the Englishmen toured. When the NSW association learnt that Monty Noble, Victor Trumper, Reg Duff, J Mackay, G Garnsey, Jack O'Connor, A Diamond, Albert Cotter, Albert Hopkins and the Reverend Ernest Waddy had signed agreement with the Melbourne Cricket Club, it called on the players to immediately withdraw their promise. Only the Rev. Waddy retracted and all the others were disqualified at the association's pleasure. The clubs held emergency meetings and all backed the association, bar the Paddington club. Paddington at first refused to suspend Trumper and Noble, but under threat of the association banning the club itself, Paddington later relented and suspended the two great players at a later meeting.

Darling then announced in Adelaide that he would not again play in NSW until the suspensions were lifted. Clem Hill backed his SA and Test skipper. Darling and Hill's threat to boycott NSW won the day. The NSWCA backed down and the suspensions were lifted. However, the battle for supremacy had only just begun. War clouds were not too far away. The relative calm of the Melbourne Cricket Club alliance with leading players was in great danger.

The first meeting of the Australian Board of Control for International Cricket was held on 6 May, 1905. Representatives of the NSW and Victorian associations were the foundation members and two of its foundation members, Ernest Edward Bean, Victorian Cricket

Test captain Joe Darling. He and the players were incensed with the Australian Board of Control. (*S S Ramamurthy*)

Monty Noble. He and Trumper were suspended by their local club Paddington over the signing with Melbourne Cricket Club. (*S S Ramamurthy*)

Association honorary secretary who worked in the Government printing works, and William Pcrcy McElhone, a Sydney solicitor who liked nothing better than total control in any debate, helped shape the image of the Board. That image, which so incensed the players of 1905, remained for many years.

SA's representatives, Joe Darling, H Blinman and G Mostyn Evans, refused point-blank to join the Board because it denied the players any voice. The South Australians also strongly objected to any interference with the financial arrangements for Australian tours of England because the Board would not define what it meant by 'financial control'. Queensland joined the Board on 22 September, 1905. It went along with the Board's decision in return for a promise that Brisbane would get a Test match when English teams visited Australia. The Board's promise of 1905 saw Brisbane get its first Test match on 30 November 1928.

In addition, the proposed 1906-7 tour of Australia was in jeopardy. The Marylebone Cricket Club declined the Board's invitation on the grounds that the Board was not fully representative of Australian cricket. SA was still out on a limb and Tasmania had not yet joined.

Joe Darling was never one to mince words. He detested the Board's attitude towards the players and was not backward in saying what he thought about the men who ran the Board. In a book published by his son, Darling is quoted thus: 'I will never forget the last interstate match I played in Sydney against NSW. SA was fielding and getting some leather hunting. The weather was extremely hot and when we adjourned for tea we found (William) McElhone and some leading notoriety-seekers present with some dead-head friends who had rushed the afternoon tea provided for the players. The waiters were very busy and, with this crowd, we could not get a look in sideways. I got up and walked over to the large tea urn, called two mates I could rely on at a pinch, and we took possession of the tea urn and served the players and kept the dead-heads waiting.'

Darling wrote that the Board meeting was a farce; that the minutes were false and the agenda had been discussed at a private gathering prior to the delegates from Victoria, NSW and Queensland arriving. Darling was present as an observer. He concluded that Messrs Bean and McElhone, along with a few others, boasted that they would 'drive out of the game all the players who signed themselves as ready to play against an MCC side organised by the Melbourne Cricket Club.'

SA finally joined the Board on 20 April, 1907, and Tasmania followed suit on 9 August, 1907. West Australia did not join until 15 October, 1914. Darling alleged that WA's late entry had been purposely delayed over fears that WA might vote against the NSW-Victoria bloc.

The 1906-7 summer saw no England team, but the following summer (1907-8) England toured Australia. However, the star players continued to resent their lack of a real voice on the Board. The friction increased when, in 1909, the Board was presented with yet another monumental hurdle, handling its first England tour. The Board refused to make the customary cash advances to the players and, to rub salt into the wound, the Board appointed Peter McAlister as the tour treasurer. The players made Frank Laver team manager and the Board bowed to their wishes. But McAlister was also made team vice-captain, ahead of Victor

Trumper and Warwick Armstrong — both vastly more experienced players; both streets ahead of the Victorian in ability and both immensely more popular. The Board went back on its agreement not to interfere with the players' tour terms by demanding 5 per cent of the first £6000 earned and a further 12½ per cent of all profits. The players were given a choice of settling for a lump sum of £400, plus all expenses, in lieu of taking the gamble of getting a better or worse pay out at the end of the tour after expenses and after the Board had taken its share.

The players had every right to be off-side with the Board. Broken promises hit the leading players clean out of bounds. Worse followed. McAlister, as tour treasurer, disclosed to all and sundry that he failed to keep any financial record of the tour. McAlister hit 815 runs at an average of 29.14 with a highest score of 85 for the tour. He failed to reach 50 as an opener in any of the two Tests he played in, scoring 22 and 19 not out in the Lord's Second Test and 3 and 5 in the Leeds Third Test.

The Board, upon being informed that McAlister had no record of the financial dealings on tour, asked Frank Laver for his tour books. Laver, who took 70 wickets to head the tour bowling averages (including 8/31 at Manchester) between his managerial duties, initially refused to show the Board his books.

Frank Iredale, Test selector in the summer of 1910-11. (*S S Ramamurthy*)

Laver offered to attend a Board meeting and answer all questions put to him on costs during the 1909 tour, but the Board refused him the opportunity. Laver had explained that his refusal to hand over the books was because 'they contain private entries and comments reserved for tour members'.

Because McAlister had been so negligent as not to have kept a written financial record, McAlister was keen to see Laver's books. While Laver pointed out his reasons for not handing the books over to the Board, he eventually allowed McAlister to borrow them. He did so in the hearing of Monty Noble, captain of the 1909 Eleven. However, McAlister was unable to construct acceptable accounts from Laver's jottings and later, despite Noble's evidence, McAlister stated categorically to the Board that Frank Laver refused to lend him his books. In reality Laver had loaned McAlister his books, but the bungling 1909 treasurer could make neither head nor tail of Laver's figures. In early 1910 Laver was again asked to hand over his books to the Board. He did not refuse, but was eventually not required to do so as the Board's officer waived the requirement. Then, at the end of 1911, it was alleged that Laver refused to hand over his books to McAlister or produce them before the Board. Late in the 1911-12 season the Board did, in fact, get to see the books, through Test skipper and selector Clem Hill, but it was still alleged that Laver had failed to deliver the goods.

In the 1911-12 summer Hill was again Test captain and selector. McAlister and Frank Iredale were his co-selectors, even though Victor Trumper had beaten Iredale to a spot on the NSW selection committee. William McElhone was clearly using Iredale as the tool with McAlister to out-vote Hill on Test selection. Trumper was not seen by the Board as a suitable choice on the Test selection panel. Trumper could not be manipulated.

Gone were the calm waters. The storm approached.

The South Africans under Percy Sherwell came in 1909-10, with

Victor Trumper returning to his most brilliant. The following year (1911-12) came John 'Johnny Won't Hit Today' Douglas's England team. The strife behind the scenes was apparent. England thrashed Australia 4-1. The Australian leading players were gearing for a battle royale.

Joe Darling, the man who would have no truck with the Board, captained Australia from 1899 to 1905; some 21 times. He quit because he said it was not fair on his wife to continue. Perhaps he foresaw more than anyone else that the Board would quickly erode the players' earnings and take total control of their destiny of the Test stage. In 1908 Darling left Adelaide and settled in Hobart. He pioneered the eradication of rabbits and for more than 25 years he worked on the committee that ran the Royal Hobart Show. In 1920 Darling introduced subterranean clover to Tasmania and he was a Member of Parliament from 1921 to his death in 1946.

Darling quit before the Board gained control. But there were still men of the Darling stubbornness to take the fight to the Ernest Beans and William McElhones of the Board. Victor Trumper, Clem Hill and Co. were gearing for a scrap as the ominous storm clouds gathered overhead.

Compared with what was soon to follow, the time from 1905, when the Board was formed, until the 1911-12 summer against the Englishmen, this episode in Australian cricket history was the calm before the storm.

12

THE 1912 DISPUTE

On 12 April, 1912, the world mourned the death of a great lady — the *Titanic*. The luxury Atlantic liner had slammed into a giant iceberg while enroute from New York to Gibraltar. Thought unsinkable, the *Titanic* lurched and sank, taking more than 1500 people with it to the murky depths. By that fateful day, Syd Gregory's Australian team was on its way to England, without six of its leading players — Victor Trumper, Clem Hill, Warwick Armstrong, Vernon Ransford, Albert Cotter and Hanson Carter. The 1912 Australian tour of England was to be Australia's most ambitious undertaking for it would involve a triangular Test series, with South Africa making up the third nation along with traditional rivals England and Australia. Australia needed its most powerful squad; without the 'Big Six' it was doomed to failure.

It was inevitable that our top Test men would face a confrontation with the Board. Ernest Bean was by then prominent and William McElhone had become the Board chairman. These two were to shape the Board's image. There was a certain element among our Test players whom the likes of Messrs Bean and McElhone wanted erradicated; not literally as with Joe Darling's rabbits in Hobart, but effectively shut away from the first-class scene, hopefully forever silenced and bereft of any power. The Board was living up to its growing reputation of promising much but leaving a trail of mistrust and broken promises.

Sydney Smith, honorary secretary of the Australian Board of Control during the Great Dispute of 1912.

Clause 9 of the Board's constitution regarding the appointment of tour manager for England read: 'The appointment of manager of any Australian team visiting England or elsewhere shall be made by the players interested and submitted to the Board for confirmation.'

The Board waived this little item and stunned Australia's Test men by appointing Mr G S Crouch of Queensland as the 1912 tour manager. The players wanted Frank Laver, a man they trusted and whom they believed had done such a sterling job as manager in England in 1909. The players, especially Messrs Trumper, Armstrong, Ransford, Cotter, Hill and Carter, thought the Board had acted illegally, under the rules of the constitution, in appointing Crouch. They met and jointly penned a letter to the Board, protesting Crouch's appointment and stating that they were not prepared to tour England in 1912 'except under our own manager, legally appointed'. Just prior to the touring side being picked, SA Board delegate G Mostyn Evans had proposed that the players appoint a manager of their own choice and pay that manager an equal amount to that which the players would receive. However, the Board's Victorian treasurer, Harry Rush, then announced that the regulation giving the players the right to appoint their own manager (Clause 9 of the Constitution) had been 'swept away'. When the Board voted for its own manager, Victorians Rush and Ernest Bean wanted McAlister, the man who failed to keep any financial records as treasurer of the 1909 tour. McAlister was not popular with the players, especially as he was seen as the Board's golden-haired boy. However, neither McAlister nor the NSW nomination, Ernest Hume (nominated by McElhone), won the post. Outraged that McElhone would not vote for McAlister, the Victorians refused to vote for Hume and the upshot was that the 'dark horse' Crouch got the job. Crouch had played a few matches for Queensland, but he had no experience of England and won the post entirely because of the bickering between NSW and Victoria.

The Board made its power play on the night of 30 December, 1911, ... the night of the Long Blades. Harry Rush moved the amendment which would have far-reaching ramifications: 'As the Board has already decided to send a representative with the team, the players be informed, as soon as the team is selected, that it will be unnecessary for them to appoint a manager.' To describe that amendment as highly provocative was the understatment of the century. Next day (31 December, 1911) chairman McElhone would not accept several amendments passed up by Queensland soldier-lawyer Colonel Justin Foxton. The Colonel said: 'But under Regulation 9 of the Board's constitution, the players have a right to appoint a manager.' Harry Rush interjected: 'Oh, we swept Regulation 9 away last night...'

The players were angry. They believed, from all available evidence, quite rightly, that the Board had no legal right to change the regulations of the constitution merely to satisfy their own needs. The Board's attitude in appointing their own man to manage the side was intolerable to the Big Six. They were quite prepared to go along with the Board sending its own representative, providing the Board paid that gentleman's expenses. The Big Six also wanted to appoint their own manager. They favored Frank Laver. The Big Six were as stubborn as the Board. They would not back down, even if it meant that Australia's hopes in the forthcoming series were doomed if they did not tour. The six players' boycott was brought about by administrative bungling, a good deal of jealousy and a seemingly total lack of conciliation and reasoning by the Board.

The contents of the letter signed by the Big Six and dated 17 January, 1912:

Dear Sir,—

We beg respectfully to approach the Board of Control in reference to the resolution carried by it at the instance of Colonel Foxton, whereby the Board proposes to send to England a representative, clothed with the powers of a manager, and to charge his travelling and other expenses against the takings of the tour, in other words, making the players pay them. That it is the intention of the Board to endeavour to invest its representative with the powers of manager is made quite clear by the further resolution, carried at the same meeting, to the effect that, as the Board has appointed a representative to go with the team, it will be unnecessary for the players to appoint a manager. We are advised that the first of the above resolutions is clearly illegal; but it is not so much that aspect of the case which appeals to us as that, if the players are not allowed to select their own manager, as provided by the Board of Control rules, a breach of faith with them will be committed. We raise no objection to the Board appointing a representative to watch its interests if it desires to do so, but we do claim that in such case all the charges of every description in connection with their representative's visit to England should be borne by the Board, and no portion thereof should nor can fairly be chargeable against the takings of the tour. We respectfully contend that the players are entitled to appoint their manager, and that, as was done last time, fourteen players should be first selected, and they should then select a player-manager, who should rank equally with others players in respect to remuneration for the tour. If this be done, and subject to the provision as to the Board's representative above mentioned, such of us as shall be selected will be prepared and glad to make the trip, but, failing compliance with our requests, we have to inform you, with much regret, that none of us will be available for selection, or to play if selected. We would have waited for the team to be selected before approaching the Board but for the fact that the selection, we understand, is not to be made until after the fourth test match, and in our interests, as well as out of courtesy to your Board, we deemed it advisable to let you know our views and intentions as early as possible.

We are anxious, if selected, to go to England with the 1912 team, but we respectfully but firmly decline to go except under our own manager, legally appointed, and paid in the manner indicated. Will you be good enough, in acknowledging receipt of this letter, to let us know when same will be dealt with by the Board of Control?

(Signed) C. HILL, V. TRUMPER, W. W. ARMSTRONG, V. RANSFORD, A. COTTER, H. CARTER.

The secretary Sydney Smith wasted no time in replying to the Big Six. He replied in a letter to Clem Hill on 22 January, 1912:

Dear Sir,—

I have to acknowledge the receipt of your letter, dated the 17th instant, signed by yourself, and Messrs. Trumper, Armstrong, Ransford, Cotter and Carter, and will, as requested, place same before the Board at its next meeting, which, in all probability, will be held early next month.

I would, however, like to point out that you are in error when you state that the travelling and other expenses of the Board's representative are to be paid by the players, and that the players are not to be allowed to appoint their own manager.

In the first place, the team which is being sent to England by the Board as the governing body of cricket in Australia, in accordance with the agreement entered into with the Marylebone C.C., has nothing whatever to do with the arrangements, the Board taking the whole of the responsibility. Certain terms, which will be communicated to each individual member on selection, have been decided on by the Board, and each member will then have the opportunity of declining the Board's invitation if he is not satisfied.

In the next place, the Board has in no sense abrogated Clause 9 of

Ernest Bean, secretary of the
Victorian Cricket Association and
Board member.

Clem Hill, Test skipper and
Australian selector. He fought co-
selector Percy McAlister during a
meeting to select the team for the
fourth Test. (*S S Ramamurthy*)

the constitution, but has only expressed its opinion that, as a
representative of the Board will accompany the team, the
appointment of a manager is unnecessary; so that it follows that, if
this opinion is not voiced by a majority of members of the team, they
can still nominate a manager for confirmation by the Board.

Personally, I do not see why the positions could not be carried out
by one person, acceptable to the Board, as well as to the members of
the team.

Whilst the Board is anxious at all times to send the best team
possible, still, at the same time, I am sure it will not permit any
number of cricketers to dictate the terms and conditions on which a
visit is to be made, or if a manager is appointed the terms and nature
of his engagement.

Yours faithfully,

(Signed) SYDNEY SMITH, Jnr.

The seemingly over-zealous Sydney Smith, who was to become one of
Australia's foremost cricket administrators, Board secretary from 1911
to 1926 and president of the NSW Cricket Association from 1935 to
1966, must have floored the Big Six with his letter. The Board had not
then seen the letter, yet the last paragraph summed up the Board's
attitude: 'Whilst the Board is anxious at all times to send the best team
possible, still, at the same time, I am sure it will not permit any number
of cricketers to dictate the terms and conditions on which a visit is to be
made, or if a manager is appointed the terms and nature of his
engagement.' If Smith was flexing his muscles, having barely been in
the job 12 months, it showed in a not too subtle manner. The players
knew then that they must come back cap in hand and relent or kiss their
international careers goodbye.

It does not amaze me that Clem Hill was the main spokesman. After
all, Hill was then Test skipper and an Australian selector. He would
soon sit down with co-selectors Percy McAlister, not a favorite among
the Test men for having beaten both Hill and Trumper to the vice-
captain's job on the 1909 tour, and Frank Iredale to pick the Australian
team for the Fourth Test against England at Melbourne. McAlister was
immediately critical of Hill's captaincy. Hill hit back in his own
inimitable style.

'The Australians wouldn't have gone to England under you,
McAlister.'

McAlister sneered: 'I'm a better captain than you and Trumper put
together. You're the worst captain I've ever seen.'

Hill was outraged. He thought McAlister a good Sheffield Shield
player, but somewhat of an imposter on the Test stage.

'If you keep insulting me, McAlister, I'll pull your nose,' Hill
retorted angrily.

McAlister sensed he was getting the upper hand. He continued in
provocative tone: 'I repeat . . . you're the worst captain I've ever seen.'

Hill could take no more. He grabbed for McAlister across the table,
then he slapped the Victorian across the face. McAlister claimed he was
struck while his hands were down. Hill dropped his hands and said: 'My
hands are down now, my friend.'

McAlister rushed to Hill's side of the table and the pair were locked
in mortal combat. They wrestled and punched for fifteen minutes,
spattering the room with blood, some of which stained the clothing of

Iredale and Sydney Smith. In the end, McAlister was lying on his back with Hill standing over him. Iredale and Smith moved in and separated the combatants. Hill left the room with McAlister yelling 'coward' mockingly as Iredale and Smith slammed the door. The *Australasian* printed a blow-by-blow account of the fight. Iredale, when asked how long the fight lasted, said: 'About twenty minutes, I should think. It all began as quick as lightning. They were both game and determined, however, we are all very sorry about the whole affair, and I don't think anyone regrets it more than the participants.'

Hill had wanted Charles Macartney in the team, but McAlister's reply was that if 'you must have Macartney, then leave yourself out.'

The Victorian Cricket Association produced a pamphlet dated 27 March, 1912, and distributed it to its members. It read in part:

'At a special meeting of the Board subsequently held, on 2nd February, the letter of the six players was received, and the Secretary's reply, as above, was endorsed. The Board likewise unanimously determined at this meeting, at the suggestion of Mr Hill, that the selection committee should be asked to choose as many certainties for England as they could agree upon on the following night; and the Board also decided that each of the players, when selected, should be informed of the terms and conditions adopted by the Board, be furnished with a copy of the agreement he would be required to sign, and be asked to state, within ten days, whether he was willing to join the team on these terms.

The reason this resolution was adopted was that in 1909 the members of the team unduly delayed replying to their invitations, whilst two of them refused to sign the agreement. In the event of refusals it was considered that those who filled the vacancies should have reasonable time to make arrangements.

It has frequently been published that the whole of the usual duties of the manager were taken away from him, and allotted to the Board's representative. This is not correct. A perusal of the above mentioned agreement will clearly show that the duties of the Board's representative in no sense encroach upon those previously assigned to the manager.

The selection committee subsequently met and chose ten players for England. These were the whole of the certainties they could agree upon, and they decided to delay picking the remainder in order that they might have further opportunities of watching the form of likely men. This is the usual practice, both here and in England.

One of those selected (Dr Hordern) declined the invitation, and three (Messrs Bardsley, Minnett and Carkeek), accepted within the ten days fixed by the Board. On the tenth day (Monday) Messrs Armstrong, Ransford, Carter, Trumper and Cotter replied that they would "give a definite answer when the selection of the team had been completed". The chairman of the Board (Mr McElhone) had previously received a communication from Mr Warner, captain of the English team, stating that he would be in Sydney on Tuesday, and asking that the Board would stay its hand till Wednesday, to give him an opportunity of again seeing these players and urging them to accept unconditionally the Board's invitation.

At the direction of the chairman, the hon. secretary informed these five players that it was impossible to allow the matter to remain in abeyance until the whole team had been completed, and that, failing a definite acceptance by the Wednesday, the invitation would be considered as declined; and on Wednesday the following reply was received from each:—

"I am in receipt of your letter of the 19th instant.

"In reply I beg to state that it is my intention to accept the invitation, but I reserve to myself the right to withdraw such acceptance if anything should arise prior to the departure of the team, rendering such withdrawal, in my opinion, necessary."

As this answer was distinctly conditional and not an acceptance of the Board's invitation, the chairman instructed the hon. secretary to reply to that effect, and to add that unless a definite and unconditional acceptance was received during the course of the day (Wednesday) the invitation would be deemed to have been declined, and the selectors be notified accordingly. The chairman and the hon. secretary waited in the hon. secretary's office till 10 p.m. that night, but no replies were forthcoming.

On the following morning (Thursday) Mr Warner again saw the chairman, and asked him to let matters stand over till noon that day, to give him another opportunity of seeing these six players, as he still had hopes of getting them to accept unconditionally the Board's invitation: This the chairman agreed to do, and he was informed by Mr Warner later on that he had after some difficulty located the six players, but had failed to come to an understanding with them. He had, however, arranged with them to see the chairman. In the afternoon Messrs Armstrong, Hill, Carter and Cotter waited on Mr McElhone, and asked that Mr Laver's conduct be submitted to an independent arbitrator, and intimated that they would abide by the latter's decision. They were informed that this request could not be entertained. During the interview the question of the non-production of the books retained by Mr Laver was discussed, and it was admitted by Mr Armstrong that there was nothing of a private nature in them, and that they should have been produced.

From the foregoing particulars it will be seen that, although the Board of Control decided that the players should give a definite reply within ten days, the chairman of the Board, (William McElhone) in view of the approaching Triangular Tests, the Board's obligations to the Marylebone C.C., and at the expressed wish of Mr Warner, on behalf of the committee of the Marylebone C.C., took upon himself the responsibility of granting the players three extensions of time. His leniency was, however, not taken advantage of. The same statement was made to him as was made to the Governor of New South Wales, the Premier, and others who intervened — viz., that if the Board would not confirm the appointment of Mr Laver they would not go.

Before the team was finally completed Sir Joseph Carruthers, president of the NSW Cricket Association, who had intervened with success in the cricket trouble of three years before, wrote to Mr Hill as captain, and offered to again intervene, but received no reply to his letter.

It is clear from these statements that the position was forced on the Board by the six players concerned, as under the terms of the invitation the whole of the players' rights were conserved for them, just as they had been in the previous tour in 1909 when they accepted their invitations unconditionally, and when, after the team's completion they nominated their manager for the Board's approval. The Board is unaware why this course, which is the proper and constituted mode of procedure, was not carried out on the present occasion.

Finally it is significant that those who have been rabidly opposed to the formation of the Board now affirm that a Board of Control is indispensable. They object only to the personnel, and desire a properly constituted Board. They want a Board that will not insist upon being thoroughly informed as to all the financial transactions of a tour in the old country; a Board that will in all cases submit its decisions for the approval of the leading players for the time being. And this means that they desire to bring the present Board to the same end as the old cricket council, and that the old and discredited system that permitted of a few players exploiting the tours for their personal gain shall again prevail.

If the cricketing public of Australia were to allow the game to be sacrificed on the altar of greed in this way it would be a calamity. What has been called the players' ultimatum proves clearly that profit is the one thing seriously considered by them. The Victorian public have been deceived by the local press which has by rank partiality, misstatements and suppression of important facts, bolstered up a case for a handful of players who care nothing for patriotism unless it can be made to pay, and pay well.'

The Beans, the Rushs and the McElhones have been replaced, but the row of 1912 caused so much ill-feeling that the wounds have yet to heal. The Australian Board of Control for International Cricket started the ball rolling in 1973 by changing its name to the Australian Cricket Board. That name change was at the instigation of Sir Donald Bradman. The Board wanted to change its image.

Just a year after the Board changed its name to the ACB, it faced a situation as potentially dangerous as the 1912 dispute. Test captain Ian Chappell suspected the Test selectors were about to axe Victorian opener Keith Stackpole from the imminent New Zealand tour. Chappell called a meeting of senior players at Adelaide Oval during the Third Test against NZ in January, 1974. The six players pledged to decline the NZ tour invitation if Stackpole was not included in the team. The selectors knew of the scheme and eventually Stackpole was picked. As it turned out Stackpole had a disastrous NZ tour, scoring 10, 27, 4, 9, and a pair of spectacles (0, 0) in his last Test appearance at Eden Park, Auckland.

In 1980 we were about to fly to England for the Centenary Test match at Lord's. As one of the selected players I wanted my wife and son to travel on the same aircraft as the team. Out of courtesy I informed the Board, only to be told that such an arrangement was impossible. Another player could be picked to take my place, I was told. The Board relented only after I wrote them a letter, which the ACB insisted upon, outlining that my family would in no way 'intrude' upon the touring party while on board the aircraft and that my family would not enter the team bus on arrival at Heathrow and would not visit the team hotel.

Some years before, ACB secretary Alan Barnes, now retired and writing the history of the Board, made that famous remark: 'There are 500,000 young men ready and willing to take the place of any Australian Test player. . .' That statement came during the Ian Chappell reign as skipper, when the players were asking for a better deal. We thought that $2400 for a 5½ month tour of England (as we were paid in 1972) was insufficient.

It puzzles me that the letter signed by the Big Six (dated 17 January, 1912,) and sent to Board secretary Sydney Smith cannot be found among the ACB records. During research for this book I contacted the Board. They made a thorough search for the original letter, but to no avail. All the old Board papers were parcelled up and sent to Victoria when the ACB shifted its base from Sydney to Melbourne in 1981. However, neither the NSWCA, the ACB nor Alan Barnes, former NSWCA and Board secretary, knows of the whereabouts of that letter. Certainly the letter would be of great value to a collector and of inestimable value to the Board.

To understand the players' frustration in having their independence snatched from their grasp, we could do worse than note the case of Dr William Gilbert Grace, the Great Cricketer. In 1873-4 the Melbourne Cricket Club sponsored an English team, led by Grace, to play in Australia. WG was paid £1500, plus expenses, while his fellows, amateurs and professionals, each scored £170 apiece which, in itself, was a tidy sum in those days. Professionalism was very much in full swing in WG's time, both in England and Australia, but the Great Cricketer was considered to be the most upstanding amateur among amateurs. In Australia it was the Melbourne Cricket Club which organised several of the early visits to Australia by English teams. In addition, the club also helped plan itineraries for Australian tours of England. However, the Australian players ran the tours while in the Mother Country. They looked after the finances and the players split profits at the tour's end. If the tour lost money, the players covered the losses. The arrangement worked well, although pressure of the district clubs, impoverished and forever seeking a way to financial security, finally brought about the formation of the Board. Both the Melbourne Cricket Club and the leading players became frustrated and outraged. I wonder if W G Grace would have enjoyed playing Test cricket in the days when the Board took control. In 1891-2 he led England in Australia. WG's tour payment was £3000! That was £50 more than Victor Trumper received for his benefit match in 1913 — then an Australian record.

When the Big Six challenged the Board in 1912, it was the Melbourne Cricket Club which the players looked upon to take control of the game. The VCA's pamphlet clearly revealed where it stood in the dispute — steadfastly behind the Board. The VCA hoped to vindicate the Board's stand and point out the inequities of a system of Australian touring teams abroad whereby the senior players took the lion's share of profits and the up-and-comers received a pittance in comparison:

'It may be denied, but it is none the less true, that young and talented players were, from time to time, taken to England on much less than full shares of the profits. It is a thoroughly established fact that a rising young star, who subsequently won his way to prominence and great fame, had originally received the paltry sum of £79; and the £100 that was eventually added to that amount by those in whose hands control then rested did not bring his share to within a fourth of what was received by the leaders in the venture. This and other facts led a well-known cricketer to exclaim in 1902, in an unusual outburst of frankness: "Australian XI! — call us a joint stock company, and you hit it in one!"

'Money became the dominating influence in numerous instances. From old balance-sheets, now in possession of members of the Board, it is known that men were chosen on condition of their accepting half shares, whilst more capable cricketers who declined less than a full share were left behind. Two players were to have received £200 for their services, but one proved so brilliant a success that the sportsmen amongst the company compelled the greedier of their associates to allot him a shareholder's full dividend.'

Certainly in 1899 Victor Trumper was added to the selected team just before the team sailed. He was included on the understanding that he accept a half-share, plus expenses. Soon after the team arrived in England it was unanimously decided to extend Trumper's half-share to a full dividend. There is no available evidence about any other player but Trumper accepting to tour on a half share.

The VCA pamphlet continued: 'It is even asserted that one man paid a premium of £200 for the privilege of belonging to a team. Whilst it is a well-known fact that one man was voted £12 12s on the way back from a trip, which amount was made up of £1 1s from each of his 12 associates, and this was all he received over and above his travelling and hotel expenses. These and other matters connected with the system of management of Home trips called for radical treatment.'

The Melbourne Cricket Club objected strongly to the VCA's pamphlet and issued a reply in August, 1912. Under the secretariat of former Test off-spinner Hugh Trumble, the Melbourne club pointed out that the player who had received only 12 guineas at the end of a tour had requested that he be not paid because he did not want to harm his amateur status.

'It involved Mr W H Moule (now Judge Moule). What happened was that Mr Moule was selected for the 1880 Australian eleven on his merits, and thereafter an agreement was sent to him to sign, giving him an equal share in the venture; but as he then contemplated staying in England and was anxious not to endanger his status as an amateur, he declined to sign it, refusing to take anything more than his expenses — a position which so far from being forced on him, was rather resented by some members of the eleven. As to the £12. 12s incident, the facts are that, on the disbanding of the team, the other twelve members of the team subscribed one guinea each to buy Mr Moule a memento of the trip, which memento was purchased and still exists.'

The club also pointed out that in 1878 one player insisted upon having £200 certain rather than risk a share of the profits. In 1896, two players agreed to divide one share between them in special circumstances. In 1893 one player agreed, with the approval of the Australasian Cricket Council, to take £200 and it is believed thereby made more out of the tour than his fellow players. In 1899 Trumper, who on his promising form was selected as an extra man after the team was completed, originally agreed to take £200 and his expenses: but the members of the team, within a few weeks of his arrival in England, put him on an equal footing with themselves.

'After 1899 nothing of the sort happened; the members were chosen by the selectors appointed by the various Associations and went on equal terms. Yet the (VCA) pamphlet, first of all, misrepresents the facts and then proceeds to malign and slander a body of men whom, on the whole, Australians are justly proud and finally comes out with the following extraordinary statement —

"The management of the game once more descended into the shady region of cliquism and favoritism, where it wallowed until the year 1905, when, in the interest of true and pure sport, and in order to put a stop to the abuses indicated, and to give all deserving players equal opportunities of getting into big cricket, the Association proposed to support the establishment of a Board of Control that should wrest the government of international cricket from the hands of men who had unequivocally shown that their chief and almost their only desire was individual aggrandisement."

'There can be no hesitation in denouncing as an unpatriotic calumny the assertion that the leading members of Australian Elevens before 1905 cared for nothing but making money out of the trip; although it is absurd to suppose that men, who were very often risking chances of advancement and incurring loss of time and salary, should not do their utmost to make the tour financially successful, it is certain that their first consideration was to win the Test matches — the only matches which, in the long run, Australia really cares for — and that teams were selected primarily from that point of view. The great majority of the Australian cricketing public now, to their sorrow, realise how much more satisfactory was the selection of Australian Elevens by men who had had successful experience in England. These men, themselves certainties, were independent in judgment and were in a position to form a sound opinion as to the chances of promising players reproducing their form in England ... moreso than has been the majority of selections made by the selectors appointed by the Board of Control.'

'Probably the reason why over so many years there were comparatively so few abuses is that Australia had the good fortune to be served by a succession of great cricketers, who were also men of great personality. Murdoch, Darling, Noble and many others were not merely great cricketers, but were born leaders, and they established a world-wide fame for grit, so that it has hitherto been an axiom that Australian cricketers are never more dangerous than when they seem beaten, and the Club publicly and emphatically protests against men like these being slandered and held up to undeserved obloquy by misrepresentation, which shows a want not merely of patriotism, but of common decency.

'The public may think over phrases such as "the interest of true and pure sport" and "all deserving players having equal opportunities of getting into big cricket", and recollect how this era has been marked by persons, whose right to selection was at least doubtful, selecting themselves for successive Australian Elevens, and by the exclusion of Mr Laver from even the Victorian teams.

'The public can say, too, whether the one fact most clearly standing out with reference to the selection of the team for Australia for last season's Tests is not the want of judgment, or whatever else it was, on the part of the majority of the Australian selectors, who refused their co-selector Hill, the captain of the Eleven, that fine player Macartney, whom he and nine-tenths of the cricketing public were most anxious to see chosen.'

(Macartney was 12th man for the First, Second, Third Tests, omitted for the Fourth in Melbourne, in the wake of the Hill-McAlister row, and was reinstated for the Fifth Test in which he batted No. 8, scoring 26 and 27. It was Trumper's last Test).

The Melbourne Cricket Club further emphasised its belief that the Australian sporting public, or nine-tenths thereof, deplored having an Australian Eleven without the Big Six.

'There is not one who has not shown his grit and ability under adverse circumstances in that greatest of all nerve-trying issues — a Test match. It is not surprising that these men stuck to Mr Laver to the bitter end, for they knew, as the public have not fully realised, what a great injustice was being done to him. Nor is it surprising that they took a manly and straight forward course, and did not wait until the team was finally selected before letting their position as to Mr Laver be known.'

In the turbulent 1970s, players also wanted a better deal. Our Test men were aware of the past whereby Test teams to England were very often good money spinners for the players when profits were shared at the end of a trip. They also knew that these pioneers of the Test stage also risked losing out if the tour was a financial flop. As you will read later in this chapter, the 1912 tour agreement had an alternative; either take your chances in a share of the profits (if agreed, you sign the First Schedule) or you sign the Second Schedule whereby you accept a tour payment of £400 in lieu of a share in the profits. In 1968, my first tour, we received about $2000; in 1972 it was £2400 (both tours were of about 5½ months' duration) and by 1980 it was $3000 for six weeks. The sizeable increase was brought about I suspect, because of greater gates from the mid-1970s onwards and World Series Cricket, which not only brought many great Test cricketers together under the Australian sun, but also the expertise of the most marvellous advances in television. Ca eras worked from every conceivable angle. The Nine Network had microphones inserted underground near the stumps. You could distinctly hear an umpire call 'over' or the players speak and shout and sometimes cuss. It not only brought famous faces into the loungeroom, but also their voices, and the people loved it.

Night cricket, not the mere advent of Kerry Packer's WSC, was the real revolution. Cricketers became instant celebrities. The first night match at the SCG attracted more than 40,000 fans. It was a tremendous spectacle. Surely many of the people who attended turned up for the novelty of cricket being played under lights. Night cricket drew a wider, perhaps a totally new audience. Teenagers and housewives suddenly became avid cricket fans. The West Indians' exuberance must have helped to a large degree. They are, in the main, natural athletes. Often I think of a West Indian as being made of rubber. They seem to be able to glide across the ground, pick up and throw in the one action — all with grace and style. Our Test men soon began to believe the oft repeated saying: shake a palm tree in the Caribbean and at least one genuinely quick pace bowler will bounce out to replace an ageing one to restore the feared Windies attack to its most fearsome. Nowadays our Test men are paid pretty well in comparison with the Test players of the

Ian Chappell era. But today there is much more money filling the ACB coffers. Packer won his fight to win television rights. His WSC may have lost what I'm led to believe was in the vicinity of $12 million, give or take the odd million, but Packer has seemingly recouped his losses and turned what many thought would end up a nightmare for the TV magnate into a dream perhaps even he would not have dared envisage.

But back in the 1970s, when Chappell or a colleague went into print about the lack of payments to Test players, he was given a going over by press and public. In Adelaide, and I suspect on other grounds, gatemen were receiving more money at weekends than the players. Gatemen come under some form of actors' union and double and triple rates apply on certain days. When such a relevation was made the players got no sympathy, in fact many players gave the first-class game away purely and simply because they could not afford to go on. In Trumper's day, payment for Shield matches was far from a king's ransom, but the carrot which dangled in front of their noses was a trip to England and a share in the profits at tour's end. The formation of the Australian Board of Control for International Cricket in 1905 put many of those noses right out of joint.

At the end of the final Test match against the West Indies in 1975-6, a meeting took place at the Hilton Hotel, Melbourne. Those attending the meeting were Australian captain Greg Chappell, Ian Chappell, the then ACTU president Bob Hawke (now Prime Minister) and ex-Test batsman and shrewd businessman Bob Cowper. Something was in the wind; perhaps a players' union. That union never got off the ground. Kerry Packer jumped at the chance to form a breakaway group and the revolution which stunned the cricket world to its foundations hit the traditionalists for a towering six.

Test men today are playing an enormous number of international matches. Former Australian captain Kim Hughes has already played 20 Tests more than Don Bradman played, yet Hughes made his debut at Kennington Oval in 1977 while Bradman's career spanned 20 years.

Today the ACB is run as a business and a multi-million dollar business it has become. There are still hitches to overcome and there still appears to be a gap between the players and the administrators but at least that gap has narrowed. The Board has learnt from bitter experience that good relations with the players are vital. WSC was a bitter pill for it to swallow, but some five years after the peace pipe was smoked the wounds of the battle had healed. The smart administrators have buried the hatchet; so too did the players who were involved.

A smarter administration in 1912 could have so easily averted the Big Six blow-up. The Board could have compromised in such a way that no loss of face would have eventuated. But the Board — or rather the more persuasive members — were so obsessed with total control that any form of compromise would have been seen as weakness and causing the ultimate destruction of the body.

There were rumblings in 1912 that the Melbourne Cricket Club was scheming to field an Australian Eleven independent of the one led by Syd Gregory — an eleven which would include Trumper, Hill, Armstrong, Ransford, Cotter, Carter and the skipper of 1909, Monty Noble. It was never brought to pass and perhaps it was just as well, because such a rebel tour would have raised the ire of the Marylebone Cricket Club: such an austere body could never work with two conflicting interests from the Antipodes. However, had the First World War not come along, a private organisation might well have taken on the Board and won as did Kerry Packer 65 years later.

All the Big Six wanted in 1912 was a fair deal. The night of 30 December, 1911 virtually ensured that they would never get one.

The press at the time had a veritable birthday. Editorials, letters to the editor and feature articles over the Big Six littered newspaper columns.

Victorian delegates to the Board, Ernest Bean and Harry Rush, issued a paper on 7 September, 1912, giving their opinion of the relative merits of the 1912 touring team. In many ways it was a pitiful account. Messrs Bean and Rush rationalised to the extreme, blaming bad weather, bad publicity and especially hitting out at the Melbourne Cricket Club which, they alleged, had an inflexible attitude towards the players and had blamed the Board for the Big Six not touring England. It appears highly likely that Messrs Bean and Rush were greatly worried about the public attitude towards the Board to have produced such a paper for the public record.

The disastrous 1911-12 tour in which England thrashed Australia by four wins to one was the foundation stone upon which Messrs Bean and Rush based their defence:

'It will be remembered that Gregory and Co. left Australia to the accompaniment of an almost unanimous howl of adverse criticism from the Press of Melbourne; and some old players, whose opinions ought to have been more nearly correct than events have proved them, joined in the chorus of abuse. Only a few weeks previously, what had been regarded as the cream of Australian cricket had sustained a series of

Signatures of the 1912 team – minus the striking Big Six of Trumper, Hill, Cotter, Ransford, Armstrong and Carter. (*S S Ramamurthy*)

G R Hazlett and Warren Bardsley, two of the younger members of the ill-fated 1912 Test team to England. The Aussies were beaten 2-1. (*S S Ramamurthy*)

four decisive defeats on the fast, true wickets of Australia but the Melbourne Press, with proper patriotism, did not publish a line in criticism of their displays. It reserved its abuse for the young players, the majority of whom were going to battle against England for the first time. The following extracts are examples of what then appeared in the Press:

The *Age*, 27 February, 1912 — 'The team will leave Australia with the reputation of a third or fourth-rate combination, in no sense representing Australian cricket. This fact is as well known in England as here. The Board's precious team will leave Australia repudiated by the Australian people and will return covered with derision.'

The *Herald*, 26 February, 1912 — 'The curtain is about to be raised on the biggest farce that has ever been known in the history of the game. Australia will be represented in the Triangular matches by positively the weakest combination that has ever left our shores. The team is totally unrepresentative and must never be known as an Australian Eleven.'

The *Argus*, 27 February, 1912 (by Old Boy) — 'When people . . . looked at the new team they gasped . . . The public does not relish the prospect of Australia being represented in England by a second-rate team.'

The *Argus and Australasian*, 29 February, 1912 (by Felix) — 'These few delegates who have done this thing must be regarded as neither more nor less than wreckers of Australian cricket . . . If these wreckers are permitted to have their way, cricket will have a set-back in this country that it will not recover from in twenty years . . .'

Harry Trott, The *Age*, 27 February, 1912 — 'The team selected will have no chance in the Triangular matches . . . Apart from these two batsmen (Gregory and Bardsley) I cannot see who of the others can be looked to get runs . . . Not much can be expected from Kellaway.'

W Bruce, The *Age*, 27 February, 1912 — 'The team can in no way be considered representative.'

J J Lyons, The *Age*, 27 February, 1912 — 'There is no one in the team who really stands out in any department of the game. It is doubtful if a weaker team ever left Australia.'

'Mr Lyons probably spoke from his personal experience of, and former connection with, weak teams. Cricket records reveal the fact that he, and also Mr Trott, visited England with the teams of 1888, 1890 and 1893. The first lost 14 matches, the second 16, and the third 10. Only one Test was won in the three visits and the 1890 tour is noteworthy for the fact that for the first and only time in the history of cricket an Australian team in England lost more matches than it won.'

The Bean-Rush report continued: 'After the termination of Australia's second Test match against South Africa, the *London Daily Cronicle* wrote — "The Australians are clearly a formidable Test side and must be held as most dangerous opponents. They have twice beaten South Africa in quite as decisive a fashion as England has done, and they have shown just as good all-round cricket as ourselves. Then, they held their own with us at Lord's. Clearly they are foemen worthy of our best steel. Of course, if the weather changes and England v Australia be played on a bowler's wicket, under flukey conditions, anything can happen."

'In regard to the alleged vindictiveness of the Board, we will quote the remarks made by Mr W P (William) McElhone, Chairman of the Board of Control at a banquet recently, held at the Sydney Town Hall in his honor — "Many hard things had to be done, but nothing was done which was not absolutely necessary if the Board was to carry out the work for which it was formed. There were many sad hearts when it came to a parting of the ways, and his heart was the saddest of them all. He hoped now to have peace, and that no private bodies of any nature would ever try to regain the control of cricket".'

Control — the very word raises the ire in free men.

There had to be a controlling body. Unfortunately while most first-class and Test cricketers of 1912 believed in such a body, be it the Melbourne Cricket Club or the Board, the players, especially the Big Six, did not have much respect for many of the Board members. There were many personality clashes and Harry Rush's 'sweeping away' Regulation 9 was the final straw. If the players needed an excuse to take on the Board in front-on confrontation, Rush's action was the ammunition they required.

The Melbourne press were very much on the players' side. However, elsewhere, especially in Sydney, the Board had things much their own way. The old Sydney-Melbourne rivalry reared its ugly head once more. Sydneyites, more than anyone, wanted the Board to stay. Many feared the Board might go the same way as the Australasian Cricket Council.

At a Victorian Cricket Association meeting on 8 January, 1912, it was pointed out that some Board members considered that the Board was in the position of Trustee and did not possess the power, under Rule 1 of the Board's constitution, to pay the salary of a representative to accompany the team, and that all it could pay was expenses.

Rule 1 of the Board's constitution: 'The objects of the Board shall be to arrange, regulate, control and finance the visits of Australian teams to England and elsewhere.'

Chairman William McElhone ruled that under this clause the Board did possess the power to appoint and pay a representative.

The senior players had had enough. In 1909 two players — Victor Trumper and Warwick Armstrong — refused to sign the tour contract. Trumper and Armstrong argued that they would not sign the Board's contract until such time as they had received advice from their legal advisers in Australia.

Exchanges of letters between team manager Frank Laver and Board chairman McElhone began before the team sailed aboard the RMS *Orontes*. Laver had required £100 advance, which was duly granted. Then certain players desired advances on their tour allowance. A further £300 arrived in the form of a bank draft. However, Frank Laver then telegraphed McElhone asking for more money, in order to be able to cover expenses while in England. Mr McElhone replied by letter; dated 23 March, 1909: 'No arrangements have been made for any further advances to be made in England, and I cannot understand why, in view of the advances already made, an amount of five or six hundred pounds, or anything like it, should be required upon arrival, and I am sure, unless strong reasons are given by you, the Board will not agree to do so. If this sum is necessary to enable you to properly conduct the tour, then I think it is to be regretted, especially in view of your telegram above referred to, that you should have left it till the last hour to acquaint the Board of the fact.'

Unbeknown to Laver, until, that is, McElhone sent him a telegram at Fremantle, WA, just before the RMS *Orontes* set sail, the Board had arranged for its London representative, Dr Poidevin, to arrange a loan in England to provide advance funds. Laver had threatened to raise a loan with his London bankers. So bickering over money had begun between the Board, in control of an Australian team for the first time, and its manager Frank Laver, one of the old school who toured England in 1899 and again in 1905 as player-manager.

Just before the team assembled in Adelaide for the trip to Fremantle and beyond, McElhone asked Laver to procure the signatures of five players — Vernon Ransford, Percy McAlister, Warwick Armstrong, Hanson Carter and Victor Trumper. Laver was living in Melbourne, yet McElhone could not obtain the signatures of Trumper and Carter who both lived in Sydney, McElhone's place of residence. Eventually all, but two — Trumper and Armstrong — signed the 1909 contract.

In 1912 the Board's contract allowed for a player to opt for £400 tour payment or a share in the profits after expenses. Those players wise enough to opt for the £400 did well, for the tour incurred a loss of £1300; a flop financially and on the field. Minus Trumper, Hill, Armstrong, Ransford, Cotter and Carter, Syd Gregory's team played 36 first-class matches. They won 9 games, lost 8 and drew 19.

In the Tests Australia played six matches, won 2, lost 1 and drew 3. However, the two wins were against the lowly South Africans. England easily won the Triangular series. The Australians picked a side which included two great batsmen in Charlie Macartney and Warren Bardsley. Macartney scored 2207 runs at 45.04 with a highest score of 208; but Bardsley did better with 2441 runs (highest score 184 not out) at the good average of 51.93. After that the batting fell away, with Charlie Kelleway on 1300 runs at 30.95. Roy Minnett, to whom the *Johannesburg Sporting Star* paid a compliment in criticising the Big Six in their stand against the Board, hit 734 runs at a poor 19.83 per innings. Macartney topped the bowling averages with 43 wickets at 16.34 runs apiece, but the lion's share of the workload was done by left-arm paceman Bill Whitty (109 wickets at 18.08) and Gervys 'Gerry' Hazlitt, whose right-arm medium-paced cutters brought him the rich haul of 101 wickets at 18.96. Hazlitt died at the age of 27, just four months after Victor Trumper.

Mr Grouch was paid £400 to manage the team and the players were given the option of accepting a like payment or taking their chances with a share in the profits, after expenses.

By 1975 the word 'control' was in the past — not buried, only erased from the Board's name. The contract Ian Chappell's Australian team signed for the 1975 Canada and England tour was a lengthy document which left no stone unturned to ensure that the Board had complete control.

A clause (number 6) stated: 'The Manager shall have control of the players and all necessary arrangements respecting accommodation, travel, meals, medical attention etc. shall be made by him. No player shall have any authority to nor shall any player incur any financial obligations whatsoever on behalf of the Board or the team.'

The *Sydney Daily Telegraph* reported on 14 March, 1912, a meeting of the NSWCA at which the association upheld the Board's stand by 22 votes to 8. Chairman McElhone said he had told Pelham Warner, the

England captain of 1911-12 and the man hoping to persuade the Big Six to back down and tour England, to tell Clem Hill that so long as the players nominated someone of ability who was respected, so long as he was not Mr Laver, the Board would accept him as manager.

Victor Trumper speaks: 'I want to refute a couple of statements made by Mr McElhone, one being that the Melbourne Club wanted to control cricket. As a player I was not aware of that, nor were the rest of the players. I would fight against the Melbourne Club or any club taking control. The players want a Board to control. We believe there should be control, and that there must be control. But as one of the six players in dispute with the Board, I regard the action of the Board in electing a representative as illegal and a direct breach of faith with the players. The appointment of a representative, in our view, was a start towards appointing a manager. We could have accepted the invitation and then not gone, but we had been advised that had we done so we could not have been penalised. But that was not sport and so we followed other procedures.

'With regard to Warwick Armstrong and I not signing the Board agreement for the 1909 tour, Mr McElhone asked me to agree to go on certain conditions regarding finance. We did not sign the agreement, but acted up to it.

'It was a matter of amusement to the players on the last tour (1909) that Mr McAlister kept one book and that of the size of a small pocket-book. And while McAlister would not give Laver a blank cheque, Laver was always prepared to give him one to pay expenses.

'I had not heard anything in England derogatory to Australian players, either on or off the field.

'We (the Big Six) would not have insisted upon Laver if a majority had been in favor of another man. If a little tact had been shown and the newspapers not made so much of it, there would not have been so much sledge-hammer business, the best team would have gone and the whole difficulty would have been smoothed over.'

So the motion, supported by Victor Trumper (Gordon club), of no confidence in the NSW Board representatives — Messrs McElhone, Smith and Sinclair — was defeated 22-8.

The strength and cunning of solicitor McElhone shone during debate. He was too clever for the laymen. Trumper smelt a rat, but his was just one vote. The loss of the no confidence motion in the NSW delegates to the Australian Board of Control for International Cricket came on the night of 13 March, 1912 — just 12 days after Trumper played his last Test innings.

13

THE AFTERMATH

In 1913 a group of Australian cricketers sought and were refused permission from the Board to undertake a tour of North America. Under the leadership of Austin Diamond, but at the instigation of Edgar Mayne, the players, many of whom toured England in 1912, went in spite of the Board. The team included Charlie Macartney, Jack Crawford, Warren Bardsley, Sid Emery and Arthur Mailey. Macartney again excelled, this time heading Bardsley (1934 runs at 43.95) with 2390 runs at an average of 45.92. Crawford took 213 wickets and Macartney, 189.

Incredibly, the Board took no action against Diamond's men when the side returned from tour. Further, the Board gave its permission for a team to visit New Zealand in the 1913-14 season. However, it took exception to the manner in which the New Zealand Cricket Council conducted its negotiations directly with Mr Arthur Sims (later Sir Arthur), who led the team. The side included Victor Trumper, Warwick Armstrong, Vernon Ransford, Frank Laver and Monty Noble. From 1914-15 the Melbourne club entered district cricket in Melbourne and gave up its one Board seat to the Victorian Cricket Association. It appeared that by 1914 the animosity had ended between the Board and the players. However, the North American tour (1913) and the New Zealand tour (1913-14) showed that the players still had a bit of fight. The senior men, such as Trumper, revelled in another tour whereby they could manage their own affairs. While it seems that the bitterness between players and the Board had largely dissipated before the Kaiser War (the First World War) the hatchet was finally buried when William McElhone retired during 1914. A team was selected to tour South Africa for the 1914-15 season. Hill, Trumper and Ransford were unavailable due to business affairs and Trumper's health, too, was a major factor in his decision to stay at home. By all accounts the reasons given by this star trio were genuine.

However, it is interesting to note that the 'rebel' 1913 team to North America did not contain one of the Big Six and Diamond's men escaped being hauled over the coals.

The 1914-15 Australian team saw Warwick Armstrong appointed captain. Bardsley was named vice-captain and the others were Tommy Andrews, Charlie Kelleway, Macartney, Jack Ryder, William Carkeek, Algie 'Johnny' Moyes, Bill Whitty, Bert Folkard, Roy Park and Frank

Victor Trumper (left), Edgar Mayne and Hanson 'Sammy' Carter aboard the S S *Niagara*. Mayne was a member of Austin Diamond's 1913 'rebel' team to the U.S. but Trumper and Carter had to opt out due to business committments. (*South Australian Cricket Association Collection*)

Baring. The side was to have spent four months in South Africa, playing five Tests. However, the war put paid to the tour. Apart from Hill, Trumper and Ransford, others unavailable were Bert 'Ranji' Hordern and John Massie, while Eric Barbour and Gerry Hazlitt withdrew from the selected team.

Johnny Moyes was among five players who never again were asked to play for Australia. Moyes later became a radio commentator and writer. His commentaries were always concise and constructive.

But what happened to the main characters in the greatest Australian tragedy?

Victor Trumper:
Trumper had effectively played his last match on the Test stage when he opted out of the 1912 tour, for he was unavailable for the South African tour, which was destined never to take place because of the war. However, Trumper went to New Zealand in Arthur Sims' team. Sims, who had hit a century in partnership with W G Grace many seasons earlier, put on 433 for the eighth wicket with Trumper against Canterbury at Christchurch at the rate of 144 runs an hour. Trumper batted brilliantly, hitting a masterly 293. It was his last great knock.

Ailing health and business worries, perhaps too much in combination, plagued Trumper. Already kidney disease had struck and he was dying. A little more than 12 months after belting that magnificent 293 in Christchurch, Trumper was dead. He died in the same year he and his wife, Annie, planned to go together to England for a holiday. He had promised her the trip and was eagerly looking forward to it, even speaking enthusiastically about the forthcoming trip to his wife while in hospital the day before he died.

Trumper toured England four times, in 1899, 1902, 1905 and 1909 and only once did he tour the Mother Country when the Board had control. Even then he refused to sign the Board contract. In 1912 he compromised the disappointment in missing the England tour by taking a private touring team to Tasmania. The war heralded the end of an era, but moreso the passing of Victor Trumper sounded the death knell for an age of cricket that was of the highest possible order.

Clem Hill:

Hill was the most outspoken of the Big Six. That was certainly understandable. At the time of the Big Six's letter to the Board, Hill was the Test captain and Test selector. He acted as the spokesman, having naturally more political thrust than any of the others. Hill was named captain of the 1912 team, but declined the invitation. He never again played Test cricket after the 1911-12 Australian summer, but after the war Hill turned out for SA occasionally, before horse racing took up most of his time. He was steward at the Adelaide Racing Club then, at the age of 60, he was appointed handicapper to the Victorian Amateur Turf Club. When aged 68, Hill was thrown from a tram in a Melbourne traffic accident and died from injuries sustained. The year: 1945. His body was taken back to Adelaide for burial.

Warwick Armstrong:

Armstrong was named captain of the Test team picked for South Africa in 1914-15. However, he had to wait until after the war to return to the Test stage. Ernest Bean was one Board member who could not forget the 1912 row. For almost a decade, Armstrong and Bean were veritably at each other's throats.

The crucial time for Armstrong was in 1920-21. He began brilliantly, hitting 157 and 245 not out for Victoria against SA, followed by 158 against England in the Sydney First Test. In the Second Test he took six wickets and hit 121 in the Third Test, thus contributing largely to Australia winning the Ashes. But Bean wanted Armstrong's head. The day before the NSW-Victoria Sheffield Shield match at the Sydney Cricket Ground, Armstrong did not attend training and was seen at Randwick Racecourse. Just before the match began, Armstrong withdrew. The Victorian selectors reacted by dropping him from the side to play an England XI the following week in Melbourne. Angry Armstrong supporters organised a protest meeting and set the time to correspond with the Saturday of the England match. The meeting took place at 3pm. Bean responded in his own inimitable style, refusing to allow the protesters the usual pass-out tickets, which meant they would have to pay to return to the ground after the meeting. England hit 445 runs for the loss of only 5 wickets for the day, showing the selectors' folly in leaving Armstrong out. At the next meeting of the VCA, Dr Roy Park, the State team doctor, told Bean and other executives that Armstrong had suffered severe bruising to his leg and that injury had caused his late withdrawal from the NSW match. When Armstrong went to the crease in the Fourth Test, with Australia five for 153, Bean allegedly stood at the gate gloating, but Armstrong had the last laugh, hitting a memorable unconquered 123. He returned to the dressingroom a hero only to find Bean, a teetotaller, drunk in the pavilion. Armstrong won the Test captaincy to England in 1921, losing only two of the 39 matches — equalling the record set by the magnificent 1902 side.

He worked for a whisky firm and was said to have been fond of the odd nip. Armstrong wrote some caustic articles for newspapers on various Test matches and when he died in 1947 at the age of 68, he left a wife and son and £90,000 in his will.

Vernon Ransford:
Ransford was bowled by Frank Woolley for 9 at the SCG on 1 March, 1912. He never batted again in a Test match. Ransford played his last Test innings on the same day as the great Victor Trumper. He continued to play for Victoria after the First World War and retired from first-class cricket in 1927. In 20 Tests Ransford hit 1211 runs at 37.84, with one century (143 not out against England at Lord's in 1909). In 1938 Ransford became secretary of the Melbourne Cricket Club, beating Don Bradman in a ballot apparently because the MCC committee 'wanted one of their own'. He succeeded Major Ben Wardill and Hugh Trumble in that post, a position he held until he retired through ill-health in 1957. Ransford never regretted his decision to stand down from the 1912 touring team. He died in 1958.

Albert 'Tibby' Cotter:
As with Trumper, Hill and Ransford, Cotter never played another Test after 1912. He missed selection in the 1914-15 South African tour team and did not tour the US and Canada in 1913 nor with Arthur Sims' New Zealand tour in 1913-14. The Jeff Thomson of his time, Cotter sprayed the ball about, but he was of express pace.

In 21 Tests Cotter took 89 wickets and had the knack of shattering stumps as well as batsmen's nerves. His last Test match was against England at the MCG, from 9-13 February, 1912, when Jack Hobbs (178) and Wilfred Rhodes (179) put on the world record opening stand of 323. Cotter had the unflattering return of 0/125 off his 37 overs and he was dropped from the final Test in Sydney. Cotter's last Test match was the last time all of the Big Six — Trumper, Hill, Cotter, Carter, Ransford and Armstrong — played together on the Test stage.

Tibby Cotter was a trooper in the Australian Light Horse. In 1917 he raised his head above the trench, as if the verify what his periscope had told him, and was shot dead by a sniper. Cotter died on the battleground at Beersheba. He was just 34.

Hanson Carter:
Carter was the first of the Australian Test wicketkeepers to squat on his haunches as the bowler turned to move in to bowl. He was also the last Test cricketer to wear the open-slatted pads, so preferred by Victor Trumper, when he batted.

Born in Halifax, Yorkshire, Carter had the distinction of being the only Yorkshire-born cricketer playing in the 1921 Headingly, Leeds, Test match, and Carter was representing Australia! He toured England in 1902, 1909 and 1921. He played first-class cricket for 27 years and at the age of 54 he joined Arthur Mailey's team in North America. Don Bradman was also in that tour team, along with his wife Jessie, and that tour doubled as a honeymoon for the Bradmans. Sadly Carter lost the sight of an eye when a ball popped up and struck him a fearful blow during one of the games in New York. Carter, as with Armstrong, was one of the rebel Big Six, who returned to play Test matches after 1912.

He revelled in telling stories about Victor Trumper and even during the years of Bradman at his most spectacular best, Carter would point skyward: 'There's Victor . . . now we can talk about the rest.' For a time Carter worked with Trumper in a sports store in Sydney, although Carter's trade was in undertaking, a business he took over from his father. It was Carter's sad duty to make all the arrangements for Trumper's funeral in 1915. Carter died in 1948.

Frank Laver:
Laver, the meat in the sandwich during the 1912 dispute, dropped out of international cricket immediately following the row. He continued to play for his Melbourne club, East Melbourne, until a few years before he died in 1919.

In Tests Laver hit 196 runs at 11.52 and took 37 wickets at 26.05, with 8/31 against England at Manchester, easily his best performance. He toured England in 1899 and as player-manager in the 1905 and 1909 teams. The 1912 dispute effectively ended the friendship between Laver and Percy McAlister, which had lasted 14 years. They had been close friends at East Melbourne where, in the 1892-3 summer, Laver struck gold in terms of runs, hitting a record 352 not out and scoring more than 1000 runs for the season. In 1903-4, Laver belted 341 not out against Fitzroy; his friend McAlister amassed 173 and the innings reached a Melbourne club record of 2/744. He never quite reached those heights as a batsman on the Test stage, although he hit six first-class hundreds, including 164 for Victoria against SA at Adelaide in 1904-5.

He wrote *An Australian Cricketer on Tour*, dealing mainly with the 1899 steamship travel to and from England and the matches of the 1905 tour. It is a valuable record of the early tours. Laver took many photographs of his trips to England and presented each of the tourists with a collection of photographs at the end of the 1905 and 1909 tours. He died in the north of Australia at the age of 50.

Ernest Bean:
Bean, a powerful member of the VCA and as we have seen a rather vindictive character, took Percy McAlister's place as a Test selector after the First World War. Bean became VCA secretary in 1917, a post he held until ill-health forced him to retire in 1925. His public row with Armstrong did not endear him to cricket followers, but the administrators were seemingly of a different breed. Bean became patron of the VCA before he died in 1938. He had been unsuccessful in his fight against a decision recommending players a bonus of £10 after a profitable post-war Test series. Bean's lot were beaten by thirteen votes to twelve. His portrait in a large gilt frame presides over VCA meetings.

William McElhone:
McElhone retired from the Board in 1914 but continued to give service to the NSWCA, becoming a life member in 1927. He was NSWCA president from 1920 until 1931. A Sydney solicitor, McElhone relished a debate and often bamboozled delegates at Board meetings with the sharpness of his mind. McElhone was Sydney Lord Mayor in 1922. He died in 1932.

Harry Rush:
Rush was the man who literally rushed in where the more level-headed Board men feared to tread, with his infamous amendment to

Regulation 9 of the Board's constitution. Rush was a VCA delegate to the Board until 1927. He died in 1928.

Sydney Smith:

Smith survived better than most. He went on to serve the NSWCA for a record 61 years. He was Board secretary from 1911 to 1926. He managed the 1921 and 1926 Australian teams to England and died at the age of 92 in 1972.

Perhaps the Board's most significant public relations ploy was to rid itself of the word 'control'.

Fifty-six years after the row, Board chairman Bob Parish was sitting in the team coach as Bill Lawry's 1968 Australian team motored through the lush green English countryside en-route to the next venue. Parish was speaking into a tape machine, describing to his son recent events and the beauty of Mother England: 'Truly wonderful this country . . . truly wonderful. Money just can't buy it . . .'

In 1977, Doug Walters, who had been a member of Lawry's 1968 side and was on the coach that day with Parish, sat down in his seat as his bus moved off from Melbourne's Old Melbourne Inn bound for VFL Park. This was the first practice for the World Series Cricket Australians. There was an air of expectancy, even a little apprehension, for the Australian press appeared very much on the Establishment side. Kerry Packer's rebels were on the outer. It was vital that we put on a good show. There was no room for hesitancy. We were now professionals . . . at long last in every sense of the word.

Walters waited for a lull in the chatter. He always had a wonderful sense of timing:

'Truly wonderful this. . . and Mr Parish, money can buy it!'

14

THE BENEFIT

News of a benefit match for Victor Trumper delighted Australians. Warwick Armstrong and Vernon Ransford lauded the idea. 'If anyone deserves a benefit match, it is Victor Trumper,' Armstrong said. Monty Noble said: 'For many years Trumper has been among the great players of Australia and I should be delighted to do anything I possibly could to further such a benefit.' Deputy chairman of the South Australia Cricket Association and Board member Mr G Mostyn Evans said: 'Cricketers in South Australia view with delight the proposed testimonial match for Trumper.' He said, 'I feel safe in saying that any South Australian cricketers chosen would make a special effort to play and that the SACA would gladly co-operate in any way possible to make the match the success, financially and otherwise, that it deserves to be.'

Only days before Trumper's benefit match at the SCG an article appeared in a newspaper with the headings:-

TRUMPER'S TALE
HUNTING FOR 'FOUR ALL THE TIME'
GREAT BATSMAN TELLS HIS OWN STORY
NATURE VERSUS THE BLACKBOARD

Asked why he bats like no other man, Victor replied: 'Oh, I don't know. I thought I would like to do it that way because it seemed easy.' Trumper had the habit of hitching up his trousers as he walked to the batting crease. He also hitched them up between fours, perhaps he was continually hitching up his trousers during a lengthy innings, for Victor revealed that he was forever on the lookout to hit fours. The writer described Trumper as the 'greatest hunter of fours in the game — the Nimrod of cricket. Had Trumper been an English public schoolboy it is just possible that conventionalism, while it would have still made a fine batsman of him in the ordinary sense, would have destroyed the native wit and ingenuity that have had their own sweet way and made him the pride of two cricketing worlds. It would seem that in his case the application in the making of a cricketer of the golden medical rule, ''leave it to Nature'', has been eminently successful. With a bound he reached the pinnacle of fame because, to draw a conclusion from his own story of his career, he could not help it.

'Others have had to plod wearily year after year keeping religiously to

Right: Victor Trumper in his benefit year, 1913. This is an autographed photograph.

E HAWKINS & CO   V. TRUMPER   COPYRIGHT

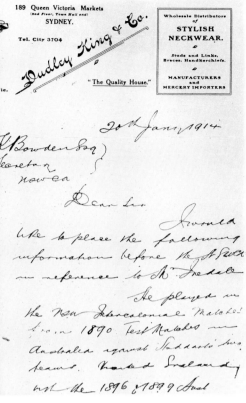

Two pages from a Victor Trumper letter to the NSW Cricket Association suggesting a testimonial match be organised for Frank Iredale. The letter is dated 20 January 1914 and is written on Dudley King & Co letterhead.

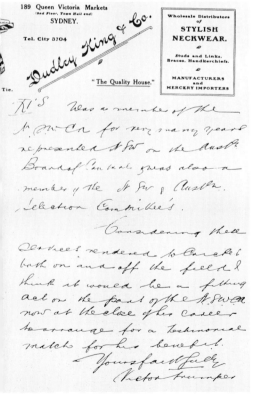

the book, and have gained the top only by their unconquerable perserverance, and yet you must not mention them, stars as they are in their own useful way, with the mighty Trumper.

Take Rhodes, for instance: 'Eight years ago his place on the batting list was last, now he is one of the orthodox, steady, imperturbable mainstays of England and is first in.'

The writer asked Trumper why he played as he did — did anyone coach him, give him a tip, reveal to him the possibilities of batting in an entirely new way at once picturesque and uniquely effective?

'No, not exactly,' Victor laughed, 'I only played that way because I wanted to. I was after fours all the time and I hit the ball where I thought I could get four off it, no matter where it was pitched.

'Some fellows put their left leg across to some balls. I thought it would be easier if I put my right leg over, so I just did it. Everybody, you know, stands differently.'

Trumper said there were players and others of the old school who had told him what he should and should not do, but 'I followed my own natural bent.' He had continued to go on after fours in the way which seemed easiest for him.

'You know,' Victor continued, 'I like to feel free and easy (as he stood in his office, sleeves rolled up, he stretched his arms out to show how he loved to be loose and comfortable in his hunt for "four all the time". (Trumper is like the sailor in Pinafore, he wants to be as free as the mountain bird). 'Of course, I did not do what they told me.'

'They say I am pig-headed (Trumper looked as if he didn't believe a word of it). If a man has got an idea, let him cultivate it. Just the same as Bosie (the England leg-spinner Bosenquet who invented the Bosey or wrong 'un). He got one; he took it on and worked it out. It comes natural to you.

Sometimes a man has a stroke — a beauty; four every time — and they say it is a fluke.

'There was Charlie McLeod, who used to play forward to Richardson (Tom Richardson, Surrey and England bowler) — you know how fast he was — and snick him for four.

'They said it was a fluke, until he had made about 200 with it at various times. That was unfair. It was a good stroke. It came natural to him and he cultivated it.'

Trumper mentioned the English player Radcliffe (George Radcliffe, Yorkshire) who cultivated a most unusual stroke. 'To him the stroke was perfectly natural,' Trumper said. 'He used to hook the ball over his shoulder, something after the fashion of a navvy shovelling dirt — but he got them just the same.'

Amazingly enough, Trumper's attitude to Test cricket was less than carefree; certainly his mental approach did not reflect the glorious array of uninhibited strokeplay which caused friend and foe alike to call Trumper the greatest batsmen of the Golden Age of Cricket.

'Test cricket is a very hard, serious matter. It means that the team which makes the least number of mistakes wins. It is not pleasant from a purely cricketing point of view. There is not so much pleasure in the cricket itself; it is the fight in it. If you want 200 runs, you have got to set your teeth — yes, and grind them, too — to get them. You must not get out; you must stay there, if it takes weeks. My word, it is serious.'

Asked whether these 'serious trials of endurance' should be curtailed,

Trumper was vehemently opposed to not playing Tests out.

'No, not having them played that way, it would not be such a fight. Limit the time and you would have too many snatch victories. Men would go in and have a bang. That would mean risks and that is not Test cricket, not as we understand it in Australia.'

Trumper admitted that there was difficulty in England playing games to the death, on account of the great program of county matches. In Trumper's day Tests in England were played over three days. When rain intervened the match was invariably drawn. (In the 20 Test matches played over Trumper's four England tours — 1899, 1902, 1905 and 1909 — eleven were drawn. Australia won five and England won four). However, Trumper said if games had have been played to the death in England — or played longer than the allotted three days — it would mean that in the event of Surrey and Lancashire meeting, Jack Hobbs, Ernest Hayes and John Hitch on one side and Reg Spooner, Harry Dean and perhaps Jack Sharp on the other would be absent.

'The result would be that the people would not go to see the county match and if you left these players out of the Test matches they would not be representative trials. I'm afraid the time limit would have to be applied in England.'

Victor Trumper admitted during the interview that he preferred playing cricket in England than in Australia.

'My word, I would,' he said. 'Why? The climate. You can sleep better. You wake up fresher and you feel more inclined to chase sixers than you do here. That is the reason why the Englishmen last longer than we do. Many of them play ten years after we are done with. That's the climate. Take last Monday (the first match between NSW and WA of the 1912-13 summer), why it was like a Turkish bath. What about it today?'

It was 99.1 degrees F.

Trumper proceeded to deliver a short lecture on things not always being what they seemed, with special reference to the fact that cricket in such temperatures was not nearly such an alluring pastime as the people who lolled about on the Hill, or stretched themselves out in the stands, made out.

Trumper in 1913 had strong opinions of cricket and cricketers. He told the correspondent that neither England nor Australia was improving its cricket. Comparing Pelham (later Sir Pelham) Warner's Ashes-winning sides of 1903-4 and 1911-12, Trumper said Warner's first team was the better, despite its winning the rubber 3-2 as against a 4-1 victory in 1911-12.

'The Australians are not so strong all round as they once were,' he said. 'When I first played in big cricket there was Hughie Trumble, Monty Noble, Ernest Jones and Bill Howell. Could they compare the best four available of late years with this batch? After them came Frank Laver and Charlie McLeod; any of these six could start bowling in a Test match.'

What about Hordern and the googlie? 'In his class,' Trumper responded, 'Hordern is good.' Trumper was talking about Herbert 'Ranji' Hordern, the first of the great Australian leg-spinners. He was nicknamed 'Ranji' because of his dark complexion. The players named him after the great England batsman, Ranjitsinhji.

This Victor Trumper letter was written to an aspiring schoolboy cricketer on 3 February 1913 and gives an insight into the great cricketer's committment, care and concern for the game. Trumper espouses the healthy life and warns the young man not to become too obsessed with cricket at the expense of a business career. The young boy became Mr R H Coningsby and he later donated the letter to the South Melbourne Cricket Club.

The googlie or the ball now referred to more commonly as the wrong 'un was the ball that its inventor, Bosenquet, first bowled to Trumper in Australia in 1903-4. It was against NSW. The first wrong 'un he sent down clean bowled the master batsman. From then on, Trumper was rarely fooled.

He said the Bosey, or wrong 'un, as a delivery was a bit of a mixture: 'When it is good, it is blooming good, and when it is bad it is rotten. There is nothing in between.' The correspondent wrote: 'Trumper evidently regards all varieties of attack in the same spirit as the dusky princess who sang, "All Coons Look Alike to Me".'

Was there any kind of bowling that worried you? asked the reporter.

'Well . . . um . . . er . . . No.'

Trumper put England's superiority in 1911-12 down to the splendid bowling of Frank Foster (32 wickets at 21.62) and Sydney Barnes, who many believe was as great a bowler as Bill O'Reilly. Barnes took 34 wickets at 22.88 in that series, with Foster getting Trumper out twice in the rubber and Barnes dismissing him four times, including twice in Victor's last Test at the SCG from 27 February to 1 March, 1912. Significantly, neither Foster nor Barnes figured in Trumper's dismissal during the First Test — the only Test of the series that Australia won. Trumper hit 113 and 14, falling to Frank Woolley in the first innings and Johnny Douglas, stand-in skipper for Warner, who was taken ill early in the tour. However, Trumper said that both Barnes and Foster were better bowlers in Australia than on their own wickets in England.

Why? 'The wickets suited them. They made the ball bounce over the batsmen's shoulders in a way that not even Jones equalled at his best (you'll recall it was Jonah Jones who slipped a fireball through Dr W G Grace's beard in 1896 and made the famous remark 'Sorry, Doc . . . she slipped.') Also, the wickets are not what they were. I think they ought to be re-made. The ground is played out.'

Our correspondent had not quite met Victor on equal footing when he asked: 'By the way, why did you give up bowling, Trumper? Oh, excuse me calling you Trumper.'

Victor beamed: 'Oh, that's all right, old man. Everybody calls me Trumper — even the newsboys.'

'Did you give it up yourself, or — '

'Got sense, I suppose. It was this way. When I was getting runs, Joe Darling would not let me bowl. He thought it would affect me as a run-getter. After that he used to put me on when it was certain a match would be drawn — just to waste time like. I got out of the way of bowling seriously after that.'

In 1899 Trumper took 1/29; in 1902, 20/415; in 1905, 0/5; and in 1909, 1/151. Against Essex at Leyton on 15 May, 1902, he bagged 5/33 off 13 overs with 4 maidens. Essex was bowled out for 178 and the Australians replied with 249, Clem Hill top-scoring with 104. Significantly, perhaps, Trumper scored only 9. His career best figures were against Cambridge when he took 5/19 off 8.3 overs. This was the match in which he hit 128 — the highest score in his fabulous 1902 season in England.

TRUMPER'S THOUGHTS ON ENGLAND PLAYERS OF HIS DAY

W G Grace was nearing the end of his career when Trumper first played against him. In fact Victor's first Test (Nottingham, 1899) was Grace's last Test.

'But he (Grace) was a master. You see,' Trumper said, 'he had progressed with the game.'

Ranjitsinhji was 'wonderful', but of all the England batsman, one stood out head and shoulders above the rest for Victor Trumper: Archie MacLaren.

'Archie was the greatest,' he said. 'All of us Australians think that. It was a pleasure to watch MacLaren bat and you know, I like to see a man who can bat on a bad wicket too. Hobbs was certainly the best professional batsman in England,' he added.

Trumper also lauded the play of Reg Spooner and Charles Fry. 'I hope we see Spooner and Fry in Australia soon,' he said. 'They would be an immense draw, if it can be arranged for them to visit Australia.'

However, war clouds in Europe were little more than 12 months away. It would be eight years before another England touring team would visit Australia. And, sadly, many great cricketers would have perished through ill-health or on the battle ground of the Kaiser War. Spooner and Fry were destined not to visit Australia.

HIS BEST INNINGS

Many people considered Trumper's century before lunch at Manchester in 1902 to be his greatest knock. However, Victor believed that his best innings was at the SCG in 1903-4 against Warner's England team. In that match, as we have seen, Clem Hill was run out and a riot started amid the crowd. Poor umpire Bob Crockett was heckled and Warner threatened to take his men off the arena. Sixty-seven years later England captain Ray Illingworth called his men from the field after an incident with his fast bowler, John Snow, on the fence at fine leg.

Trumper recalled the match, in which he hit a magnificent 185 not out. As brilliant as that was, R E Foster hit 287 for England and Warner's men won a marvellous encounter:

'Yes, I believe that 185 not out was my finest innings. We had bad luck. If Hill had not been run out — some of the Englishmen have told me he was not out — we would have put on another 50 that night and that might have pulled us through. Then, you will remember, it rained overnight and that did not improve our chances.

'Yes, I think we had bad luck in that game, but still, you know, that's all in the business.'

The Victor Trumper benefit match was held on the Sydney Cricket Ground from 7 to 11 February, 1913, between Trumper's NSW XI and a Rest of Australia XI.

The Rest batted first and it is of no moment to relate individual scores, except that the score was in excess of 350 and, when Trumper's NSW XI began, Charlie Kelleway went early. That brought Eric Barbour and Charlie Macartney together. They batted valiantly and paved the way for Victor. Clem Hill captained the Rest, which included such greats as Warwick Armstrong, Vernon Ransford, Edgar Mayne, Jack Ryder and Johnnie Moyes. Moyes may have become a marvellous Test player. He was later picked for South Africa, but the First World War stopped his march.

Trumper batted on the Saturday, sadly a day marred by rain. Yet thousands of people braved the wintry conditions to pay tribute to the

Cover of the scorecard produced for Trumper's Testimonial Match at the SCG on 7, 8, 9, 10 and 11 February 1913. With a bit of luck, Trumper scored 126 not out and everyone was delighted.

Memento of the 1913 Testimonial
Match. This was Trumper's
personal copy. (*S S Ramamurthy*)

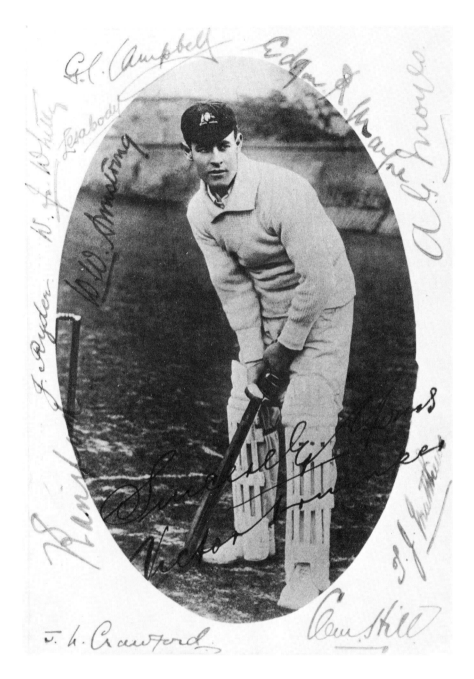

greatest batsman the game had then known. Trumper was visibly
moved. He took guard and looked wistfully around the ground.
Perhaps, for once in his cricketing life, he was not thinking clearly.
Tears welled and, as he watched Bill Whitty approach, he could not see
anything, save a blurred form. First ball was down leg side, a full toss.
Trumper swung and missed. Next ball was right on line and the ball
crashed into middle and leg stumps. The umpire diplomatically,
perhaps quite rightly, signalled 'no ball'. Trumper survived. Jack Ryder
enthusiastically appealed for lbw a number of times against Trumper,
but there was little chance of the umpire upholding the decision as cries
of 'No, not out' echoed about the ground, not just from the adoring
crowd, but from ten of Ryder's teammates!

**V.TRUMPER TESTIMONIAL MATCH
SYDNEY [7-2-1913]**

Autographs of players from both teams competing in Trumper's benefit game which ended in a draw. (*S S Ramamurthy*)

Trumper held on until stumps and the game was resumed on the Monday. It was on that day, 9 February, 1913, that Trumper again revealed his genius. He hit a brilliant, unconquered 126. But it wasn't the score that enthralled everyone, it was the manner in which he scored runs.

The game ended in a draw, but Trumper's 126 not out will forever live in history as one of the great knocks when the people dearly wanted a big score from their hero. Johnny Moyes idolised Trumper, but as a writer Moyes was very astute. He also revered Bradman; got to know the man as few men had, but still, in his writings, you felt in Moyes' heart there was something special about Victor Trumper. In his superb book *A Century of Cricketers* (Angus & Robertson, 1950) Moyes talks about Trumper's batting in that testimonial match. 'In 1912-13 at Adelaide Trumper made 11 and 0 for NSW against SA. "I'll see you in Sydney," was his goodbye to us.

'It was the difference between a Trumper who was ailing and one unchecked by bodily weakness. In his testimonial match at Sydney he went in to bat late at night and he was there at the close of play. When he resumed he expressed the view that we had treated him rather generously in the matter of an lbw decision and he proceeded to "give us a chance". I saw him, with the flick of the wrists, lift a fast rising ball from Jack Crawford on to the cycle track, which in those days encircled the ground. I saw him vary it by cutting a similiar ball for four. In the same over, Trumper jammed down on a fastish yorker and turned it away past square leg to the fence. This is not imagination, for I was fielding in the slips, and I saw it and marvelled. One of the choicest memories of my life is that I was privileged to see Victor at close quarters and to watch his wizardry.'

That match saw the emergence of Jack Ryder, who took eight wickets for 88 runs in the two NSW innings. Ryder later played in Armstrong's 1921 side and batted with Bradman at the outset of The Don's fabulous career. The tall Victorian all-rounder also became a Test selector and died only a few months after the 1977 Centenary Test match at the MCG.

Trumper received £2950.13.3 as proceeds from his testimonial match. It was easily the best financial return any Australian had received to that time.

The first such benefit was given to James Kelly, the Test keeper, a close friend and teammate of Trumper's who married Victor's wife's sister. Kelly's benefit raised £1400. The only player to approach Trumper's benefit amount was the highly popular Monty Noble, who in 1907-8 (Australia v the Rest) received £2000, although Warwick Armstrong collected £2500 by public subscription in 1921-22 and Charlie Macartney's benefit match (Rest v Australians in 1926-27) realised £2598. But it was not until the 1948-49 summer that Trumper's testimonial match record was broken. And that record went to the greatest record holder of them all — Don Bradman. Bradman's benefit match (Bradman's XI v Hassett's XI, Melbourne) brought him £9432 (gate receipts £5185).

Trumper was elated with the huge amount given him for his testimonial. A dinner in his honor was held at Paris House, Sydney, on the night of the first day of the match and everyone was overjoyed that Trumper overcame his early nervousness and hit a brilliant century in the NSW first innings.

Victor Trumper's personal, autographed menu card from a dinner in his honor held at Paris House, Sydney, 7 February 1913 – the day the benefit match started. (*Tom Nicholas*)

But in September, 1914, Victor ran into another brick wall. His health and business were both in a poor state and he was summonsed to appear in court.

Thomas John Houghton brought an action against Victor, claiming £111.7s for alleged commission as agent and working secretary for Trumper before, during and after the testimonial match. The action was heard before a judge (Mr Justice Pring) and jury in Sydney's No. 1 Court.

Houghton claimed commission at the rate of 10 per cent on the sum of £1113.13s.2d collected by the citizens' committee, formed by Houghton at the request of Trumper, and for work done by Houghton

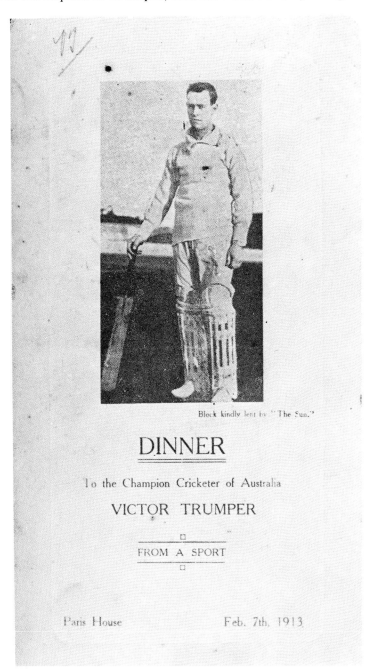

The cover of Trumper's menu card. Note the initials 'VT' in the top left hand corner. Victor passed the card around for signing by most players in the match. (*Tom Nicholas*)

Block kindly lent by "The Sun."

DINNER

To the Champion Cricketer of Australia

VICTOR TRUMPER

□

FROM A SPORT

□

Paris House   Feb. 7th, 1913

in connection with the testimonial match — but not on the net sum received by Trumper (£2980).

Houghton told the Court: 'I worked for five solid months for Mr Trumper and have not received the price of a postage stamp for my services.'

Houghton said in evidence that he earned his living as an organiser, advertising agent and journalist. 'Early in December, 1912 I met Mr Hanson Carter at his place of business, Oxford St., Woollahra, and later I saw Mr Trumper, who told me the match would be a failure if it was left to the cricket association. Trumper also said that Mr Bowden, NSWCA secretary, would do his best to make it a failure. Houghton then alleged that Trumper had told him: 'You are just the man I want to run it for me. You form a committee and I'll give you 10 per cent on all I get. If it is left to the association, I won't get as much as Charlie Turner got.' (C T B 'Charlie' Turner, the great spinner of the 1880s collected £331 in his testimonial match — NSW v Rest, SCG in 1909-10.)

Houghton then alleged that he had said to Trumper: 'All right, I'll do my best.' In order to get stuck into the task, Houghton asked Trumper for names of people who might assist him in forming a committee. Trumper had allegedly written names of such people of the back of an envelope. 'I interviewed those people and issued a circular convening a meeting of Victor Trumper's friends and admirers to be held on 16 December, 1912.'

Mr Justice Pring: 'Have you that circular?' — 'No; it can't be found.'

Trumper denied that he had ever promised payment of any kind to Houghton, however, he did confess to having met Houghton at the beginning of December, 1912. He denied saying to Houghton that if the matter were left to the NSWCA it would be a failure, or that Mr Bowden would do his best to make it a failure. Victor told the Court that he did not say: 'Don't worry; you'll get paid all right.'

When asked whether he had promised Houghton any money, Trumper said: 'No. Commission was never mentioned. It was to be simply a present.'

Houghton then verbally attacked Trumper in Court, with: 'I am going to ask you something that will perhaps tickle you a bit. Did you ask me to start that subscription list with a certain sum of money?'

Trumper: 'No, I did not.'

Houghton: 'What! You will get into trouble directly.'

Mr Justice Pring: 'You must not threaten the witness, or you'll be getting into trouble, yourself.'

Houghton: 'What for?'

Mr Justice Pring: 'For doing something that is very improper and wrong.'

Houghton: 'Oh, I beg pardon. I didn't really know. (To Trumper) Did you ask me to start that list with the sum of twenty guineas in the name of a certain gentleman?'

Trumper: 'No, that was your suggestion to me.'

Case dismissed.

Trumper's business interests had all failed. He was by now earning a modest living as a commercial traveller. Realising that Victor was incompetent in matters of money, the citizens' committee asked that Trumper's benefit money be set up in trust by the NSWCA. Certainly such a move was not unprecedented. In 1906, Syd Gregory was given just 12½ percent of the £630 benefit proceeds and the rest was placed in the hands of a trust set up by the association.

In Trumper's case, writes Philip Derriman in his history of the NSWCA, 'the money was controlled by three trustees, nominated by Trumper and approved by the association. One of the trustees was E A (Edwin) Tyler, for many years the association's treasurer. Another, surprisingly, was William McElhone.' The third trustee was Harry Jamieson. In June, 1913, Trumper wrote to the NSWCA asking for an advance of £46, but the association refused on the ground that the money could be dispensed only by the trust. The trust was not wound up until the mid-1960s, a few years after Victor's widow Sarah Ann (Annie) Trumper had died. New trustees — Sydney Smith, the NSW secretary, and Frank Maitland Cush, a public servant who boarded Don Bradman when he first began playing with St. George upon leaving his home town of Bowral — were sworn in to replace McElhone and Tyler on 20 April, 1938. McElhone died on 22 April, 1932, and Tyler on 24 October, 1937. (Incidentally Frank Cush and his wife had the young Don Bradman staying with them right up until The Don married Jessie Menzies in 1932.)

Derriman writes that Trumper attended the monthly association meetings until 26 October, 1914. His reason for not attending any meeting after that date was 'probably that he suffered a decline in his health. According to his wife it was in October 1914 that she first noticed symptoms of the disease which caused Trumper's death eight months later. In January, 1919, the NSWCA erected brass memorial tablets for Trumper and Albert 'Tibby' Cotter in the SCG Members' Pavilion.

'They were added to a row of similar tablets which had been erected for other great NSW cricketers: Duff, Murdoch, the Gregorys and Ferris. The tablets were removed during renovations in 1982 and recently were still waiting to be re-erected elsewhere. However, the association believed Victor deserved a more substantial memorial at the SCG and, in January 1920, it opened the Victor Trumper Memorial Fund. Trumper had not been dead five years, but it seems the war years had dulled the lustre of his name, for donations came in slowly. By April, 1920, the fund had inched up to £58 and by July, to £141. When it was eventually closed in March, 1921, the fund totalled only £229. Originally, the association intended using the fund to erect a grand drinking fountain at the SCG. In August 1920, however, the two officials of the association in charge of Trumper's benefit money, McElhone and Tyler, reported to the NSWCA that Trumper's widow and her children were in financial trouble. McElhone revealed that he, Tyler and the third trustee, Jamieson, had made themselves personally liable for £600 still owing on a home that Mrs Trumper had bought. Tyler reported that Mrs Trumper had 'little or no furniture in the house'. He suggested that instead of erecting an expensive memorial to her husband, it would be better to help her and her children. This, then, is the explanation for the simple plaque which many people over the years have considered a cheap memorial for so famous a sportsman. The plaque is unquestionably cheap: it cost the NSWCA only £16. However, the association was able to give Mrs Trumper £213, the balance of the fund.'

Trumper in his Help Street, Chatswood, garden in 1913. This is a postcard now in the possession of Charles Trumper. (*Charles Trumper*)

15

TRUMPER'S LAST GREAT KNOCK

'The Big Ship', Warwick Armstrong and Trumper stride confidently to the crease in England, 1909.
(*S S Ramamurthy*)

Victor Trumper's last great innings was played on Saturday, 27 February, 1914. The Australian score stood at 5/104 overnight, in reply to Canterbury's 92. But with Trumper, Warwick Armstrong, Jack Crawford and Vernon Ransford in reserve, the packed house at Lancaster Park, Christchurch, eagerly awaited the batting of Trumper, especially, and the 'Big Ship', Armstrong.

Arthur Sims (later Sir Arthur) had brought this star-studded band of Australians to New Zealand and the crowd buzzed with the anticipation of a bumper day's cricket when Trumper walked to the crease. Armstrong had fallen for 31 and Trumper joined his skipper, Sims.

The correspondent for the *Lyttleton Times* wrote: 'It was when Trumper came in that the crowd sat up to watch proceedings intently, and everybody hoped that the champion would get past the critical stage and make a big score. There appeared to be no critical stage for Trumper. He opened out on Bennett with some perfect strokes to the off, placed right between two fieldsmen who, time after time, would converge on the ball but would fail to get it owing to its marvellous pace. One could have imagined that it was a purely exhibition effort. From driving to cutting and back to leg glides, the batsman seemed to have a supernatural knack of finding a clear avenue to the boundary. He monopolised the batting.'

Trumper, in batting with Sims, made his captain eternally grateful, especially as Vic was batting beautifully. Sims was later to rejoice in having batted in such a big stand with Trumper, as he had, years before, batted in a century-plus stand with W G Grace.

'Everything came to him (Trumper) and he ran to forty while Sims was making five. He was beyond criticism and one could only marvel that any batsman could maintain such a sequence, not merely of correct strokes, but of ideal scoring shots, half a dozen of which would lift the average game out of the ordinary. The centuries flew up unexpectedly, Trumper averaging one an hour. He made 50 in 26 minutes, 100 in 73 minutes, as against Sims' 191 minutes for the century, and 150 in 92 minutes, as against Sims' 150 in 236 minutes. Trumper was 200 in 131 minutes and 250 in 152 minutes. His three sixes worked the crowd up into a state of enthusiasm and those who had to dodge the flying balls shouted: ''Turn it up, Trumper!'' Still, it was not often that Lancaster Park had a world's champion 'going' properly and his placing of the

A postcard of Arthur Sims' 1914 side to New Zealand. Sims is third from left in the back row while Trumper is at far right. Arthur Mailey is seated at front left.

BATSMEN OUT	FALL WKTS	BATSMEN IN	BOWLERS WKT
DOLLING 0	1	0 SIMS 182	BENNETT 4
COLLINS 10	2	28 CRAWFORD 1	CARLTON 5
WADDY 0	3	28 EXTRAS 38	WILSON
NOBLE 36	4	94 TOTAL 651	SANDMAN 0
MAILEY 3	5	104	HICKMOTT
CODY 54	6	118 CANTERBURY	PATRICK 0
ARMSTRONG 31	7	209 1ST INNINGS 92	WHITTA
TRUMPER 293	8	642 VISITORS	
RANSFORD 2	9	649	

POST·CARD

Write here for Inland Postage only   The Address to be written here

A memento from J W Roberts 31 Stevens St Sydenham Christchurch

Mr V Trumper Sims' Australian Cricket Team

Postcard of the scoreboard Australia v. Canterbury, 27 February 1914, showing Trumper's last great knock of 293 and Arthur Sims' 182 in a total of 651. NZ bowler Joe Bennett said Victor Trumper could have made his runs with a walking stick that day!

Reverse of the scoreboard postcard. It reads: 'A memento from J W Roberts 21 Stevens St. Sydenham, Christchurch. Mr V Trumper, Sims' Australian Cricket Team.'

ball was an educative treat. Everybody would have liked to see him play out the day, but when he skied one from Bennett at 293 he was undoubtedly hitting a little wildly. It was a great and long-to-be-remembered innings. The batsman never lifted anything he did not intend to lift and he hit so hard at everything that it was bound to travel. If one had to praise a particular stroke, it was the late cut.

'It was so late at times, that on one occasion his bat gave Boxshall a good crack on the gloves.'

Trumper and Sims flayed the attack to the tune of 433 in 180 minutes (Trumper 293, Sims 184 not out).

Among the Australian team were Arthur Mailey, Frank Laver, Monty Noble and Herbie Collins. Armstrong and Noble took their wives on tour and at the conclusion of the Canterbury match, Noble spoke of the first time he had visited Christchurch and that Australians looked upon that city as the home of New Zealand cricket. He also praised Frank Laver saying, 'He is one of the finest men I've met' and Frank had been 'vilified by men who ought to have appreciated the good qualities of the man'. Noble was obviously referring to the 1912 dispute, of which Laver was the veritable meat in the sandwich. 'Fortunately,' continued Noble, 'most of us have pretty broad shoulders and desire only to play the game as good citizens of Australia.'

What our correspondent from the *Lyttelton Times* did not mention was that a small boy, not in his teens, approached Victor just as he began to walk to the crease. The boy asked Victor if he would use his bat. 'All right, sonny, take mine back to the dressingroom,' Vic said. Herbert Collins, watched the entire episode, having been dismissed off the bowling of Joe Bennett the previous day. 'Bennett, one of the best bowlers in the Dominion, opened to Trumper and saw his first ball hit over the sightboard for six. When 90, the shoulder of the nipper's bat broke. Trumper picked up the piece and gave it to the umpire. He played on with half a bat to make 293. Bennett and other players facetiously told Trumper to pull a stump out and play with it instead of a broken bat. Bennett declared that Trumper could have made his score with a walking stick.'

Trumper was dropped a number of times during his innings, as was Sims. The unlucky bowler was Bennett on one occasion. At stumps, Australia had reached nine for 651. This whirlwind 293 was Trumper's last great knock in first-class cricket. However, he did manage another double century (211) in a one-day fixture against Southland at Invercargil, on 11 March, 1914. Because of the nature of the fixture, a one-day match, it was not deemed first-class. In another second-class match, Sims' Australians plundered 922 runs, with Jack Crawford hitting 354. Trumper headed the tour batting aggregate and averages with 1246 runs at an average of 83.0. The Australians played eight first class matches, winning six and drawing two. They also played eight other games, winning two and drawing six. Warwick Armstrong took the lion's share of the wickets (89), Mailey chimed in with 48 and Noble, 30. Collins, the opener who resembled Humphrey Bogart, scored 687 runs at an average of 45.8.

But at the end of the day, the display of pure batting genius was when Trumper hit 293. It was truly his last great knock.

16
TRUMPER MASTERPIECES

Herbert Collins played for Paddington and New South Wales with Trumper and did not play a full summer of first-class cricket until the 1912-13 season. Victor Trumper was then a State selector and he urged his co-selectors to perservere with Collins. Trumper was then the State captain and he led the team in Hobart against Tasmania. Vic said to Herbert as he was going in to bat: 'See that you don't let me down.' Collins hit a brilliant 282, then a record score, and Vic was as delighted as if he had scored the runs himself.

Just before the game got underway, Trumper had the fingers of his right hand jammed in the door of a car. His fingers were badly bruised and swollen. He did not intend batting, but the crowd wanted to catch a glimpse of Trumper's mastery, however inconvenienced he might be. Vic relented and batted to allow Collins to get more runs. Trumper came to the crease and immediately began to unleash some majestic drives. He could use only his top or left hand, the one used for control rather than power. Yet he left the bowlers and fieldsmen dumbfounded and the crowd in no doubt of his genius. He balanced the bat until point of contact and placed the ball where he liked, finishing with a superb 80.

Only once have I seen such batting. In 1970-1 the South African Barry Richards was playing for South Australia against NSW at Adelaide Oval. In the first innings Richards suffered a broken right thumb. In the second innings he batted one handed, as did Trumper almost 60 years before, and Richards carved up the attack in similar vein, driving beautifully to hit an unconquered 40-odd. Richards was one of the great batsmen of the modern era, but political troubles at home prevented him from playing more than just four Test matches. That year for South Australia he hit 356 (325 in a day) against West Australia in Perth — an attack which included Tony Lock, Dennis Lillee and Graham McKenzie.

In the 1906-7 season Trumper played one of his grandest knocks. It was a treacherous Melbourne 'sticky' and Vic proved his mastery on this glue-pot. Jack Saunders, the left-arm Victorian and Test fast bowler, delivered his first ball of the match to Trumper. The ball pitched leg and missed off stump by a whisker. Vic beamed down the wicket at Saunders, bent over with his hands to his head: 'Well, Jack, I might as well be caught as bowled.' Ominous words. Trumper took to

Trumper waxes lyrical; the foot of this photo reads: 'There's a saying old and rusty/But it is ever true/ 'Tis never trouble trouble/Till trouble troubles you./ V Trumper 7th May '12.' (*Richard Watson Collection*)

Trumper leaves the SCG after falling for 1 in the First Test Australia v. England 1903. England led by 292 after the first innings and Trumper almost turned the game Australia's way with a magnificent, unbeaten 185 in his second innings. (*Tom Nicholas*)

The Australian team of 1903-4. Standing, from left: A Gehrs, W W Armstrong, W P Howell, H Trumble, A J Hopkins, C McLeod, V Trumper. Sitting: J J Kelly, C Hill, M A Noble (captain), R A Duff, S E Gregory.

Saunders and flayed the Victorians in turn, all the while his comrades were falling, especially to the bowling of Saunders. Trumper scored an amazing 101 out of 139 runs scored while he was at the wicket. Trumper made his 101 in 57 minutes, hitting one six and 18 power-packed fours. He reached 64 in 31 minutes and 73 in 40 minutes in an innings of rare brilliance. NSW eventually reached 263 and won the match, in which Saunders bagged a total of 12 NSW wickets, but the game was made ever memorable for Trumper's knock.

We have discussed at length Trumper's 104 against England at Old Trafford in 1902 in the chapter devoted to his diary. Perhaps an even better innings was the one he played against Pelham Warner's 1903-4 side at the Sydney Cricket Ground. The first innings was a disaster. Trumper was caught at slip by Reg Foster, falling away to his left and holding the ball in his outstretched left hand, off the bowling of Arnold.

Monty Noble's side, having won the·toss, were struggling. Trumper went for 1, Duff for 3 and Clem Hill for 5. Then Noble rescued the innings with a solid 133. He was backed by Warwick Armstrong (48) and Albert Hopkins (39). the team managed to make 285. But the wicket was hard and true and the Englishmen easily overtook the Australian tally with Reg Foster hitting a marvellous 287 and Len Braud, left-arm spinner and batsman, compiling a good 102. England hit up a massive 577. Then it was Australia's turn to try and turn the match around. Sid Gregory and James Kelly walked to the crease with Australia 292 runs in arrears. It would be a tall order to make the Englishmen bat again, let alone make sufficient runs to set Pelham Warner's men a reasonable target. As Warner wrote in *How We Recovered the Ashes* (Chapman and Hall, 1940), 'It was very evident,

The England team of 1903-4. From left: Knight, Hirst, Hayward, Tyldesley, Rhodes, Bosanquet, Arnold, Braund, Lilley, Warner (captain), Foster. (*Pelham Warner Collection*)

from the first ball of our opponents' second innings, that they meant to make us pay heavily for victory, if indeed victory was to be ours. But we too were equally determined to make the most of our initial advantage and for a long time it was a stubborn fight, good bowling keeping the batsmen quiet even on that past-pluperfect-prestissimo wicket.' Noble kept his big guns — Trumper, Hill and Duff — away from the new ball, opening up with Gregory and Kelly, who had batted at the fall of the eighth and ninth wickets respectively in the first innings. Duff batted in the No. 3 spot, Hill at No. 4 and Trumper at No. 5. Gregory and Kelly batted well, hitting 36 before Kelly went, bowled by Arnold for 13. Duff joined Gregory and the pair pushed the total up to 108 before Gregory was caught behind by Dick Lilley off the left-arm spin of Wilfred Rhodes. Rhodes kept an impeccable length and the batsmen found him difficult to get away. Australia lost its third wicket at 191 when Duff was snapped up at forward short leg off Rhodes for a back-to-the-wall 84.

Then Trumper strode to the crease to join Hill, who was then 37. It was 3.40pm on 15 December, 1903. Gradually the pair got on top and although George Hirst took the new ball for the final over before tea, Hill and Trumper survived. After tea Hill was subdued, playing dourly and carefully. Trumper, after a quiet start, began to unleash his range of strokes. Len Braund came on against Trumper. For his first two deliveries, Trumper positioned himself perfectly to cut and hammered each one in turn for four, backward of point. The third ball was wide down leg side. It beat Trumper's flailing bat and keeper Lilley and went scuttling away for four byes. Braund's fourth ball was well up and Trumper danced down the wicket and hit it like a tracer through cover — another four.

The fifth was played sedately back to the bowler and the sixth Trumper drove firmly past mid-off. The batsmen had run three when

Pelham 'Plum' Warner leads his team on to the SCG during the First Test of the 1903-4 season. Trumper's second innings of 185 not out has been acclaimed as his greatest ever Test knock. Note the sloping cycle track which encircled the SCG at the time. (*Pelham Warner*)

George Hirst threw to the bowler's end. Braund accepted the shy at the batsman's end, where Trumper was running. The ball missed the stumps and the batsmen ran again, looking for the fifth. However, Hill had run a good deal past the stumps at the bowler's end. It was a dangerous call by Trumper and the return from Relf to Lilley was perfect, right over the bails. Lilley broke the stumps and, on unanimous appeal from the Englishmen, umpire Bob Crockett at square leg raised his finger. Hill was run out! He had run way past the stumps and believed he had made good his ground. Hill was surprised and annoyed by the decision. He did not say a word in protest to Crockett, but slapped his pad with his bat, looked up towards the heavens, shrugged his shoulders, shook his head and left for the pavilion. The crowd was incensed. They began chanting 'Crock, Crock, Crock!' booing and hissing as Hill walked disconsolately towards the gate.

Pelham Warner was upset and he became even more so when he heard the groans and hisses of disapproval from the Members' Pavilion.

Warner walked towards the members in an effort to restrain them. Instead, the booing intensified. Monty Noble had joined Trumper and the three cricketers sat on the grass in the middle, waiting for order to be restored. Warner told Noble that if the demonstration against Crockett did not cease, 'I will be compelled to take my men from the field.' The noise abated and the game continued, but as soon as the first ball had been bowled, the crowd increased the tempo of their annoyance: 'How much did you pay Crockett, Warner?' and 'Have you got your coffin ready, Crockett? Which gate are you leaving by, Crockett?'

Sir William McKell, one time Governor-General of Australia and an avid cricket follower and one who regards Trumper as the greatest batsman of all time, was at the ground that day. He was 93 (at the time of writing) and vividly recalled the demonstration against Crockett: 'Clem Hill was clearly in, but he was given out and the crowd heckled. Funny really it wasn't as bad as Warner made out. A fellow standing next to me accidently dropped his bottle of beer (an empty one) and it fell down onto the cycle track which surrounded the SCG in those days. It made a crazy tinkling noise as it rolled down the track and everyone cheered. Others followed suit and with the hundreds of bottles rolling down the track, the heckling and cheering, the ground erupted.' Warner wrote that he had acted wisely in not withdrawing his men from the field: 'People in England, however, can have no conception of the yelling and hissing that went on that afternoon right up to the drawing of stumps; even such hardened Test-match players as Hirst and Rhodes were quite upset.' When the players left the field at stumps, Crockett was escorted under the protection of two burly plain-clothes detectives. The Englishmen and Crockett were hooted loudly.

Australia's opening pair Reggie Duff and Victor Trumper (right) stride onto the Adelaide ground during the 1903-4 season.

Frank Iredale wrote in the *Daily Mail* that Warner's action in walking to the pavilion had, in fact, incited the demonstration to fever pitch. Warner wrote: 'In answer to Mr Iredale I would like to point out that the row had already begun before I started on my fruitless journey to the pavilion.'

The demonstration took precedence, but between the tea interval and stumps, Sydney and Warner's men saw Trumper at his very best. Rhodes bowled with three men in the country, at long-on, long-off and deep extra cover, a field which would have done any modern captain proud in limited-overs cricket. Rhodes, alone, managed to keep Trumper relatively quiet. All the other England bowlers were, as Warner put it, 'roughly handled'. Trumper scored with almost every stroke and he played every shot imaginable; the cut, the drive, the leg glance and the stroke of his own invention where he went right back on his stumps to force the ball off the back foot wide of mid-on or through the off side. The leg-spinner Bosenquet had Noble stumped by Lilley for 22 and Warwick Armstrong held on with Trumper to stumps with Australia five for 367. Trumper was 119 not out, Armstrong 14. In the 100 minutes since tea, Trumper thrashed 112 runs; 64 in the final, glorious 40 minutes. Warner wrote that for the first time on the tour his attack had been severely dealt with and that, without Rhodes, he would have been at the end of his tether.

The fifth day, 15 December, 1903, saw 20,000 people turn up at the SCG to watch the Test. Trumper was the big drawcard, but everything depended on the Australian middle- and lower-order batsmen staying with him. Armstrong fell to Rhodes for 27, but Albert Hopkins proved a staunch ally for Trumper, who was fighting along in determined fashion, knowing full well that a score in excess of 200 for England to chase on a worn track might turn what appeared to be a dismal defeat into a miracle win. The innings ended at 2.45pm, with Trumper unconquered on 185. His contemporaries and the spectators who saw that knock regard it as Trumper's greatest.

Thanks to the genius of Trumper, Australia scored 485 in its second innings, leaving England 194 to win. England had lost four for 82 when George Hirst joined opener Tom Hayward. Before he scored, Hirst

Warwick 'The Big Ship' Armstrong.
(*News Ltd*)

pulled a ball hard but straight to Frank Laver at square leg. He spilled it. Poor Bill Howell, the bowler; poor Frank Laver. In 1902 Fred Tate missed a vital catch and all England blamed him for Australia's remarkable three-run win. The Hayward-Hirst partnership realised 99 runs and when Hayward was stumped by Kelly down leg side off Jack Saunders for 91, England was as good as home, with just 13 runs to win and five wickets in hand. Hirst made 60 not out. The match had the grand 287 by Foster, the 102 by Braund and the 133 by Noble, but Trumper's gallant 185 not out was one of his masterpieces, perhaps his greatest innings, especially with the team in a seemingly hopeless position at the start of the second innings.

Warner later wrote that if anyone could have stayed with Trumper he would have beaten Reg Foster's record score of 287.

The Second Test match of 1903-4 was played on the Melbourne Cricket Ground. It was Wilfred Rhodes' match, having a total of 15 wickets for 124 on a treacherous sticky wicket. That final analysis came despite his having eight catches missed! England batted first, scoring 315, then Australia faced the might of the England attack on a wicket which was left exposed to the overnight thunderstorm. Trumper dominated the innings. It was one of his best on a bad wicket. He scored 74 out of Australia's paltry 122. Victor immediately attacked Rhodes and it was an innings which Monty Noble described as a 'complete triumph of the bat over the ball on such a "glue-pot".'

By the Third Test in Adelaide, Trumper was in superlative form. It was 15 January, 1904, when Trumper and his trusty partner Reg Duff walked onto the beautiful Adelaide Oval. The pair hit out brilliantly with Duff surprisingly outscoring Trumper. The *Adelaide Register* of Saturday, 16 January, 1904, takes up the story: 'With continued fine weather, which is now promised, it will be still good next week. Lord Tennyson (the Governor-General) and Sir George Le Hunte (the State Governor) were present at the bowling of the first ball and did not leave until late in the afternoon. The play may be divided into two stages. Australia had the upper hand until the tea adjournment; afterwards the English bowling asserted itself and the record was spoiled or improved, according to the standpoint of the supporter.

'While Hill and Trumper and Duff were going, the spectators were in ecstasies. One has heard of the "champagne of cricket" and, after three hours of this delightful trio, one can understand the feelings of the coiner of the phrase. Duff was the most dashing and, although his was not a chanceless innings, it was full of merit. Magnificent strokes to all points of the ground he made, and he has never been seen to finer advantage in Adelaide. Trumper was quieter than usual. There was no hesitancy, no suggestion of inability to cope with the bowling; but a set determination to take no risks. Absolute control of the bat over the ball was the predominating feature of his display and with the dose which he administered to his opponents was a seasoning of brilliancy that added piquancy to the taste.

'He was over three hours making his 113, probably one of the slowest centuries he has ever compiled. Trumper, who occupied fifty minutes in making 20 runs, warmed up Arnold with a couple of fine boundaries and the bowler went off at 81. Rhodes took up the attack, but the onward progress of Australia was not checked. No maiden over was bowled during the first hour, which produced 88 runs. Duff was playing magnificent cricket and scoring at the rate of a run per minute. He went out freely to Bosenquet and at 63 should have paid the penalty; but Lilley let the ball bounce out of his gloves. It was a bad miss, for Duff was a couple of yards out. A big sweep to leg, the ball rattled against the pickets and 100 was posted in 68 minutes. Warner earned applause for a capital piece of fielding on the boundary. Right on lunch George Hirst broke through Duff's defence and hit the stumps. This was a splendid start, 129 in 88 minutes (Duff bowled Hirst 79, Trumper not out 47). The scorebook was still without a maiden and no one over yielded more than 9 runs.'

In this innings Trumper played along sedately. It was perhaps the one time when Victor allowed others to dominate. Clem Hill blasted 42 of the pair's first 90 runs after lunch in an hour. Victor had hit 46, taking his score to 93. Their batting had the crowd of about 8000 in raptures. Hill was, as usual, effective; Trumper, although batting as if he wanted the century more than anything in the world, charmed spectators with his classic style. The crowd had built up to 10,000 by the time Victor reached his 100, his second of the series, in 2 hours 46 minutes, hitting 11 fours and not giving the semblance of a chance.

The *Referee* continued: 'Trumper at 113 had a narrow escape. He cut Fielder past point and bolted but Rhodes, at cover, fielded splendidly and returned. Lilley ran up from short stop. But the batsman scrambled back. Hirst had one over before tea and, as at luncheon time, it was fateful to Australia. His fourth ball Trumper pulled into his stumps. The outgoing batsman had a wonderful reception as he returned to the pavilion. Throughout his innings Trumper played well within his strength and from first to last never made a bad stroke. He hit a dozen balls to the boundary and was in occupation 3 hours 9 minutes. The partnership (Trumper and Hill) put on 143 runs in 101 minutes.'

Wilfred Rhodes, England's staunch opener and spin bowler.

George Hirst and England captain Pelham Warner at Adelaide during the Third Test of 1903-4.

Yorkshire and England all-rounders
George Hirst (left) and Wilfred
Rhodes during the 1903-4 England
tour of Australia. (*Pelham Warner*)

The Second Test at the MCG,
England batting. Pelham Warner
and Tom Hayward at the wickets;
Hayward cuts Howell for four.

Australia won the match by 216 runs, with Trumper hitting a classical 59 in the second innings, but his knock of 113 will go down as his most sedate and perhaps his most responsible in Test cricket.

For Paddington and Gordon, in Sydney first grade cricket, Trumper was as much a legend as he was on the international scene. One match in the 1902-3 season, the summer succeeding his incredibly brilliant tour of England where he hit 2570 runs, Victor played an innings of such radiance and brutality that it made more than headlines in the local newspapers. Victor hit 335 runs in 165 minutes, playing for Paddington against Redfern at Redfern oval. It is now more than 82 years since that Trumper masterpiece was played but there are people alive today who vividly remember Victor's knock. Sir William McKell recalled the innings just months before he died: 'The local Chinese shopkeepers rushed to put shutters over their windows when Victor starting to belt them over the fence. In those days there were no sixes. A hit over the fence was five and after the stroke the batsmen strolled through to opposite ends.'

Commenting on the innings some time after the match, the notorious, but much-loved King of Barrackers, Yabba, rarely known as Stephen Harold Gascoigne, said: 'In one over — a six ball over in those days — Vic and Dan Gee got three fives each. It was a case of one hit and one walk down the wicket. The uninitiated would have thought they were walking a single. I shall never forget the hit that landed on the boot

England won back the Ashes in the Australian summer of 1903-4 as well as hitting up a world record score of 769 in a game against New South Wales. Poor Victor had 111 runs hit off his medium-pacers. (*Pelham Warner*)

Victor Trumper in the summer of
1903-4. Shopkeepers rushed to
board up their windows when they
heard Trumper was batting and
liable to loft huge shots right out of
the ground.

Cricket in the bush, circa 1903.

factory. But another went right out of the southern end of the Park
¬nto the balcony of a two-storey terrace of houses. Another landed
right out and nearly went into the Australian Eleven Hotel (since
demolished) bar in Elizabeth St. All traffic was held up. The stroke that
Victor brought up his 300 was also a "lost ball". It went into a carrying
yard. Vic then retired, but old Mr Ironsides induced him to return to
make 350; he got 225. By this time the 'keeper had taken to bowling. He
pitched one up and Vic ran 10 yards down to it, fell and got tangled up
with his bat. Needless to say, he was out. By this time Dan Gee was 150.
He got 10 in the next over. Then he also fell down. I think it was from
fatigue. If there was one fan around the ground there was 10,000. They
were 20 deep everywhere. Traffic had no chance of getting past. M A
Noble, the Australian captain, did nothing but walk outside the crowd,
watching to see in what suburb the ball was inclined to lodge. The side
was all out for 618 in one afternoon, which is, I think, a record score for

THE MENU CARD. APRIL 22, 1904.

Cover of the menu card for a dinner welcoming the victorious England team back home from Australia. Pelham Warner's Ashes-winning team was given a grand welcome in London. Note the dead kangaroo in Warner's bag. The Englishmen won 3-2 in a marvellous series. (*Pelham Warner*)

grade. They didn't start until 2.15pm and were all out before six.' Yabba said he believed there were only six lost balls.

'If there had been sixes in those days goodness only knows what Victor would have scored, as he would have been retaining the strike. Even under-armers were bowled in a desperate attempt to get him out. This was the first time I had seem them since Humphreys, the English lob bowler, got wickets against Australia when I was a boy.'

Yabba didn't live to see Test captain Greg Chappell order his young brother Trevor to bowl the infamous under-armer in 1981. Gascoigne died in 1942, aged 64. Yabba was born in Redfern but in his adult life hawked rabbits around Balmain in his pony and cart. He apparently acquired the universally known name of Yabba from a rather corrupted version of his call 'Rabbo, wild rabbo for sale'. Gascoigne watched many Trumper innings before the Great War, but Yabba's fame did not come until after the war. When a slow batsman scored after a period of stonewalling, he yelled: 'Whoa there! He's bolted.' He had the crowd in raptures. One day in Sydney when Maurice Tate (son of poor Fred who dropped that catch to sink England's hope in the Trumper match at Manchester in 1902) put on his third pair of boots at the end of a tiring day: 'Eh, Maurice, thank goodness you're not a centipede.'

Yabba saw Trumper and Gee hit up 517 for the first wicket and he saw the Trumper shot which carried the ball more than 140 metres through a window of John Hunter's Boot Factory, a building later purchased by South Sydney Leagues Club. The club later demolished the building and built modern premises. Yabba said there were, in the end, nine fieldsmen on the fence, including the lone slip. The only men close in were the bowler and wicketkeeper. Trumper was not asked to pay for the broken window. Instead he was entertained lavishly by the shoe company executives and taken on a tour of the factory. The broken window was put on display at South Sydney Rugby League

Trumper's greatest power-packed innings was probably in the Paddington-Redfern club game during the summer of 1903. Trumper thrashed 335 in two and a half hours in a team total of 618 including one huge hit which sailed almost 140 metres (150 yards) and smashed a second floor window of John Hunter's Boot Factory. Company executives lavishly entertained Trumper, took him on a tour of the factory and later donated the broken window for public display! Vic didn't have to pay for the window. Right: Close-up of the famous window taken some years later. Below: An artists's impression of Trumper's huge hit. (*Pollard Publishing*)

Club, but today no one at the club knows of its whereabouts. It is interesting to reflect that the club's motto (bearing a white rabbit on a red and green background) is 'South Sydney Rabbitohs'. Yabba would be proud.

Herbert Collins was also present at that famous Paddington-Redfern match. He recalled that lawn bowlers on a nearby rink, including the NSW Premier James McGowan, had to abandon their match because of the number of Trumper 'fivers' sailing over from Redfern Oval and endangering the lawn bowlers. The bowlers joined the thousands at the cricket match.

(Coincidently, Victor Trumper III and Dan Gee III played in the same school team for Manly Christian Brothers' College in 1957.)

A few days later a report in the *Sydney Mail* made illuminating reading: 'The extraordinary performance of Trumper in making 335 in about 2¾ hours at Redfern Oval in the last round of matches caused hundreds of people who do not follow local cricket as a rule to inquire on Saturday morning where the Paddington Club were playing, what time do the grade matches commence and what was the quickest way to get to Hampden Park (now known as Trumper Park). To those who are not aware of the fact it may be mentioned that the Paddington Oval lies in a hollow; it cannot be approached from any direction without walking down hill. It was a great sight, so I am told, for I was not present when operations commenced, to see the people like so many swarms of bees making for the ground. All points of vantage were occupied early and often, the balconies of the adjacent houses were in great demand and also the few surrounding trees. People from all parts of the city and the suburbs were there with the one object — Trumper was expected to play another innings of 335 in 2¾ hours and they wanted to see something sensational. And they saw it. But for an important engagement I would have been one of the 5000 who were present. I got there at 3.45pm. I listened for the cheers that came not. Apparently Sydney district had won the toss and Trumper had not yet gone to the wickets.

'On arrival at the ground it was found that the almost deathlike silence was due to the fact that, with the exception of Kelly and Marshall, all were out and the total had not reached the half century. Small wonder therefore that Paddington stock was a drug in the market. The unexpected had happened. Trumper, Gee, W R Iredale (brother of Frank), M A Noble and his brother, Alick Bannerman (brother of Charles) and the others were out. Those same men who had accumulated 618 for nine wickets, and had beaten Redfern by an innings and 443 runs, were out for under 50. The last two men, Kelly and Marshall, played up splendidly and brought about a double change in the bowling. At 97 the Australian "stumper" (J J Kelly) was caught for 42, his companion was not out 24 and the innings closed at 97.' One of the Sydney club's wreckers was Jack Marsh, the Aboriginal fast bowler. Our correspondent wrote: 'It was a triumph for those who have urged the selection of Marsh in our representative elevens to see him bowl Trumper for nine. Trumper admitted that it was a good ball — it was a full toss; he tried to hook it, at the last moment the ball dropped and struck the foot of the stumps. The darky's next victim was Iredale — not F A — and a few stages later he claimed Bannerman and Carty.' Trumper must have had drawing power in those days akin to the days of

Former Test and Victorian medium-pacer Max Walker examines the bat Trumper used during the 1907-8 series in Australia. The bat is now in the S S Ramamurthy Collection. (*News Ltd*)

Bradman, although Bradman rarely disappointed his fans. He nearly always got a score, usually a big one. Trumper never (apart from his 1902 tour and the 1910-11 series against the South Africans in Australia) scored with anywhere near the consistency of Don Bradman.

The Fourth Test of the 1907-8 series at Melbourne saw Trumper bag a pair. Despite Victor's two ducks Australia won the match by a massive 308 runs. The game finished on 11 February, 1908, and the final Test in Sydney was not scheduled to start until 21 February.

So with a few days up his sleeve, Victor travelled to a sheep station in Western Victoria. He stayed there with friends of his wife, Annie. Somehow he got roped into playing a local cricket match. He did not give his surname as that would have given the game away, especially after the local skipper asked: 'Would you care for a game of cricket, we're one short?' Victor, Annie and their friends were picnicing near the local oval and Victor beamed: 'Okay, I'll play.'

'Can you bat?' asked the skipper.

'Oh, a bit,' replied Trumper.

'Okay, you can bat at number 10.'

Victor's team batted first and he went in after a middle-order collapse. Victor farmed the strike brilliantly and set the oval alight with his strokes. He hit a superb century and his team won comfortably. After the match, the skipper approached him. 'I say Mr Victor, would you care to play for us next week?'

'I'm sorry, I can't. I have to be in Sydney to play in the last Test!'

Trumper played in the final Test and batted at number seven, scoring 10 and a marvellous 166 in the second innings — another masterpiece. Australia won a tight match by 49 runs, winning the series 4-1. Victor's Test scores were 43, 3, 49, 63, 4, 0, 0, 0, 10 and 166. It shows the character of the man that he played in that country match after having just bagged a pair — and three ducks on the trot in Test match innings.

Another great innings of Trumper's was played on the Adelaide Oval against Percy Sherwell's South Africans. He hit 208 not out on 10 January, 1911, finishing with 214 not out. In The *Register*, Adelaide's correspondent 'Point' wrote next day: 'For 20 minutes before luncheon Trumper was strictly defensive and clearly feeling for the pace of the wicket, which was unusually slow for Adelaide. As the batsmen said, the ball squatted and did not come along fast from the pitch so that they found themselves unable to play some of their customary shots.

'Before luncheon not a single four was scored. During the interval Trumper apparently thought out the problem, decided that the wicket was true and made up his mind that while he would have to play back more often than was his wont, he would have a go at the ball. He immediately started to score fours and he began at 2.15pm, so he continued for the rest of the afternoon.

'Many of his strokes were remarkable, possible only to a man with such wonderfully keen eyes and so subtle a pair of wrists. He cut, drove, raised his left foot and hit to square leg without ever hesitating or being in doubt; but his most striking strokes were those when he picked up over-pitched balls and landed them to the on boundary. Pegler, who in the main kept a good length, was simply stupified when, handling a new ball, he found himself knocked for three fours in one over and saw Trumper, without any movement of the feet, land a well-pitched-up

Victor Trumper's team to West Wyalong, Easter 1911. Trumper is seated in the middle without cap, his brother Syd is seated front left. (*Tom Nicholas*)

ball nearly over the fence. Other batsmen stay for longer or shorter periods and make useful scores, but Trumper, like the brook, went on merry all the time and at the end of the day was still unconquered.

'The dashing right-hander never gave the semblance of a chance and his brilliant batting aroused the spectators to a pitch of enthusiasm never surpassed on the Oval. Fancy a man scoring 159 in a Test match (second innings of the Second Test — Australia v. South Africa, Melbourne from 31 December to 4 January, 1910-11) and then the first time he picked up his bat again making 208 not out in another Test! It was not only the big score, but the electrifying way it was compiled that impressed the crowd. Clem Hill said it was the best knock he ever saw and Sherwell, the South African captain, said after stumps were drawn that he had come to Australia to see cricket.'

Trumper's 214 not out and 28 in the second dig could not prevent South Africa winning the match. It was South Africa's first Test win over Australia. South Africa scored 482 and 360; Australia 465 and 339 with the Springboks winning by just 38 runs. But at the time the critics were hailing Victor's innings as the greatest Test knock of all time. They likened it to Charles Bannerman's 165 in the First Test ever played against England at Melbourne in March, 1877, and Clem Hill's 188, against Stoddart's England team at the MCG in 1898. Hill scored that total out of Australia's 323. He had rescued the innings which at lunch was in tatters at 6/58, against the bowling of Tom Richardson, Johnny Briggs and J T Hearne.

Victor's great knock was his seventh Test century. He was destined to hit just one more century on the Test stage — 113 against England on his beloved SCG in December, 1911.

At the end of the Adelaide Test match, South Australian Cricket Association secretary J A Riley wrote to him congratulating Victor on his great innings and asking him if he would accept a memento. It is not known what memento was offered, but I have a copy of the letter and it is reproduced here.

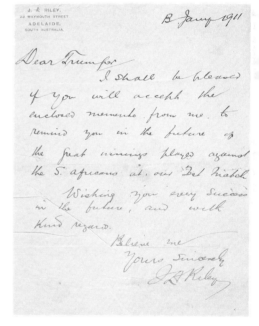

The letter from Mr J A Riley to Trumper in 1911.

17
TRUMPER'S TECHNIQUE

The Trumper grip. Note the comfort of the hands, their closeness and the absence of all strain. Trumper grip is high on the handle, suggesting that perhaps he was ready to take the long handle to the bowler but this was his normal grip. This photograph and the series on pages 184 to 188 are from *Fry and Beldam's Great Batsmen – Their Methods At A Glance*, Macmillan 1905.

Sifting through a series of photographs of strokes made by Victor Trumper, taken by Beldam and probably in 1902, one gets the impression that the great batsman's immediate appeal was his poise and style.

His feet appeared to be in position. He used a long handle bat, often during his career a hand-made one from Gunn & Moore. Hands close together, with his top hand very near the top of the handle; a grip today which would suggest a batsman was going to have an almighty slog. But when Trumper batted he took the 'long handle' to all comers; be it George Hirst, Wilfred Rhodes or, arguably, the best bowler in Test history, the trundler of quickish leg-spin, Sydney Barnes. In an interview in 1913, Trumper said he sought a four every ball faced. He had an uncanny knack of placement; something seemingly inherent in only the very great batsmen such as Trumper, the greatest of them all, Don Bradman, and, among the moderns, South African Graeme Pollock and Australian Neil Harvey. Perhaps the West Indian Viv Richards has also this gift of placement. Richards, too, has a poise, a certain commanding air about his batsmanship which lifts him out of the ruck amid the 'ordinary' and places him among the elite in cricket history.

Note Trumper's grip: hands close together high on the handle. There is no rubber handle grip. Victor liked to 'feel' the bat handle. Rarely did he wear gloves. If he did one was worn on the right or bottom hand. He rubbed resin on the handle binding to enable a better grip, his bottom hand a good four inches higher than the shoulder of the bat. It is interesting that Don Bradman also liked to 'feel' the handle of the bat. Bradman wore the open palm style of gloves. Trumper favored the open-slatted batting pads and usually wore a cap, rather than the white washer hat. However, he often donned floppy headgear in the field on a hot day.

His stance was not classic, in the sense of being totally relaxed and upright. Trumper had a slight crouch, with his back leg slightly bent at the knee. His right foot was not parallel with his back foot, but pointed in the direction of cover. But it was a stance which gave the impression that he was ready for action. Herbie Collins, Australia's Test captain in England in 1926 and who played in the Paddington and New South Wales teams for some time with Trumper, tells us that Victor 'although not strong physically had hands and wrists like iron'. He had a high backlift, starting at about point and sweeping outward and upward, thus enabling him to swing the bat down straight and through the line of the ball.

Anything short and Trumper immediately played back and across, his right hand shifted down to the shoulder of the bat. Yet by the time he made contact, his hands were together and in total control of the shot. Trumper was a particularly fine cutter and puller of anything short. He was, perhaps, one of the first internationals to pull a short ball from outside the off stump, rather than cut it in the more sobre, orthodox fashion of batsmanship before the Golden Age.

Also a fine hooker of fast bowling, Trumper (in the following series of photographs) gets into perfect position. Body inside the line of flight and he hits the ball down. This particular shot is more in keeping with a pull stroke as the ball did not rise as high as was intended and Trumper hits it just in front of square leg.

His off and cover driving were, to his contemporaries, poetry in motion. Note the high backswing and the glorious follow through, weight admirably transferred from the back to the front foot, everything in position for a perfect execution of the off drive.

Trumper steps down the pitch, preparing to take the long handle to the bowler. (*Pollard Publishing*)

Plate Six   Plate Seven

Plates Six and Seven show the straight drive, where he has jumped down to the pitch of the ball. Again high backlife, eyes intently fixed on the ball and a full sweep of the bat.

Plate thirteen shows the finish of a forcing stroke to the off side. Trumper seems cramped as the ball may have either cut back or was too close to his body to effect the shot other than in an awkward manner. Plate Fourteen shows the finish of a forward stroke, rather like the good old fashioned 'flat bat' shot, so effective on slow wickets which afford little bounce.

Plate Thirteen   Plate Fourteen

Trumper was a master of the pull-drive. He would advance down the wicket to an in-swing or off-spin bowler and loft the ball high over mid-on. There is no attempt to keep the ball down, but Trumper's head is well down. Plates Fifteen and Sixteen are good examples of Trumper's technique for this stroke.

Trumper also liked to hit high, wide and handsome over mid-on,

Plate Fifteen   Plate Sixteen

against medium pacers and fast bowlers, while all the time hitting the ball with his weight on the back foot. Again Trumper makes no attempt to keep the ball along the turf. In Plates Seventeen and Eighteen, we see the style and note the characteristic free fling of the arms away from the body in Trumper's follow through.

Plate Seventeen   Plate Eighteen

One of his specialties and favorite shots was the late cut. Trumper was able to effect this shot to deliveries which were short but quite close to his body by maintaining his arms close to his body. Normally a batsman finds this shot difficult to play, unless it is wide of the off stump. Trumper could play the late cut to balls only fractionally outside off stump. In Plates Nineteen and Twenty overleaf we obtain a good view of the way he played the stroke, eyes forever on the ball and hitting down on the ball with head right over the delivery.

Plate Nineteen   Plate Twenty

Plate Twenty One gives us an idea that not all Trumper shots were elegant. Here he plays a crude cut off the front foot with his upper body almost parallel with the ground. Plate Twenty Two is a better example of the finish of the late cut; this time played off the back foot.

Plate Twenty-one   Plate Twenty-two

Trumper's square cut is shown in Plate Twenty Three. He has given himself plenty of room and hammered the ball past point. The finish of the square cut in Plate Twenty Four is virtually a repeat of his follow-through for the late cut. The ball has been pitched wide and, in his endeavor to reach it and give the stroke power, his left foot had left the ground.

Plate Twenty Five shows Trumper cutting off the front foot. The next plate shows the shot midway through his follow through. Rarely do you see a player effect this stroke nowadays. Among those of the modern era, Victorian Lindsay Hassett played this shot well.

Plate Twenty-three   Plate Twenty-four   Plate Twenty-five

Plates Twenty Seven and Twenty Eight are perhaps the two most exciting cricket action shots ever captured on film; albeit George Beldam took them during an interval of the Australians v Surrey game at Kennington Oval, in 1902. They are quite obviously posed photographs but it depicts the style of Trumper in all its grandeur. It shows all too clearly why so many players of his time regarded Trumper as the greatest batsman of them all. Just studying these two photographs one envisages Trumper jumping down to drive Rhodes over the fence at Old Trafford or at Sydney and just how stylishly and effectively he decimated the Canterbury attack at Lancaster Park,

Plate Twenty-seven   Plate Twenty-eight

Christchurch, in February, 1914 hitting 293 in just 180 minutes. Take Plate Twenty Seven. Wrists of iron? Hands of iron? The rippling muscles in his hands and wrists reflect enormous strength, the very thing Collins illuminated.

The drive past mid-on in Plates Twenty Nine and Thirty further illustrate Trumper's concentration and free swing of the bat.

Plates Thirty One and Thirty Two give us a good view of Trumper's style in jumping out to drive.

Plate Twenty-nine

Plate Thirty

Plate Thirty-one

Plate Thirty-two

It is a pity that cameras could not clearly show the men of Trumper's era batting in the middle. We have to be content with posed photographs such as these, or faded and often blurred photographs taken at long distance where it is difficult to pick out the players on the field let alone be given insight into the shot played and where the ball was in relation to the position of the batsman.

Victor played with the Second Carltons, an old Sydney club, for a season or two before joining South Sydney. He played alongside Charles Bannerman, the batsman who hit the first Test century, against England in the first Test ever played at Melbourne in 1877. Bannerman had coached Trumper for some time, but thought Victor's style a little 'too flashy' and continually scolded Victor for chasing balls too wide of off stump. Noble said Trumper was a 'law unto himself'. 'You could talk to him and coach him; he would listen carefully, respect your advice and opinions, and leaving you, would forget all you had told him, play as he wanted to play, and thereby prove that, although you might be right, he knew a better method. It is necessary for most batsmen to play the game for a few overs before unfolding their strokes. Not so with Victor. He was off at the jump, making an amazing stroke off a ball which would probably have clean bowled most of his comrades. His defence was his offence. If, on a bad wicket, a left-hander was troubling anyone, he would immediately set about knocking him off, and generally succeed in doing so.'

To Trumper attack was the only way. On his magnificent 1902 tour of England, when he hit 11 centuries at 2570 runs, Trumper played out only three maiden overs.

Against the spinners Trumper did not bother to detect which way the bowler was turning. His simple yet effective method was: if it was short, go right back on the stumps. That way he had time to follow the spin. If it was well up: jump down and hit the ball on the full or half-volley.

Noble writes that Trumper's method of scoring quickly against the medium-pacers was revolutionary. 'Instead of playing forward in the orthodox way, he would surprise the bowler by getting across the wicket and, with a straight bat, would hit a good length ball on the rise from the pitch outside the off stump with great force and along the ground between mid-on and mid-wicket.'

Nowadays Viv Richards is often seen playing a similar stroke. Richards is particularly severe on medium-paced bowling and often moves into position a la Trumper to execute this highly productive shot. If anyone of the modern era wanted to see a player of the Trumper mould bat then I suggest Viv Richards is the closest thing to him. Richards is a destructive batsman who loves nothing better than hitting the ball hard and taking the attack to the bowler. He sometimes gets bogged down and this often leads to his downfall.

The best Australian batsman after Trumper and before Bradman, although he played Tests with Victor from 1907-8, was Charlie Macartney. Macartney, in his book *My Cricketing Days* (Heinemann, 1930), tells an extraordinary tale about Trumper's batting. 'Trumper brought off the biggest hit I've seen. A yorker from Frank Laver was the ball he selected for the hit, and with no apparent effort he seemed to pick it up with the bat, and it finished on the roof of the northern pavilion at straight hit. I have seen bigger hits by lunging, but this was a fast-footed one, necessitated by the pitch of the ball.'

Such a stroke is seemingly impossible. If it were a yorker it would be impossible to lift the ball, let alone hit it high over the bowler's head and land it on the member's pavilion at the MCG. Macartney, as did all the players who had anything to do with the master batsman of their time, revered Trumper. He recalled the time in 1907 when he snicked one to Paddington keeper James Kelly: 'I made a square cut hard, and clearly touched the ball, Jim Kelly making the catch. On a unanimous appeal the umpire gave me not out. The umpire was the late James Laing, who stood at that time in interstate and international matches. At the moment I did not know exactly what to do. I could not very well go out, so made up my mind to have a wild hit at the next ball. I did, and it went out of the ground over two fences! That completed the over. Victor Trumper came over to me and said: ''Don't throw it away; you will be given out many more times when you are not out than you will not out when you are out.'''

It is clear from that anecdote that Trumper was not, what they call in the trade, a 'walker'. Obviously in Trumper's day it was not the done thing to walk if the umpire had given you 'not out'. Perhaps, they considered that an insult to the umpire. Incidentally, in my time (1967-1980) I never met a genuine walker; or a batsman who walked from the scene every time he considered that he was out whichever way the umpire went. However, there was one celebrated England batsman, considered a walker, who walked in the minor games when in the 90s or whatever score (depending upon his form at that stage) and yet stood unmoved in a Test if he got a faint nick. The renowned walker causes more strife than the likes of a Trumper or a Bill Lawry. They left it to the umpire.

Trumper had one peculiar shot, known as the 'dog-shot'. He used it when hitting out at a yorker. He would raise his left leg and, just as the ball was about to cannon into middle and leg stumps, his bat would come down like lightning and hammer the ball away past square leg like a rocket. According to his contemporaries, Trumper played the ball so late that many a bowler appealed for LBW and was left red-faced as he watched the ball career across the turf and into the square leg boundary.

The mere audacity and supreme confidence of Trumper's batting gave him the reputation of world's best. His batting enthralled and his generosity amazed. Macartney tells of the time that Trumper hit 212 for Paddington against Central Cumberland in 1906-07. It was Trumper's final innings for the season and he finished with a season's average of 85. The man with the top average usually received a handsome trophy. Macartney had yet to bat for Gordon against Redfern at Chatswood Oval and his final innings was to be played the following Saturday. Midway through the week Charlie strolled into the Trumper and Carter Sport Depot.

'Hey, Vic how many runs will I have to make on Saturday to beat your average for the season?' Macartney wrote that 'without the slightest hesitation Vic reached for pencil and paper and after ascertaining what my figures were, and the number of innings I had played, stated that I would require so many to do the trick. When my side batted on the last day, I was fortunate enough to make 224 not out, which made my figures greater than his. He was the first to congratulate me the next week: ''Well you did it, Charlie, and a bit to spare.'''

18

GREAT CRICKETER DEAD

Time stood still on Monday, 28 June, 1915, for the family, friends and thousands of admirers around the world of Victor Trumper. That morning, at 10 o'clock, the great batsman died.

Many young men had been killed in the horrific Gallipoli campaign and the newspapers were full of the tragedy. But Trumper did not go to war. He was already battling kidney disease. Trumper's death at the age of 37 stunned the nation. Australia's most brilliant and charismatic batsman had gone. The cricket world was in mourning. While war news took precedence over almost every other happening, news of Trumper's death was emblazoned on the newspaper placards in front of newsstands throughout London, GREAT CRICKETER DEAD.

An illustrated weekly, the *Sydney Mail* was full of the landing at Gallipoli and of the subsequent operations in the Dardanelles. There were pages of photographs of gallant Anzacs who had given their lives or were wounded. A single-column photograph and 19 lines was all that Trumper could be given. But it was a feeling tribute. Australia had lost its greatest sporting hero to that time:

'Victor Trumper was the greatest batsman Australia had produced and the most accomplished in the history of the game in any country.

'The solid qualities of Tyldesley and Hobbs, the magnificent skill of Hill and Darling, even the wizardry of Ranjitsinhji, paled before a wonderful grace and orthodox poetry of motion that lifted batting to a standard that had not entered into the dreams of those who imagined they had seen all that cricket had to offer when Grace and Shrewsbury or those already mentioned had been at the wickets. He was a modest, good-living young man.

'His courage in his illness was the natural revelation of a Christian character.'

The *Sydney Referee's* cricket correspondent 'Not Out' said poignantly: 'The war hits us hard; but this blow has a sadder touch than any we may have felt when our other heroes of the athletic world have died on the field of battle. Trumper's name in cricket will never perish. He was the artist of cricket from toes to finger-tips. He was a man of bright, winning personality, upright and generous to a fault, as was recognised by those responsible for placing the proceeds of his testimonial match under trustees, for himself, and after him for his widow and children. I cannot conceive of his having had any enemies,

A sad day: Cricketers march ahead of Victor Trumper's cortege from Circular Quay to Waverley, Wednesday 30 June 1915

for he was a spotless youth in character and habits. May the turf rest lightly over his grave.'

Trumper's funeral took place on Wednesday, 30 June, 1915. The funeral was one of the largest and most impressive ever afforded a sportsman in Australia. The cortege left Victor's Chatswood home. The Reverend E H Cranswick of St. Paul's Church of England, Chatswood, read the service and subsequently delivered a singularly appropriate eulogy at the graveside at Waverley Cemetery. Hundreds of cricketers past and present marched four abreast with Trumper's body from Chatswood to Fort Macquarie, where it was met by hundreds more.

The cortege comprised a four-horse hearse, four carriages and a floral carriage. Victor's body was placed in a solid oak casket with handles after his remains were removed from St. Vincent's Private Hospital. He was interred in the Church of England section of the Waverley Cemetery.

Neither Annie Trumper nor his mother, Louey, attended the funeral. They were far too distraught. The chief mourners were Victor's father, Charles; his two brothers, Charles and Sid; his uncle Thomas; brothers-in-law W Briggs, J Briggs and George Smith; and T Love, James Kelly, G Love, J and V Kavanagh and H West.

Near Regent St., Paddington, the procession halted and those who had marched joined special trams and went as far as Charing Cross. There they left the trams and formed in line again, leading the procession to the cemetery and down through winding paths to the beautiful site chosen as Victor's final resting place — a high spot near the cliffs, overlooking the blue Pacific.

Thousands of people had stood in silence as the cortege passed. Men, women and children had wept openly. Men from all walks of life had joined the procession, sportsmen from throughout Australia journeyed to pay their last respects. Politicians, plumbers, carpenters, men who scarcely knew him but had perhaps received his autograph, a free piece of cricketing equipment while he was in the sports store business or three-pence towards his entrance to a match, joined the sad throng. Even the Taxation Commissioner, Mr William Whiddon, was there, along with the Minister of Railways, Mr Hoyle, and a host of Senators.

Queensland Cricket Association's Mr G Crouch was there; you'll recall it was his selection as manager of the 1912 Australian team for England which caused Trumper along with five contemporaries to withdraw from that team.

Reverend Cranswick gave a lengthy service at Trumper's graveside after Trumper's pallbearers finished their task. The reverend exalted Trumper as son, husband and father. He described him as the hero of all assembled and to thousands of others.

'Victor possessed many noble qualities and these made him the great sportsman that he had been throughout his career. He played the game as it should be played and though he will be remembered for many things, nothing could be greater than his wonderful spirit of sportsmanship.'

There was not a dry eye as the coffin was lowered. Hanson Carter had performed his last service for his friend and one-time business associate Victor Trumper. It was Carter the Test wicketkeeper who, as an undertaker, organised the funeral. It was a massive task. Even these days having to bring the cortege from Chatswood on the North Shore of Sydney Harbor would not be easy. But in 1915 there was no Sydney Harbor Bridge. The coffin had to be transported across the harbor and lifted into another horse-drawn hearse at Circular Quay. Special trams for the hundreds of mourners had to be arranged. Everything had to happen like clockwork.

Carter did the job as efficiently as he kept for Australia in a tense Test match. This funeral must have weighed heavily on his mind, for Carter revered Trumper. Years later he would often extol the virtues of Trumper's genius as a batsman, pointing skyward and saying: 'That's Vic. The others are here,' indicating a plane about the level of his eyes.

Tributes and wreaths came from throughout Australia and England. The NSW, Victorian and South Australian Cricket Associations sent wreaths, as did the Australian Board of Control for International Cricket (now the Australian Cricket Board), the Melbourne Cricket Club, the NSW Rugby Union and NSW Rugby League, all Sydney district clubs and personal friends, of which Victor had many. Messages of sympathy came from the South African Cricket Association and the Tasmanian Cricket Association.

Trumper was survived by his wife, Annie, daughter Annie Louise, 9, and Victor junior, 18 months.

Victor had suffered scarlet fever in 1908 and many thought that attack contributed to his subsequent kidney condition, nephritis. The condition, chronic parenchymatous nephritis, was known in the day as Bright's Disease. Victor was in great pain just prior to his death and he suffered uraemic convulsions for 14 hours before he died. Annie Trumper wrote to friends in England a couple of months after Victor died. She decribed in her letter that she first became worried about her husband in October, 1914. 'The season had just commenced. He had played all Saturday afternoon and on Sunday I noticed his ankles were a little swollen. It worried me at the time and I threatened to bring in the doctor.

'Victor begged me not to worry, he was all right, but after great

Victor Trumper's children, Nancy and Victor II outside their Help Street Chatswood home less than 12 months after Victor's death. (*Tom Nicholas*)

An appreciation to Victor Trumper, struck just one day after his death. (*South Australian Cricket Association*)

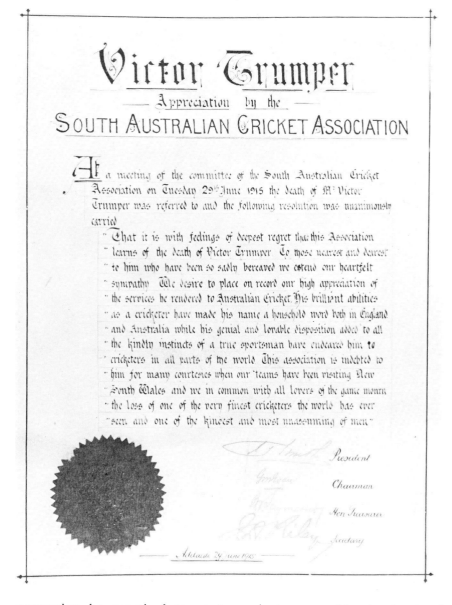

persuasion he promised to go to a doctor, an old schoolmate. I was anxious all day for him to come home, as he was usually bright and happy when coming home. He said: "Nothing serious is wrong with me. Probably a cold on the kidneys" and he would have to diet himself for a while. He knew I had an awful dread of Bright's Disease. Of course, all his worry about business did not help him and unfortunately he had tons of worry since he first commenced business. At times he seemed tired, but looked well and I thought it was worry all the time. Vic trusted everybody. He was too honest for business and trusted everybody to the last degree. He said he would never go into business again and I thought that was the end of his worry.

'In March, 1915, we went to Collaroy Beach, not far from here, for a fortnight, I thought it would do the children and my poor Vic good, but we were there only two days and he did not seem at all well, the sea-air being too strong for him. At once we came home and I made Vic seek

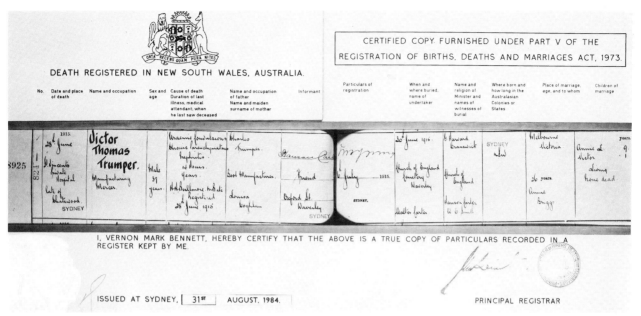

Excerpt from the Registrar of Births, Deaths and Marriages shows that Victor Trumper died 28 June 1915 of 'uraemic convulsions . . . nephritis (Bright's disease)', in layman's terms, kidney malfunction.

the advice of a specialist, who ordered him to bed. That was the beginning of March, and he was in bed for three months and got along beautifully. He was always naturally cheerful and was in great spirits when all the swelling disappeared.

'He was very tired of bed and insisted on the doctor allowing him to get up. The doctor was afraid, it was the beginning of June, rather cold, and he was afraid of a chill. Evidently he did get the chill somehow and swelling commenced to appear again. The doctor ordered him into hospital (which I think was a mistake) for treatment with ''steam'', which could not be done at home, on 21 June. The doctor thought he was going to pull through but my poor Vic, on Sunday night, 27 June, at about 10.30pm, to their great surprise in the hospital, took a nasty turn, became unconscious and remained so until he died at 10am on Monday, 28 June.'

That previous afternoon Vic and Annie were talking enthusiastically about their planned visit to England. Vic's many friends had organised the England trip soon after they had heard he was in hospital. They were to have paid for Vic and his family to travel to England as they considered such a trip would prolong his life for a number of years. However, they had realised his health would never again be sufficiently good for him to grace the cricket field. Vic had promised Annie another England trip (they went together in 1905, Vic's third visit). He loved England.

Annie continued: 'They had sent him word of the promised trip that morning and he was delighted telling me about it. That same afternoon, his last afternoon, Vic told me he had such a lot to do for me and the children. He said he would not rest until he saw his boy an ''Oxford University Boy''. How he loved that baby nobody knows and to lose that ''Daddy'' at 18 months! What a father to lose and what have the children lost! Nancy was always ''Mummy's girl'' but baby loved Vic and always wanted his daddy. You would love baby Vic, he is so affectionate. Surely after eight years God sent him as a consolation for what was coming. We hope he will be spared to me. His grandparents say he is the picture of his daddy when he was a baby. A thorough boy and full of sport already. I really don't think there could be another Vic although you could not imagine a son of Vic being anything but good. Anyway I shall try and do my very best for them.

'Poor Nancy, of course she can always remember him. Rather quiet in her way, not much to say, but a great comfort to her mother now. I know she frets a great deal about her daddy at times. He was never known to have been cross with her.'

Trumper's memory is perpetuated by a grey marble plaque affixed to the back of the Sheridan Stand at the SCG, Trumper Park, (formerly the Hampden Oval in Paddington) and the Trumper Stand, the main grandstand at Chatswood Oval.

Talk to the oldies about Trumper and their eyes glisten with pride.

The Trumper Pavilion at Sydney's Chatswood oval. There is also a Trumper Park in Paddington and a plaque on the Sheridan Stand at the Sydney Cricket Ground.

There are few left who even saw Trumper play. But those who did remember him vividly — a saintly figure.

The late Sir Neville Cardus, whose cricket writing was in the super-class and whose prose approached an almost Shakespearean quality, wrote in glowing terms of Trumper when he heard the sad news of Vic's death:

'The death of a cricketer before age has fallen on him is sad; it is even against nature. Well may he look down on the fields from his chill hall of immortality, far removed from the jolly flesh and blood of his life, and cry out "Another day in the sun and wind and I am not there, I am not there".

'All the little intimate delights belonging to cricket, a man's flannels and his bat, his own boyish enthusiasm for a summer game — surely these are things which ought to hold a cricketer to the friendly earth till he is tired of them?'

The news of Trumper's death shocked English cricket circles. Pelham Warner (later Sir Pelham), who led the 1903-4 England team to Australia and also the 1911-12 side said: 'Trumper was the most unassuming cricketer in the world, and at one time was its finest batsman; but he spoke as if he had never made a run in his life.'

Newspapers agreed upon the brilliance of Trumper. The *Daily Chronicle* said in tribute: 'No one among the famous Australians had such remarkable powers. His ability to make big scores when orthodox methods were unavailing lifted him above his fellows.' The *Daily Mail* said likewise: 'He was Australia's greatest batsman. Certainly he was the most brilliant, particularly on bad wickets, where his skill and daring enabled him to score.'

On 10 July, 1915, Mrs Helen Cooper of Chatswood wrote to the *Sydney Referee*. Her husband Bransby Cooper played one Test match for Australia — the very first Test — scoring only 15 and 3, but Australia won that encounter with England on the MCG by 45 runs. In 1869 Cooper scored 101 for Gentleman of the South v Players of the South, hitting 283 runs in partnership with W G Grace in 220 minutes. Cooper died in 1914. But his wife, Helen, never forgot Victor Trumper's affection for other people:

'An old man in Sydney with only one leg, on hearing of Trumper's illness, made his way to the hospital hoping to see him. He was informed by the officials that no one was allowed to see him but his wife and mother. Nothing daunted, he managed to climb the stairs and almost reached the door, when the attendant told him it was impossible to allow anyone in. "Oh!" he pleaded, "just let me see the lad, if only for one minute. I cannot let him die without one word." His condition was so low that the poor old man's request had to be refused. On being questioned as to why he was so anxious to see him, he said, "Well, I was laid up in this hospital for six months and Victor Trumper was the only one who ever came to see me. He never missed a week that he did not come to cheer and comfort me and I would like to have seen his face, if only just to look in the door." That was one of the many acts of kindness that Victor was constantly doing for others.'

A veteran cricketer of Goulburn, W Walsh, was at Trumper's funeral. 'The waters were calm, glorious sunshine overhead and the blue sky flecked by fleecy clouds. The coffin was borne from the hearse to the grave by Monty Noble, Tibby Cotter, Hanson Carter, Syd Gregory, Warren Bardsley and another. I was subsequently informed it was Warwick Armstrong, although I failed to recognise him. They were his worthy allies in the contests on the various cricket fields of the world and it was fitting that the final post of honor should be alloted to them. Clem Hill was absent, but we all felt that he was there is spirit, for he had a great regard for Victor. As the coffin was being lowered, Monty Noble showed much emotion, and so did Warren Bardsley. The scene was pathetic and I think appealed to most of us as a practical sermon of life. All the mourners have gone home and I am alone looking out over the ocean. Victor died of Bright's Disease. His kidneys wasted away.'

> "There is no death!
> What seems so is transition;
> This life of mortal breath
> Is but a suburb of the life Elysian,
> Whose portal we call death."

The great Australian off-spinner, Hugh Trumble, who made the last of his five tours of England with Trumper in 1902, made this tribute:

Pelham Warner, England captain in 1903-4 and 1911-12 said that at one time Trumper was the world's finest batsman.

'There is no doubt in my mind that Victor Trumper was the finest batsman that ever lived. This was the opinion of most competent judges in England.

'In one match at Kennington Oval I was conversing with W Read, William Murdoch and John Shuter (the old Surrey captain), just after Trumper completed one of his finest innings. When we asked one another, "what do you think?" all agreed that he was the greatest batsman ever seen. These men were contemporaries of W G Grace at his best and knew what they were saying. With Trumper at his best, any other batsman at his best would give him the palm. A ball an ordinary first-class batsman would be content to stop, Victor would score runs off. I have bowled to a number of first-class batsmen, but none could do as many tricks with the ball as he. You could not bowl a length at him. He was so resourceful and quick on his feet. When you thought you sent down a good length ball he would quickly step back, making it short. He had wrists like iron. Yes, Clem Hill and Alf Noble would take their hats off to him. He was the same on all wickets, there was no stroke he could not play.'

Trumble said the essence of the contract on the three day game in England called for runs being made quickly to enable the side time to bowl the opposition out. 'Victor would obtain a century promptly, thus enabling us to get the other fellows out and win.' Trumble said Victor Trumper would have made a fine bowler had he not been such a great batsman. 'He was a great outfield, catching and returning the ball perfectly. He was the finest fellow on the side, always a trier, and thoroughly fit. He was the best-hearted fellow that ever lived, considerate to all, especially the younger players.'

Trumble was Australia's first great spinner. He played 32 Tests, taking 141 wickets at 21.78 and on the 1902 tour he took 140 wickets at 14.87. In his final Test match at Melbourne in the 1903-4 season against Warner's England side, Trumble spun Australia to victory with 7/28, including a hattrick, a feat he performed on the MCG against England in 1901-2. He bowled to all the great batsmen of cricket's Golden Age and it is a glowing tribute indeed that Trumble ranked Trumper head and shoulders above the rest.

Clem Hill did not make it to Trumper's funeral, but on the night of Monday, 28 June, 1915, he told the *Adelaide Register* by telephone: 'Poor Vic. He was Australia's greatest batsman and a white man. He never realised his own greatness. He always played for the sake of the man at the other end. Runs came in every direction when he was at the creases, but he did not play for himself. He was always out to do the best for his side. Yes; he was a marvel. Fourer after fourer. He would make any wicket look easy. When runs were wanted he could always be relied on. Poor old Vic!'

Nearly four years after Victor's death, tribute to the memory of the great batsman was paid by members of the Victorian Eleven visiting Sydney for a Shield clash with NSW. It was the afternoon of Thursday, 23 January, 1919. Victorian captain Edgar Mayne, a former Test comrade of Trumper's, placed a wreath on Victor's grave at Waverley Cemetery. A card with the following inscription: 'In loving memory of our comrade, Victor Trumper — from the Victorian Eleven,' was placed on the grave.

Two days later tablets were unveiled at the SCG in memory of

January 1919: Former Trumper Test colleague Edgar Mayne, captain of Victoria, places a wreath on Victor Trumper's grave as his teammates stand in silent witness. (*South Australian Cricket Association*)

West Indies captain John Goddard and teammates placed a wreath on Trumper's grave in December 1950. Many visiting teams took time out to visit Victor's grave in Waverley Cemetery.

Trumper and Albert 'Tibby' Cotter, who was killed by a sniper's bullet in 1917 during the First World War.

Many visiting teams took time out to visit Trumper's grave as the years went by, including John Goddard's West Indians in the early 1950s and on 2 November, 1977, Bob Simpson laid a beautiful green and gold garland wreath on Victor's grave to commemorate the centenary of his birth. Together with representatives of the NSW Cricket Association, Trumper's relatives and a handful of old comrades, Simpson, who had been hauled back into Test cricket in the wake of the World Series Cricket insurgence, paid tribute.

The *Sydney Morning Herald* devoted an entire editorial column to Trumper on Saturday, 25 January, 1919, hailing Edgar Mayne's men for their kindly gesture when given another opportunity to throw the mighty weight of the pen behind and in support of Trumper's gallantry and sword-like batting, which thrilled thousands throughout the cricket world from when he first set foot on the Test stage in 1899 until Frank Woolley caught him off the bowling of Sydney Barnes for 50 in the 1911-12 Australian summer.

The account was titled TRUMPER'S SPIRIT:

'The members of the Victorian Eleven performed a graceful and an appropriate act when, on the day of their arrival in Sydney, they placed a wreath on the grave of Victor Trumper. Trumper was one of the greatest batsmen that ever lived, and of all cricketers the most accomplished artist. The combination of hand and eye with him was so perfect that he could successfully do what others would know better than to attempt, and he could do it with an appearance of consummate ease. Men when they gossip of cricket always recall certain great innings, the day when Graham on a bad wicket hit the fastest bowler in England all over the field, or when Gregory made

Scoresheet of Victor Trumper's last Test innings – 50 in 119 minutes against England, 28 February, 1912. It was fitting that his last Test stroke went for four runs and that he was then caught off the incomparable spinner Syd Barnes. (*NSW Cricket Association*)

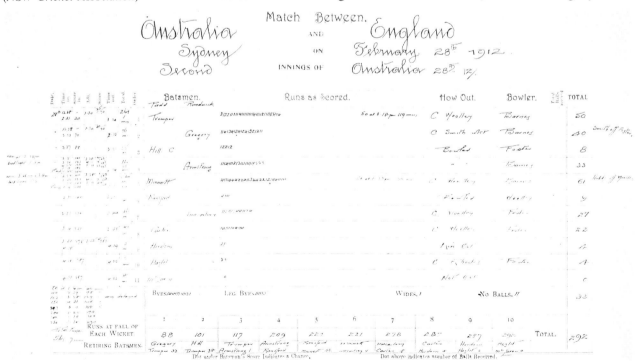

his two hundred and Australia still lost the match. But every comparison comes back to the fine delight of watching Trumper at his best when every variety of bowling came alike to him. He stands out alike from the sensational batsmen and from the consistent members of a team who may be trusted to wait for the right ball and score from it. While he was batting everything seemed so easy that nothing was sensational, and every ball was the right one. There were men of similar gifts among the English cricketers; Ranjitsinjhi, who, under an alias, is now figuring as an orator among the Indian princes, and R E Foster, who made his greatest score in the match which Trumper strove vainly to retrieve. But no batsman ever gave to onlookers or fellow-cricketers such a clear sense of perfection. One of his opponents, Knight, of Leicestershire, has described in the "Complete Cricketer" how "that slender figure, wan and drawn of face, cadaverous but spiritualised with the delicacy of ill-health, glides to the wicket. Not violently nor recklessly like his comrade Duff, nor with the careworn anxious deliberation of Noble, does he reach the heights, but insensibly and unconsciously lifts us with him to where winds blow cool and the outlook is infinite". Many recollections will come back to-day to the spectators of the interstate match, but none more frequently than the sight of those two men, Trumper and Duff, going out to wickets watched by thousands as if the fate and reputation of their country depended on them. Wise men will say again, as, indeed, they said then, that those were the days when we were lost to all sense of reality. Others will see in this honour paid to a great athlete a proof that we are incapable of appreciating the lessons of the war. The question is not to be decided entirely by a comparison of English and German methods, or by instances of the astonishment of foreigners at the English habit of seeking out a cricket pitch and talking of cricket while they are engaged on more serious things. But some hint of the true answer is given by the homage paid to Trumper. He would never have been held in honour if he had been selfish or vain or antisocial. Men were grateful to him for the pleasure he gave them, but they admired him for his character. Ranjitsinjhi says in his book that the average cricketer is just a man with a clear eye, bronzed face and athletic figure, somewhat lacking in general information, reading little, not talking much about things he does not understand. Ranjitsinjhi was writing in a country in which the livelihood of large numbers of men is gained entirely by playing cricket. But even there his description would have to be modified to-day. He would have to add that the cricketer, though he took little part in the shaping of events, was among the first to see his duty when the call came to him.

'Interstate matches before the war had lost a little of their importance in the eye of the public. The unlearned spectator reserved his attention for the international series which had been increased by the visits of the South Africans. Retired or undistinguished players were reluctant to be spectators only for more than a limited number of afternoons, and were inclined to concentrate on those occasions on which all the greater constellations could be seen at once. But the interstate series, especially the matches between Victoria and New South Wales, have a history which must preserve them against all the fluctuations of popular attention. To-day they resume their position

Newspaper clipping headed: 'Late Victor Trumper'. The caption reads: 'The inimitable champion executing a characteristic stroke.'

as the scene at which alone cricket can be studied at its best. Not only must the future internationals be found there, but it is there that the club, the school, and the family cricketer must go to see how the game may be played. After the war people will be a little less dogmatic than they used to be about the effect of popular institutions. Whoever talks about degeneracy will remember that before the war Englishmen were said to have lost their stamina through allowing others to play their games for them, and how Homer made the same comparison between the Greeks who fought in the Trojan and their fathers. Whatever the scientific deduction should be, interstate matches have sound justification. If they did not exist there would be less emulation and less skill in the matches of double and single wicket, through which cricket has really earned its title to be the national game. Of the justification for that title there can be no doubt. Everywhere, from the wickets surrounding the cricket ground to the suburban side streets, some young or old batsman can be seen "taking his stand at the wickets in an attitude of haughty defiance", twisting himself into knots to resemble a Hordern or flinging himself forward to gain the speed of a Cotter, another name which will be gratefully and affectionately remembered to-day. We read the other day of a new game which was a form of cricket so modified that ladies might take part in it. But ladies always have taken part in cricket. It is on record that the mother of the Graces, when one of her elder sons was chosen to play in the great annual matches, wrote to the selection committee to say that she had been training another named WG at home whose defence was far sounder. Mr Snaith once wrote a whole novel to describe the ineffectual attempts of his hero to win the heart of his heroine by beating her at single wicket, and the very best picture that we know of England before the war opens with the account of a mixed cricket match between teams of men and women, most of whom subsequently fought gallantly for the Empire. It may not be patriotic to wish that cricket may be played with methods more attractive to the spectator than those which had become fashionable immediately before the war. We remember reading a description of a catch by Tyldesley, in which he was said to have thrown the ball up as if he were at play. Tyldesley was an excellent model for a young player, and cricket was never so popular or so free from disputes as when both players and, officials remembered that it was a game.'

19

THEY REVERED HIM

The greatest accolade a cricketer can receive is the universal approval and respect of friend and foe alike. Victor Trumper enjoyed enormous respect for his ability with the bat and as a man. His contemporaries — Australian, English, South African and New Zealander — held Trumper in the highest esteem. He was known as the 'immortal' Trumper. Children loved him because he was kind and easily approachable; cricketers and cricket lovers revered him for both his generosity and his special brand of batsmanship which lifted batting at the top level out of the ruck and set new standards for style. Had Shakespeare been writing of Trumper and not of Julius Caesar, he would most assuredly have penned 'the good that Trumper did lived after him for eternity'.

It is a pity that Trumper's batting was not captured on good quality film so we of the modern era could watch the brilliance of his strokeplay, the ease and grace of his footwork. We might, too, lament that we were never given an opportunity to see W G Grace on film, nor an ancient version of David Frost interviewing Napoleon or the rebel leaders of the French Revolution, or watch the first marathon runner at Olympus. Sadly, Trumper, so near our time, was yet too far. There is no quality film of Trumper batting, although I have seen some footage of the master batsman. However, the fellow throwing the ball was having an off day and Trumper, thoroughly enjoying himself, did not appear to be taking things seriously. Perhaps the crude form of movie camera in 1905 was more a source of amusement to the players than a serious means of capturing a genius at work, to be recorded for posterity. Happily, we are able to glean a good deal of Trumper's genius from the writings of his fellow players and Neville Cardus, whose penmanship was to cricket writing what Shakespeare was to the theatre.

Trumper's stage was cricket. But there were no false sets; no second chances to stay in front of his audience were he to snick a ball from Sidney Barnes into the waiting clutches of Frank Woolley at slip. Trumper did not always set tongues wagging with the enormity of his scores, albeit he hit many centuries, a few double centuries and one triple, as did Bill Ponsford and Don Bradman between the wars. It was the agility and grace of Trumper; his inimitable style which captured the imagination of a nation, indeed, of the entire cricket world.

Charles Trumper, Victor's nephew, proudly holds an enlargement of a stamp featuring Trumper released by Australia Post in 1981. (*News Ltd*)

M A 'Monty' Noble, who was about to leave the Crown Street Superior School when the boy Trumper arrived and who later played in the same New South Wales and Test team as Trumper, revered the man:

'I have no hesitation giving the palm to Victor Trumper as the world's greatest batsman,' Noble told the nation in an Australia-wide radio address on 27 June, 1936, entitled: I Knew a Man — Victor Trumper. Noble told an enthralled Australian Broadcasting Commission listening audience that Trumper was 'not only a brilliant batsman, but his brilliance usually shone out most dazzlingly under adverse conditions — that is, when his side was up against it'.

The extraordinary part of Noble's praise for Trumper was that he still regarded his long-dead comrade the greatest batsman of all time, even though Don Bradman was at his zenith. Bradman, the man whose batting deeds transcend all others in the Golden Age, between the wars or any other time before or since.

Noble continues: 'Those of us who were intimately associated with Victor were not greatly astonished that cricketing success should eventually be his portion, for it was with pride and admiration that we watched his early efforts during the period when Nature was moulding him mentally and physically — his brain, his eyes and his muscles — to such perfection of harmonious purpose that he might properly fulfil the destiny allotted to him.

'But we did not imagine that, in a few seasons, he would completely revolutionise the art of batting and that his name for ever would be associated with the initial crumbling of erstwhile cricket convention and the inglorious capitulating of orthodoxy in favour of a more versatile and virile comprehension of batting possibilities. I firmly believe that Victor's great purpose in life was to be the pioneer of a new conception of what may be described as "cricket harmony".

'Cricket in NSW at that time was languishing under the spell of orthodoxy and passive resistance, which were fast throttling the people's appreciation of the game and destroying the allegiance of its many devotees. How Victor's wonderful demonstrations shocked old ideas and brought light out of semi-darkness is well known, particularly in Australia. With his coming the old order passed for ever.'

Noble went on to say that Trumper was 'lovable, genial, modest and humble, absolutely without conceit. He was as clean in mind as he was generous in spirit. He always had a kindly thought for others, particularly for the down-and-outs. He never stopped to ask if a case were a deserving one. To him all underdogs were "poor chaps" and if he could help them by word or deed so much the better. That was the spirit that endeared him to us all.'

Frank Iredale, who played for NSW with Trumper and toured with the great batsman on his first tour of England in 1899, wrote in *Thirty-Three Years of Cricket*:

'To be near him always as it were, seemed to me to be an honour. He was one of natures which called to you, and in whose presence you felt it was good to live. His loving nature made many friends and his cheery optimism was good to see. In all my cricket years, and association with cricketers, I never knew a man who practised self-effacement so much as he. He loved the game and respected those that played it.

'In victory and defeat he was just the same — his demeanour never changed. If by any chance a player coveted a bat he used, he gave it to him. His unselfish nature was of such a breadth that it at times became embarrassing to his many friends who had to avoid his favours. I never knew a cricketer who showed his emotions so little as he did, no one could read his mind, therefore he was never understood. Everything he did was seemingly taken for granted. It was never necessary to ask him to do anything in a match because everyone felt that before the words were out of one's mouth they were conscious that he knew what you were going to say. No work was too hard for him, and if he did more than his share, no word ever passed his lips which would convey the thought that he knew.

'If there was a bad seat on the train, he was in it; if the sleeping compartment happened to be over the wheels, one always felt sure that Victor had changed his seat from somewhere else and taken the worst one. On trips to England if the steward offered an apology for the food, Victor would say: "It really didn't matter, I'm not a bit hungry." He never sought publicity and shunned any attempt of anyone to put him forward. Even in his everyday life, going to and fro to his business, he would always be found round the back of the steamer or at the end of the train where no one could see him. His nature was just as hard to describe as his cricket, because one cannot recall in one's acquaintance with men, a nature such as he had. He was splendidly loyal and a firm and just believer in what was right. He was a hard man to know because he made you so indebted to himself for the many kindnesses extended. All the children loved him because he was easily approachable and so adaptable. He thought of others so constantly that one could almost believe he lived for the rest of the world.

'I remember during the Manchester Test in 1899, we were both in the long field and during the period when a new batsman was coming in, we had our yarn. Notwithstanding the fact that he loved his trip and the experience he was going through, I felt somehow that his mind and thoughts were of his home; he loved his home and the ties that surrounded it and, though he came with us on many occasions to theatres and elsewhere, one felt that whatever may have been in the place where we were, it certainly was not the real man.

'To see him at his best, one had to go into the sanctuary of his home, his wife and child, and there the man whom the world saw but never knew was at his best. I met him on many occasions out walking in the cool of the evening with his wife, whom he loved with a tenderness which one knew was so real, and it was on these evenings that Victor enjoyed his real pleasure in life. I came out with him and his wife from England in 1905, and it was in communion with him on this trip, day after day, that I got to know him so well. It was only his real friends who knew him and I am sure the cricket world knew nothing of the real man. He looked upon cricket as a duty more than as a sport. If he punished a bowler he felt real sorry for him afterwards. In our old club — the Gordons — we had many talks of the game, but I never knew him to speak one word of his own part in it. He was so much a part in character from any other cricketer I knew, that one almost had to confine one's talk to him of cricket in the general sense. I cannot speak of him as a cricketer, because I realise that nothing I could say would do him justice. He is comparable to no one because he was the first of his line. He was the beginning and the end of a new life in cricket and when he died — all too soon — his cricket died with him. His memory,

The Trumper stamp, in good company with Sir Norman Brookes (tennis), Darby Munro (horse racing) and Walter Lindrum (billiards). This memento was presented to Victor Trumper junior by Australia Post.

however, lingers and will for ever, so long as this grand old game of ours is played. In future years we may develop great players who may achieve great deeds, but one feels somehow or other that we shall never see a man like Victor Trumper again.'

Tom Horan, who played in the First Test match at the MCG against England in 1877 and a year later was among the first official Test team (under the captaincy of Dave Gregory) to England, also made a name as a writer. Horan wrote for the *Australasian* newspaper, under the pen name of Felix.

An article by Felix on Trumper appeared in the English magazine *Cricket* — a weekly record of the game — on Saturday, 19 April, 1913:

'I remember the first time Victor put 'em on. I mean the pads, and I am referring to the first time I saw him shape at the practice nets on the Melbourne Cricket Ground. That was at Christmas-time, 1897. He did not play in that match against Victoria, but going on to South Australia he was included a week later in the NSW Eleven and performed well. While on the MCG, the veteran Harry Hilliard introduced me to him and I was struck by the frank, engaging facial expression of the young Sydneyite. After a few words he went away and old Harry said to me: "That lad will have to be reckoned with later on." My word! But do you know what particularly attracted my attention when I first saw Victor fielding? You wouldn't guess it in three. It was the remarkably neat way in which his shirt sleeves were folded. No loose, dangling sleeves which were folded back again after a run for the ball, but always trim and artistic. It is a small thing, perhaps, to some, but to me it counts and suggests a good deal.

'Let us get away from his first appearance at the nets on the MCG and take him at the time he was chosen fourteenth man to go to England with the 1899 Australian team. I remember well having a long chat about him with M A Noble, in Scott's Hotel, and I may say that M A at the time predicted a brilliant batting future for Victor. If my memory is right, these two great cricketers were at school together, only M A was a senior and Victor, a junior. At all events in the course of conversation I found that in certain matches Victor, as a boy cricketer, was barred. Opposing sides would not play if he were included against them. "As a fact," added Noble, "I have known him to be in for two days at 95 in the shade and still going strong. They simply couldn't get him out and gave up the game." That was as a schoolboy and we have a parallel in Melbourne, in the case of Warwick Armstrong, who used to be barred on some occasions when he was a member of a boys' club out Caulfield way.

'So we see that as a schoolboy cricketer Victor was great in batting. When he toured England in 1899, he was also great. If you remember, it was during that tour that he made his mammoth score of 300 not out against Sussex in six hours and 20 minutes, by play from first to last "of the most perfect character". But the crowning glory of his achievement was his brilliant success in England in 1902.

'Then it was that the welkin rang with the tumult of sustained applause, in recognition of his glorious play. Then it was that century after century stood against his name on wickets wet or dry. Then it was that he scored a century in one of the most extraordinarily exciting Test matches ever played, when 'midst the cheers and shouts of enthusiastic

Lancastrians and Australian supporters at Manchester, he walked back to the pavilion with his blushing honours thick upon him.

'My old friend Mr Byers, who went especially to England to see the Australians play in 1902, walked round the ground at Manchester, near the finish of that memorable match, and he told me that the excitement was so intense that some onlookers were white and others ashen grey.

'Everywhere the Australians travelled Victor Trumper was the "observed of all observers". That was the time, as an old Yorkshireman told me, when Sheffielders knocked off work to see Victor bat. And those Yorkshiremen had a treat in watching "the star among the stars" in the Third Test match, for he got 62 out of 80 in 50 minutes and did 'just what he liked with the English bowling'. Wisden adds — "Trumper in the course of the season, made many bigger scores than his 62, but on no occasion did he play a more marvellous innings".

Plaque commemorating Victor Trumper's listing in 1979 in the NSW Government's Hall of Champions at Sports House, Sydney.

'I have set forth something of what he has done in England, and I may add that C B Fry went so far as to quote Latin in his praise at the close of the 1902 tour. Let us now see if we can't pick up something about him on our own MCC ground. Just imagine that we are together with the veterans under the trees when Victor's name goes up on the board. There is a hum of expectancy all round the ground. "Here he comes," is the cry and the welcome is as hearty as rinkers can give. You know what that means. Soon he gets going. Presently you hear an elmer say, "By jove, that was a yorker he got to leg for 4." "Gosh there's another yorker served the same way. How does he do it?"

'Cricketers well know that the vast majority of batsmen are quite satisfied if they manage to stop a yorker. So it is not unreasonable to find themselves expressing surprise when yorkers are sent to square leg for 4. Even such an imperturbable wicketkeeper as Carkeek was taken by surprise and when asked what he thought of Trumper replied, "Oh, Trumper; what do I think about him? Why, he hits yorkers to leg for 4 — that's enough about him, isn't it?"

'Once, when he sent a yorker from Fred Collins for 4, Fred was asked what he thought about it. He scratched his nice head of hair and said, "I can't understand it."

'Victor has what you may term "prehensile fingers". If you shake hands with him you will find out. He grasps the bat like a man who means business. You rarely, if ever, find him get out through the bat turning in his hand. Those "prehensile fingers" prevent it.

·When he comes down on the yorker he gauges the timing to a nicety and, just at the right moment, he comes down on the ball with full power and has the bat at an angle which causes the ball to fly away to forward square leg. This is my opinion and I think it is correct. I have seen the celebrated Charlie Bannerman (first man to score a Test century, MCG 1877) send a yorker hard to mid-on, but never to square leg. He was a pocket Hercules and came down on the ball with great power. Watch the phalanx of fieldsmen on the off side when Trumper bats. Ordinary batsmen play ball after ball direct to the fieldsmen. Trumper doesn't. He places the ball where the fieldsman is not. Presently the captain endeavours to block Victor's stroke. No sooner is this done than the magician, with his wand of willow, places the ball in almost the exact spot vacated by the fieldsman who had gone to block the champion's stroke.

'I remember once seeing Clem Hill on the MCG send a perfect length ball from Charlie McLeod like a shot to square leg for 4. He stepped back, almost on the wicket and, with the quickness of thought, mind, wrist and bat working in simultaneous accord, the ball was on its wav to the boundary. It was a rare bit of work, the execution perfect. I have never seen a better stroke. It was only a gifted batsman who could make it. In fact, the only other batsman who could have done it is, in my opinion, Victor Trumper.

'Further round the ground you meet another veteran. "Hallo! Did you see that? Shaped for a pull, changed his mind and drove it to the off for 4. How does he do it?" This is the sort of stroke that must have puzzled George Hirst, the celebrated Yorkshire all-rounder. P F Warner said something to him about placing the field for Victor and Hirst replied, "I think it doesn't matter much where we place them for Victor; he does pretty well with all the placing." It puts me in mind of J C Shaw, the famous bowler, and W G: "Oi poots 'em where oi loikes and he poots 'em where he loikes".

'Years ago I read a brilliant article in the *Argus* by James Smith. In it reference was made to what he termed, one, two, and three-storied intellects. In cricket Victor Trumper is full "three-storey". Upstairs everytime; hence top-notcher.

'In 1903-4 P F Warner made mention of Victor as the best batsman in the world. Wisden said the same. When Warner was here last time he considered that Victor was not the Victor of yore. That may be so, but he has come on again and the splendid success which has crowned his efforts in big cricket this season must be eminently gratifying, not only to himself, but to his numerous friends and admirers. His name is a household word in Australia and in England he is known not only in London and other big cities, but in the remote villages of Yorkshire and Lancashire. Perhaps the most eloquent tribute to him (if we rightly look into it) was from the black fellow in New York, who asked Edgar Mayne, during the recent tour, "Where is Victor Trumper?".

'What is the secret of his world-wide popularity? I put it down, in part, to a charming personality, in part to the peculiar charm of his batting. His wonderful eye and quickness of foot action enable him to get out or come back just as he pleases. You will see him leave his crease and, changing his mind, get back and make a beautiful late cut that sends the ball to the boundary in a trice. See him hit a sixer without apparent effort. Just a graceful swing and away the ball goes, over the heads of the people, to the topmost part of the embankment. But, undoubtedly, in my opinion, the most astonishing stroke of all is the way he gets a fine length ball to the on side, just as Clem Hill did with the fine length ball of Charlie McLeod. Victor's batting on sticky wickets over and over again has proved of great value to his side and in this respect his supreme confidence enables him to attack with vigour where other batsmen are content to keep their stumps up and look on while Victor is scoring.

'I recall one great innings he played on such a wicket on the MCG, when he got into the seventies against Warner's team in 1903-4. It was splendid. J L Toole, in his early theatrical days, was selling tickets for one of his own performances. A hob-nailed Lancastrian bought a ticket and asked, "Is young lady dancing poetry o' motion to-night?" She was ill and couldn't appear. J L told him so. "Oh, then give me back my money. I want poetry o' motion. I don't care for t'other stuff."

Victor's batting is poetry of cricket. He combines such grace of style with versatility of stroke, that he wins all hearts. He is, indeed, a master of all strokes and his consummate excellence in timing, united with perfect soundness of judgement, render him unrivalled, allied, as these attributes are, to a flexible wrist and a punishing power unsurpassed at the present time. He has won golden opinions as a man and as a cricketer all over the world and I am sure everyone will wish him the best of luck for his testimonial match.'

Tom Horan, or Felix, never lived to see Don Bradman bat. What superlatives would Felix have bestowed upon The Don? Horan died in 1916, one year after Trumper. Horan's article on Trumper appeared after Victor's benefit match in the English journal, but it was a repeat of an article he wrote for the *Australasian* just prior to Trumper's benefit match at the SCG.

The Battle of Britain was over; a psychological advantage to the free world, survival for England. By November 1940, despite the fact that Germany was waging a terrible war which would cost many more lives, Neville Cardus's autobiography was serialised in various publications. Even the war could not keep fair-minded men thinking about the grand old game.

'In my memory's anthology of delights I have known in many years devoted to the difficult but entrancing art of changing raw experience into the connoisseur's enjoyment of life, I shall place Trumper's cricket — and thank his immortal shade for it,' wrote Cardus.

Cardus goes into length about the very thing Horan (Felix) wrote about regarding the England bowlers' despair in setting a field to Trumper. Archie MacLaren was the England captain when Trumper hit that brilliant century before lunch at Manchester in 1902. Cardus takes up the story:

'MacLaren's strategy was directed at Victor Trumper. "Keep Victor quiet," were MacLaren's orders to his team as they went into action.

Cricket memorabilia collector S S 'Ram' Ramamurthy with the 1902 Trumper diary in his Whyalla, South Australia, home. Ram has one of the finest cricket collections in the world. (*S S Ramamurthy*)

"The pitch will be sticky after lunch, then we'll bowl 'em out as quick as they come in. If the Australians are only 80 or so at the interval we've won the match and the rubber. So keep Victor quiet at all costs!'' And the subtlest of England's cricket captains, the most lordly and imperial, concentrated all his craft in reducing Trumper to immobility. The field was set deep to save the fours and length bowlers as accurate as Rhodes, F S Jackson and Tate pitched the ball where they imagined Victor would not be able to reach it.

'And the outcome of all this scheming, of all these canny protective devices of all the plots and stratagems to ''keep Victor quiet'' was that Victor scored a century before lunch.

'Years afterwards, a number of MacLaren's friends chaffed him about this extraordinary frustration of his generalship. We were engaged in a friendly dinner, after a good day's sport, and during coffee and liqueurs we harked back to the olden times. We challenged MacLaren — pulled his leg. ''Why, Archie, you must have slipped a bit when you allowed Trumper to win the 1902 rubber on a turf nearly waterlogged in the outfield. Did you place too many men deep and allow Victor to pick up the runs through the gaps near the wicket?''.

'MacLaren, who adores an argument, rose to the bait; he took lumps of sugar out of the basin and set them all over the table, saying, ''Gaps be blowed! Good God, I knew my man — Victor had half a dozen strokes for the same kind of ball. I exploited the inner and outer ring — a man there, a man there and another man covering HIM.'' (He banged the lumps of sugar down one by one, eloquently punctuating his luminous discourse).

'''I told my bowlers to pitch on the short side to the off; I set my heart and brain on every detail of our policy. Well, in the third over of the morning, Victor hit two balls straight into the practice ground, high over the screen behind the bowler. I couldn't very well have had a man fielding in the practice-ground, now could I?'''

Cardus watched that Trumper innings. The boy Cardus was just 12 years old. He concedes that the first young rapture leaves a lasting impression and that impression lasted Cardus throughout his eminent life.

'I can see Victor even now as I write; his cricket burns in my memory with the glow and fiery hazard of the actual occurrence, the wonderful and consuming ignition. He was the most gallant and handsome batsman of them all; he possessed a certain chivalrous manner, a generous and courtly poise. But his swift and apparent daring, the audacity of his prancing footwork, were governed by a technique of rare accuracy and range.

'Victor was no mere batsman of impulsive genius; he was in the purest sense a stylist of the royal blood; he hit the ball with the middle of the bat's blade — even when he pulled from middle stump round to square leg.

'As I look back on my boyhood and try to think of all the formative influences that made me a man of some awareness to the things of the imagination, I realise the power of three strangely diverse forces, each evocative of colour and romance — the music of Wagner's, Turner's canvas ''The Fighting Temeraire'' and Victor Trumper. I do not hesitate, at this high prime of my life, to write the name of Victor Trumper along with those two immortals of a higher plane of artistic activity.'

'Victor was as much an artist in cricket, as much an inspiration to an impressionable urchin of Manchester, as any Turner or Wagner. It doesn't matter, really, in what direction or calling the spirit of genius takes its flights; I would no more forget Trumper's batsmanship than I would forget gorgeous sunsets, cloud-capped mountains, sonorous cadences of verse and symphony, or the full-bloom of the rose. All these things have "immortal longings".'

Cardus pointed out that the 'modern young sceptics' would probably look into Trumper's batting average and compare it unfavorably with the averages of Bradman, Ponsford, Sutcliffe and others. Certainly taking things 40-odd years on, players such as Greg Chappell, Bob Simpson, Graeme Pollock, Bill Lawry, Norm O'Neill, Geoff Boycott and so the list goes on . . . all these men finished their careers with a better average than Trumper.

But do we compare Trumper with others merely on the score of averages and weight of runs? Certainly in Bradman's case, figures are important for The Don was not only a genius, he was a freak, the like of which we are never likely to see again. Yet there are people who look at the great West Indian Viv Richards and attempt to persuade us that Richards is the more complete player. Cardus dances down the pitch to present a perfect straight drive:

'I am concerned with Trumper as an artist, not as a scorer of match-winning runs. You will no more get an idea of the quality of Trumper's batsmanship by adding up his runs than you will get an idea of the quality of Shelley's poetry by adding up the number of lines written by Shelley.

'Trumper was a great player whether he made 18 or 180. His cricket before lunch at Old Trafford in 1902 would have been thrilling and memorable if no scoreboard had been there at all to make an assessment of the merely utilitarian value of the innings. His strokes were rapid and powerful, yet flexible and handsome. He added the bloom of wrist-work to finely balanced muscular energy. He was always on the offensive; C B Fry once said of Trumper that he played a defensive stroke "only as a last resort" Whenever Trumper played back without scoring you knew that the bowler had achieved a master-ball.'

Herbert Collins, who played first-class cricket from 1909 to 1926, played in the same Paddington team with Trumper:

'Trumper was my ideal as a cricketer, but I did not pattern my style on his. I had a good reason for not doing so. It would have been impossible even to imitate him. He was the "freak" of cricket. Without skite or egotism, he maintained that if a ball could get past a piece of wood and hit the stumps it was only a fluke. No bowler could ever claim to have taken the initiative from Trumper, who played the first over in a Test match with as little concern as he would have played an over from a tired bowler whom he had slogged for a double century. Believe me when I tell you that it was odds-on Trumper hitting the first ball bowled to him for four. That was always his objective and he gained it hundreds of times.'

Bert Collins took over from Warwick Armstrong as Test captain in the wake of the 1921 tour of England. He was a splendid skipper and in 11 Tests as captain he lost only two matches, winning five, with four drawn. Collins was also a prominent bookmaker whose spiritual homes were Monte Carlo and the dog and race tracks.

'In my first game for Paddington I played with a bat that Trumper gave to me. I was as proud as a peacock, although somewhat awed. Trumper showed me a few points with bat and ball while at the nets, but told me that my own enterprise would take me further in cricket than all the tuition. "Every man must play to his own natural style and temperament," Trumper told me.

'A player had left our team and joined another. When the teams met Trumper went to the wicket with a twinkle in his eye. His former teammate had boasted that he knew how to get Trumper out. "He's easy money for me," the fellow boasted. Trumper hit the first five balls of the over for sixes, while the sixth ball hit the top of the pickets. Two balls were lost after that display of fireworks. They were hit into the Chinamen's gardens at Hampden Oval (now Trumper Park).'

The bowler's name was Rose. He was playing for Waverly against Trumper's Paddington team on 26 October, 1907. Trumper scored 89 in 35 minutes, hitting, at one stage, 50 in 5¼ minutes. He was stumped by Hanson Carter off the bowling of Tommy Howard. His scoring strokes: 4,4,2,1,4,4,6,6,6,6,4,6,6,6,4,4,4,1,2,1,2,4,1,1.

Collins goes on: 'In those days crowds would flock to a grade match to see Trumper bat and when he was out they would troop away from the grounds, having no further interest. Trumper just grinned when this happened.'

Collins, as did so many other cricketers and fans, revered Trumper. He recalled that when he was a youngster trying to make the NSW team, Trumper was a State selector, having beaten Frank Iredale for the job.

'Trumper told me as I went in to bat against Tasmania: "See that you don't let me down." I hit 282 and that was then a record and Victor was delighted. Victor played in that match after having the fingers of one hand jambed in the door of a car. He did not intend batting, but the crowd clamoured for him. To allow me to get a few more runs, he came to the wickets and, batting with one hand, played delightful shots to score 80 runs. He balanced his bat until point of contact and placed the balls where he liked. Averages didn't count with Victor Trumper. Had he been a player seeking records, goodness knows what he would have done. He shunned publicity, but could not dodge it. His deeds could not pass unnoticed. No one knew he was about until a bat was broken or a score was wanted.

'He was one of the best throwers I have seen. One day he threw a ball from the outfield, right over the bowler's head, to be taken by Jim Kelly on the full to run a man out. Trumper could field anywhere. It was a highlight of cricket when a wicket fell in Test cricket to see Clem Hill and Victor Trumper throwing a ball to each other from opposite sides of the ground. They didn't know how to drop a catch.

'Though not strong physically, Trumper had hands and wrists like iron. He could bend a bat, while he used bats so heavy that we wondered how he could lift them.

'With all his success he remained a lovable fellow who gave advice to youngsters and his money to anyone who asked for assistance. He bought bats for kids in the parks, telling those who knew of his benefactions that in doing so he might make a find for Australia.

'There will never be another Victor Trumper.'

Charles Fry was one of the legends of cricket. A marvellous bat, Fry played first-class cricket from 1892-1921, hitting 30,886 runs at an average of 50.22. He played 26 Tests for England, scoring 1223 runs at 32.18 and at the age of 21 held the world long jump record. It was once said of him that he broke the record after having quaffed half a bottle of scotch. He played football (soccer) for England, was a Member of Parliament and served on the League of Nations. A critic once said of him that he only had one stroke: 'True,' replied Fry, 'but I can send it in twenty-two places.' He played with the great Ranjitsinhji for Sussex and England and was once offered the Kingdom of Albania. A man of great majesty. He wrote of Trumper:

'Victor Trumper is, perhaps, the most difficult batsman in the world to reduce to words. He has no style and yet he is all style. He has no fixed canonical method of play, he defies all the orthodox rules, yet every stroke he plays satisfies the ultimate criterion of style — minimum of effort, maximum of effect. Perhaps he may be explained thus: a wonderful eye, a wonderful pair of wrists, a supreme naturalness, consequent on a supreme confidence that his wrists will never betray his eye. Almost as soon as the ball has left the bowler's hand he judges its length and direction and at once determines on his stroke; thus he has practically shaped for the stroke before the ball has pitched; yet he has rarely compromised his stroke so far as not to be able to correct it accordingly to what the ball actually does after pitching.

'The gracefulness and vigour of his strokes are due to an almost perfect natural balance and to his remarkable wrist power. Even in his hardest driving his wrists do the work. His body weight comes into the stroke, but never with any labour or tug: he has a free arm swing, but this is always subordinated in such a way as not to disturb his poise.

'He has, it may be said without exaggeration, a marvellous gift for timing a cricket ball. But, above all, he trusts his eye.'

Bill Whitty, who toured with Trumper to England in 1909, dismissed Trumper seven times in five Sheffield Shield games between 1910 and 1913. Whitty played for South Australia and once clean bowled Trumper with a ball the great left hander described as the best ball he ever let go: 'It was a phenomenal ball — it swung right aross, then broke back to knock out his leg stump, with the bail flying 33 yards . . . I apologised to Victor for it all.' Next time they met, a month later, Trumper hit 201 not out in 3½ hours on the SCG.

'Trumper was the best bat I ever saw and the greatest stylist the game has ever known. He never let the ball hit his pads and was invariably on the offensive. He had a remarkable eye and believed that the ball was bowled to be hit.'

All the greats of yesteryear — Trumper's contemporaries on both sides of the world — maintained that Victor was the greatest batsman to grace the Test arena. Many of these men, such as Hanson Carter, Monty Noble, Hugh Trumble, Warwick Armstrong, Herbert Collins and Pelham Warner lived to see the modern sensation, Don Bradman. Some conceded that Bradman was a mighty player and perhaps the greatest ever, but Noble and Carter were adamant that Victor Trumper was the best of all time.

The same applied to Clem Hill and Charlie Macartney. Hill once said of Trumper: 'As a batsman, I'm not good enough to lick Trumper's boots.'

Joe Darling, Test captain on Trumper's first tour in 1899 and the 1902 tour was asked what he thought of Trumper after he had belted the Sussex attack into submission to score 300 not out: 'What do I think of him? I thought I could bat until I saw Victor!'

Pelham Warner, who captained the 1903-4 and 1911-12 England teams to Australia said: 'The world's best batsman? There's only one — Trumper!'

On 8 July, 1981, Frank Eric McElhone wrote a touching note to NSWCA secretary Bob Radford. He enclosed a copy of an essay he had written on Trumper and he wanted it to be kept in the association's library. Nineteen days later Eric McElhone died. McElhone played under Trumper for NSW in 1910-11. As with all the others, McElhone revered Trumper:

'On one occasion two schoolboy friends of mine, one of whom was Norman Gregg (later Sir Norman, eminent eye doctor), were watching Trumper batting at the SCG, from near the fence in front of what is now the Brewongle Stand, when a drunk near them muttered: "He has only one stroke." My friends asked: "What's his only stroke?" "Hitting the ball where there is no fieldsman."

'Victor had a keen sense of humour. During a match at the SCG (1910) Dr Herbert "Ranji" Hordern, Australia's first googly bowler, jokingly complained to captain Trumper for having kept him bowling for such a long spell on a hot afternoon. Victor immediately said: "Will half a crown satisfy you?" From that moment whenever Vic put Hordern on to bowl he would say "and here's your half a crown!" Trumper was a man of the highest character and principles and one of nature's gentlemen. Vale Victor Trumper!'

That great Test bowler Hugh Trumble, who toured with Trumper on two occasions (1899 and 1902) wrote in *Punch*, published 18 December, 1924: 'A Trumper appears only once in a generation. Yet what an inspiration he was! It is not too much to say that such a man makes other great cricketers. Like literature and art, the game owes much to inspiration. For years small boys used to gather on vacant allotments and try to imitate the wonderful strokes with which Victor used to pile up his centuries.

'There was something almost uncanny about him. I am certain he saw the ball while it was yet behind the bowler's palm. Before the ordinary man could have seen what the delivery was to be, Victor Trumper had sensed it and was prepared. Trumper had the most devastating effect on bowlers. When at the zenith of his powers, it mattered little how the field was placed.'

Trumble said his modesty and kindness remain a legend and no other player has drawn from the pens of the finest writers sentences that so grace the literature of cricket. One of the finest, according to Trumble, came from the pen of Daniel Reese: 'He (Trumper) left behind him a record and reputation that shine like a planet in the history of the game.'

It is, perhaps, human nature that a cricketer thinks more about the players of his era than those of the current crop or those who played long ago. Arthur Mailey was lucky, in that he bowled against Victor Trumper and Don Bradman. An impish character, Mailey was

cartoonist, journalist and butcher and once had emblazoned across his
butcher shop window — 'I bowl tripe, write tripe and sell tripe'.

He played 21 Tests for a return of 99 wickets at 33.91 and once took
4/362 for NSW against Victoria during the game in which the world
record total of 1107 was scored (1926). Mailey blamed 'that chap in the
crowd who kept dropping catches' for his lack of success. Mailey lived
near the Sydney suburb of Waterloo. He had a life-sized portrait of his
hero, Victor Trumper, on the wall in front of his bed. In 1921 Arthur
took all 10 Gloucestershire wickets for 66 runs. He later called his book
Ten for 66 — and all that.

As a mere slip of a lad, just after the turn of the century, Arthur got
his first crack at first-grade cricket in Sydney. Arthur was delighted,
especially as his team, Redfern, was about to confront Paddington,
home of the legendary Trumper. In his book Mailey describes that first
meeting with Trumper, the events leading to their meeting and the
aftermath. It is rivetting reading and I would be amiss not to reproduce
the work, if for no other reason than that both Mailey and Trumper
would have wanted it that way:

'It is difficult to realise that a relatively minor event in one's life can
still remain the most important through the years. I was chosen to play
for Redfern against Paddington and Paddington was Victor Trumper's
club. This was unbelievable, fantastic. It could never happen —
something was sure to go wrong. A war — an earthquake — Trumper
might fall sick. A million things could crop up in two or three days
before the match.

'I sat on my bed and looked at Trumper's picture still pinned on the
canvas wall. It seemed to be breathing with the movement of the
draught between the skirting. I glanced at his bat standing in a corner of
the room, then back at the gently moving picture. I just couldn't believe
that this, to me, ethereal and godlike figure could step off a wall, pick
up the bat and say quietly, "Two legs, please, umpire," in my presence.

'My family, usually undemonstrative and self-possessed, found it
difficult to maintain that reserve which, strange as it may seem, was
characteristic of my father's Northern Irish heritage.

'"H'm," said father, "Playing against Trumper on Saturday. By
jove, you'll cop old Harry if you're put on to bowl at him."

'"Why should he?" protested Mother. "You never know what you
can do till you try."

'I had nothing to say. I was little concerned with what should happen
to me in the match. What worried me was that something would happen
to Trumper which would prevent his playing.

'Although at this time I had never seen Trumper play, on occasions I
trudged from Waterloo across the sandhills to the SCG and waited at
the gate to watch the players coming out. Once I had climbed on a tram
and actually sat opposite my hero for three stops.'

(Similarly Bill O'Reilly, perhaps the greatest spinner of them all, told
me that he once sat on a tram next to a famous bowler. They never
spoke, but Bill was quite excited by it all. His hero? Arthur Mailey!)

'I would have gone further but having no money I did not want to
take the chance of being kicked in the pants by the conductor. Even so I
had been taken half a mile out of my way.

'In my wildest dreams I never thought I would ever speak to

Trumper, let alone play against him. I am fairly phlegmatic by nature, but between the period of my selection and the match I must have behaved like a half-wit.

'Right up to my first Test match I always washed and pressed my own flannels, but before this match I pressed them not once but several times. On the Saturday I was up with the sparrows and looking anxiously at the sky. It was a lovely morning but it still might rain. Come to that, lots of things could happen in ten hours — there was still a chance that Vic could be taken ill or knocked down by a tram or twist his ankle or break his arm . . .

'My thoughts were interrupted by a vigorous thumping on the back gate. I looked out of the washhouse-bathroom-woodshed-workshop window and saw that it was the milkman who was kicking up the row.

'"Hey", he roared, "yer didn't leave the can out. I can't wait around here all day. A man should pour it in the garbage tin — that'd make yer wake up a bit."

'On that morning I wouldn't have cared whether he poured the milk in the garbage tin or all over me. I didn't belong to this world. I was playing against the great Victor Trumper. Let the milk take care of itself.

'I kept looking at the clock. It might be slow — or it might have stopped. I'd better whip down to the Zetland Hotel and check up. Anyhow, I mightn't bowl at Trumper after all. He might get out before I come on. Or I mightn't get a bowl at all — after all, I can't put myself on. Wonder what Trumper's doing this very minute . . . bet he's not ironing his flannels. Sends them to the laundry, I suppose. He's probably got two sets of flannels anyway. Perhaps he's at breakfast, perhaps he's eating bacon and eggs. Wonder if he knows I'm playing against him? Don't suppose he's ever heard of me. Wouldn't worry him anyhow, I shouldn't think. Gosh, what a long morning. Think I'll dig the garden. No, I won't; I want to keep fresh. Think I'll lie down for a bit . . . better not, I might fall off to sleep and be late.

'The morning did not pass in this way. Time just stopped. I couldn't bring myself to doing anything in particular and yet I couldn't settle to the thought of not doing anything. I was bowling to Trumper. I was early and I was late. In fact, I think I was slightly out of my mind. I didn't get to the ground so very early after all, mainly because it would have been impossible for me to wait around so near the scene of Trumper's appearance.

'"Is he here?" I asked Harry Goddard, our captain, the moment I did arrive at the ground.

'"Is who here?" he countered.

'My answer was probably a scornful and disgusted look. I remember that it occurred to me to say, "Julius Caesar, of course" but that I stopped myself being cheeky because this was one occasion when I couldn't afford to be. Paddington won the toss and took first knock.

'When Trumper walked out to bat, Harry Goddard said to me: "I'd better keep you away from Vic. If he starts on you he'll probably knock you out of grade cricket."

'I was inclined to agree with him; yet, at the same time, I didn't fear punishment from the master batsman. All I wanted to do was just to bowl at him. I suppose in their time other ambitious youngsters have wanted to play on the same stage with Henry Irving, or sing with

Caruso or Melba, to fight with Napoleon or sail the seas with Columbus. It wasn't conquest I desired. I simply wanted to meet my hero on common ground.

'Vic, beautifully clad in creamy, loose-fitting but well-tailored flannels, left the pavilion with his bat tucked under his left arm and in the act of donning his gloves. Although slightly pigeon-toed in the left foot he had a springy, athletic walk and a tendency to shrug his shoulders every few minutes, a habit I understand he developed through trying to loosen his shirt off his shoulders when it became soaked with sweat during his innings.

'Arriving at the wicket, he bent his bat handle almost to a right angle, walked up the pitch, prodded about six yards of it, returned to the batting crease and asked the umpire for "two legs", took a quick glance in the direction of fine leg, shrugged again and took up his stance. I was called on to bowl sooner than I had expected. I suspect now that Harry Goddard changed his mind and decided to put me out of my misery early in the piece.

'Did I ever bowl that first ball? I don't remember. My head was in a whirl. I really think I fainted and the secret of the mythical first ball has been kept over all these years to save me embarrassment. If the ball was sent down it must have been hit for six, or at least four, because I was awakened from my trance by the thunderous booming Yabba who roared: "Oh for a strong arm and a walking stick!"'

'I do remember the next ball. It was, I imagined, a perfect leg-break. When it left my hand, it was singing sweetly like a humming top. The trajectory couldn't have been more graceful if designed by a professor of ballistics. The tremedous leg-spin caused the ball to swing and curve from the off and move in line with the middle and leg stump. Had I bowled this particular ball at any other batsman I would have turned my back early in its flight and listened for the death rattle. However, consistent with my idolisation of the champion, I watched his every movement.

'He stood poised like a panther ready to spring. Down came his left foot to within a foot of the ball. The bat, swung from well over his shoulders, met the ball just as it fizzed off the pitch, and the next sound I heard was a rapping on the off-side fence.

'It was the most beautiful shot I have ever seen.

'The immortal Yabba made some attempt to say something but his voice faded away to the soft gurgle one hears at the end of a kookaburra's song. The only person on the ground who didn't watch the course of the ball was Victor Trumper. The moment he played it he turned his back, smacked down a few tufts of grass and prodded his way back to the batting crease. He knew where the ball was going.

'What were my reactions?

'Well, I never expected that ball or any other ball I could produce to get Trumper's wicket. But that being the best ball a bowler of my type could spin into being, I thought that at least Vic might have been forced to play a defensive shot, particularly as I was almost a stranger, too, and it might have been to his advantage to use discretion rather than valour.

'After I had bowled one or two other reasonably good balls without success I found fresh hope in the thought that Trumper had found Bosanquet, creator of the wrong 'un or Bosie (which I think a better name), rather puzzling. This left me with one shot in my locker, but if I didn't use it quickly, I would be taken out of the firing line. I decided, therefore, to try this most undisciplined and cantankerous creation of the great B J Bosanquet — not, as many may think, as a compliment to the inventor, but as a gallant farewell, so to speak, to a warrior who refused to surrender until all his ammunition was spent.

'Again fortune was on my side, in that I bowled the ball I had often dreamed of bowling. As with the leg-break, it had sufficient spin to curve in the air and break considerably after making contact with the pitch. If anything it might have had a little more top-spin, which would cause it to drop rather suddenly. The sensitivity of a spinning ball against a breeze is governed by the amount of spin imparted and if a ball bowled at a certain pace drops on a certain spot, one bowled with identical pace but with more top-spin should drop 18 inches or two feet shorter.

'For this reason I thought the difference in the trajectory and ultimate landing of the ball might provide a measure of uncertainty in Trumper's mind. Whilst the ball was in flight this reasoning appeared to be vindicated by Trumper's initial movement. As at the beginning of my over he sprang in to attack, but did not realise that the ball, being an off-break, was floating away from him and dropping a little quicker. Instead of his left foot being close to the ball, it was a foot out of line.

'In a split second Vic grasped this and tried to make up the deficiency with a wider swing of the bat. It was then I could see a passage-way to the stumps with our 'keeper, Con Hayes, ready to claim his victim. Vic's bat came through like a flash but the ball passed between his bat and legs, missed the stump by a fraction and the bails were whipped off with the great batsman at least two yards out of his ground.

'Vic made no attempt to scramble back. He knew the ball had beaten him and was prepared to pay the penalty and, although he had little chance of regaining his crease on this occasion, I think he would have acted similarly if his back foot had been only an inch from safety.

'As he walked past me he smiled, patted the back of his bat and said, "It was too good for me."

'There was not triumph in me as I watched the receding figure. I felt like a boy who had killed a dove.'

20

THE STRONGEST LINK

When Donald George Bradman was born in Cootamundra, New South Wales, on 27 August, 1908, Victor Trumper's greatest triumphs were recent history. He still thrilled crowds in England in 1909, but never with the same authority as he had shown in 1902, the season in which his batting genius was at its zenith. It was little more than two years after The Don took his first stance in this world that Trumper again revealed his star qualities. The year was 1910-11 and Australia was pitted against Percy Sherwell's South Africans. Trumper was run out for 27 in the Sydney First Test, which Australia won by an innings and 114 runs. Then he had a sequence of 34 and 159 (Melbourne); 214 not out and 28 (Adelaide); 7 and 87 (Melbourne); and 31 and 74 not out (Sydney) — 661 runs at an average of 94.43.

There is a link between Trumper and Bradman; that link was Charles Macartney. What a trio. Trumper hit the first century before lunch on the first day of a Test (at Manchester in 1902). Macartney emulated Trumper's feat by hitting a superb 112 in 116 minutes before lunch on the first day of the Third Test against England at Headingly, Leeds, on 10 July, 1926. Then, four years later, Don Bradman produced an innings at Leeds which will live eternal in Test history. The Don joined Trumper and Macartney in hitting a century before lunch on the first morning of a Test. He went on to hit 115 between lunch and tea, then 89 in the final session to be 309 not out at stumps. The next day, Bradman snicked one behind and was gleefully taken by Duckworth off the bowling of Maurice Tate, the son of Fred (who had so suffered at the hands of Trumper at Old Trafford in 1902) for the then world-record score of 334.

The Trumper-Macartney link was probably never better illustrated than when they batted together in a match at Goulburn, NSW. The match was arranged as a farewell to Jack O'Connor and played on Friday, 28 March, 1913. Macartney and Trumper between them hit 347 runs. Macartney cut loose, hitting a great 116, but Trumper scored at double the rate, belting an unforgettable 231 in 90 minutes. As great a batsman as was Macartney, Trumper was the master. On the last ball of the day Victor moved down the wicket and, amid cheers and laughter, purposely hit over the delivery and was clean bowled. That was the way he played the game.

In England in 1902, a fellow came into the Australian dressingroom

Victor Trumper, the first of three Australians to hit a century before lunch in a Test. The other two were Charlie Macartney and Don Bradman. (*Mary Whitty Collection*)

Don Bradman in the late 1930s.

and offered the players the chance to use a bat (weighing 3½ pounds) he had made. Victor jumped at the chance: 'If it has a spring I'll use it.' He did and ripped off a century in even time. Once at a match on the SCG, two teenagers were sitting near the NSW dressingroom. They asked Victor to sign their bat. Victor went down into the crowd and sat with the boys. Then he said: 'Look, why don't I bat with it?' The boys were astonished, but Victor kept his word and soon after went in to bat with the boys' bat, hit the bowlers all over the SCG and signed it and gave it back to those adoring youngsters.

Trumper, Macartney and Bradman remain as the only three Australian batsmen to have achieved a century before lunch on the first morning of a Test match against England. Macartney toured with Trumper to England in 1909. They batted together before that for Gordon. Both men lived on the Sydney North Shore and Charlie often visited Victor's Help St. home and the pair batted and bowled on Victor's backyard pitch with the enthusiasm of two youngsters trying to emulate the heroes they had just watched in a Test at the Sydney Cricket Ground.

Macartney made his debut against England on December 13 on the Sydney ground. He came in at the fall of the fifth wicket and hit a sound 35 after Trumper had scored 41. In the Second Test at Melbourne, Macartney opened with Trumper. The pair hit an opening stand of 84 in the first innings (Macartney 37, Trumper 49), followed by an even brighter and bigger opening a second time. Trumper this time scored 63 and Macartney, 54, his first half century on the Test stage. Macartney revered Trumper. He, as did all of his contemporaries, believed Trumper to be the master batsman of all time.

Early in Bradman's first-grade career in Sydney, The Don was selected for a combined country team to do battle with a city team, skippered by none other than Charlie Macartney. The Don hit a sparkling 98. Macartney, writing in the *Evening News*, praised the young Bradman: 'The Countrymen's best performer with the bat was Bradman. He played a fine innings, using his feet nicely to the first grade slow bowler Morris, and playing the other types with easy confidence. He is rather weak on the on-side, however, and had a bad habit of walking away from the wicket when playing defensive strokes. The latter fault is a common hard-wicket player's error. Bradman has every probability of being a State player in the near future and, provided he overcomes these faults, will be a very classy one.' If The Don had faults, he quickly and surely overcame them for he soon became the greatest batsman in the world, even causing the contemporaries of Trumper to sit up and take notice.

There have been some very great Australian batsmen throughout the years. We should not use the word 'great' lightly. It is a select band, indeed it can only be the truly great who form the golden links of the strongest batting chain in Australian Test history.

To my mind, Bradman stands head and shoulders above the rest. Yet the greats of their own era, Trumper, Clem Hill, Charlie Macartney, Bill Ponsford, Stan McCabe, Lindsay Hassett, Keith Miller, Neil Harvey, Bob Simpson, Arthur Morris, The Chappells, (Greg and Ian), Bill Lawry and Allan Border are all links in that mighty chain.

We return to that age-old debate: Who was the greater batsman, Bradman or Trumper? In Mike Page's splendid definitive biography on

Victor Trumper, aged 20, in England for his first tour in 1899 . . . the greatest batsman the world had ever seen.

The Don, entitled *Bradman*, Page puts forward each player's case in facts and figures. Page illustrates the relative changes in lbw laws, size of stumps, size of ball, changes in rules governing covered wickets and the most telling argument of all: runs. Bradman was clearly the greatest run-getter of the two; in fact The Don was the greatest run-getter of them all. In just 80 Test innings Bradman hit a total of 6996 runs at an average of 99.94. Trumper had 89 Test innings, hitting 3163 runs at an average of 39.04. As Neville Cardus pointed out, one can't argue the relative merits of a batsman or a bowler purely on figures. Certainly few people would say that Bob Willis is a better bowler than Fred Trueman, despite Willis having taken more Test wickets. But in Bradman's case it is different. He scored his runs in rapid fashion, on all types of surfaces and he was just one boundary short of averaging 100 runs per innings over a career in Test cricket which spanned 20 years.

I naturally did not see Trumper bat, as he died 30 years before I was born. Sadly, too, I never saw The Don bat, as he retired when I was three or four years old. I've seen some mighty batsmen since The Don's time. The South Africans Barry Richards and Graeme Pollock; West Indians Garry Sobers and Viv Richards; Australians Neil Harvey, Greg and Ian Chappell; Englishmen Len Hutton and Geoff Boycott and the little Indian opener, Sunil Gavaskar. If I was asked to give my opinion as to the best batsman I have seen, I would give the palm to Neil Harvey. South African Graeme Pollock was the best player I bowled against. He hit the ball with astonishing power, as hard as West Indian Viv Richards. But unlike Richards, whenever Pollock got a start and had you on your knees, he rarely got out through a casual or careless stroke.

While compiling this book I approached Sir Donald Bradman, as ever The Don is ready, willing and able to help out where he can. When The Don agrees to help out he does so in a thorough and considerate manner. I had wondered whether during The Don's early years older players would have told him all sorts of stories about Victor Trumper. Perhaps they would have extolled all the virtues of Trumper's batting, with 'there'll never again be a player as great.'

'No, it never irked me when older players spoke so highly of Trumper and their views did not have any influence whatever,' he said.

I had asked Sir Donald whether such Trumper stories had given him greater resolve to become the greatest batsman of all time.

'I never, at any time, set out to be the greatest batsman of all time, nor did I ever have such an ambition. I merely tried to play as best I could and any comparable judgement of skill was for others to determine,' Sir Donald added.

'I think I also had enough sense to realise that each individual has his own particular skill and style and that you have to make the best you can of yourself. It is usually hopeless to try and copy others.'

Sir Donald never saw Trumper bat. But he said that the likes of Arthur Mailey, Charlie Macartney, Hanson Carter and Johnnie Moyes played with and against Trumper. They had spoken to The Don of Trumper and in glowing terms. Sir Donald said these men's adulation seemed largely due to the 'style and elegance of his batting, very similar, they said, to Alan Kippax and Archie Jackson. Having played with the last two named I must admit they were beautiful to watch'.

However, The Don conceded that style does not necessarily bring efficiency and consistency.

'Style is hard to define. Of the modern players (David) Gower is probably the best example. Greg Chappell certainly had an imperious quality about his batting that his brother Ian lacked. But which one would you have rather had in your team when the going was tough? I seem to remember (Neville) Cardus once writing on this aspect and the comparison he used was that an eagle looked much more beautiful in flight than an aeroplane but could not possibly match it for speed.'

A G (Johnnie) Moyes was a fine cricketer, who played for South

Australia and Victoria and was selected in an Australian team, but a planned South African tour did not take place because of the First World War. Moyes later became a prominent writer and broadcaster. He played in the 1913 Victor Trumper testimonial match and never forgot the Trumper show after Victor believed the umpire had given him a 'let off' just before stumps the previous night. Moyes wrote: 'He proceeded to give us a chance. I saw him, with a flick of the wrists, lift a fast rising ball from Jack Crawford on to the cycle track, which in those days encircled the playing area. I saw him vary it by cutting a similar ball for four. In the same over, he jammed down on a fastish yorker and turned it away past square leg to the fence. This is not imagination, for I was fielding in the slips, and I saw it and marvelled. One of the choicest memories of my life is that I was privileged to see Victor at close quarters and to watch his wizardry.'

But Moyes also came to terms about Bradman. As Bradman's career neared its end, Moyes wrote: 'Trumper was brilliant, but so was Bradman and no one who saw him in his greatest days of the thirties could hold any other opinion. In seeking runs he was more ruthless than Trumper, but the character of the game had changed before he came into it, and heavy scoring had become the fashion. He not only followed the fashion, but created a new one, setting up a record which will probably never be equalled. Both were born to be great. Both lifted cricket out of the ruck — if we accept what Noble wrote and what we saw ourselves in the days when Bradman's approach was being heralded. Both had the power to charm, to draw the allegiance of the crowd and to hold it.

'The difference was the times in which they played. In Trumper's day cricket was a game and those with whom he played were content to bask in the light of the reflected glory, to give him full praise and often adulation. They were happy in their own success, rejoiced in his, and they loved him as a man.

'In Bradman's day cricket had already become commercialised and was played more tensely, as he found at once. Others did not take kindly to his success; there was not the generosity which featured in Trumper's day, one reason being that the genius of Bradman brought into his lap some of the ripe plums which might, they thought, have been theirs. The result was that many disliked Bradman, chiefly because of his success, and because, as a shield against pinpricks and criticism, he built an iron curtain of reserve. I knew and loved Victor Trumper. I know Don Bradman and my affection for him has grown with the years.

'Who was the greater? No one can say. I have tried to stress the similarity in ideas between the two men of genius. If we take a step further we must, I think, agree that on very bad pitches Trumper was a greater player, one reason being that he played more often on the rain-spoiled pitch, learned how to counter it, had the skill to do so. He has never been equalled in skill on a 'sticky' by any Australian. Bradman had no experience of such pitches before becoming a Test batsman. Doubtless he had seen wet matting hanging on the fence to dry, but he had no opportunity of learning the art of sticky-wicket batting. At the same time, Bradman's record in England shows clearly enough that many of his critics have done him less then justice, for he could outplay all others, English and Australian, on the English turf. This is a fact and you can't argue about facts; nor can you discard figures when they are of the Bradman quality.

'If anyone tried to choose an international side on averages or to pick the best eleven on figures he would get a queer answer; but when a man, on all types of pitches, scores 117 centuries in 334 innings in first-class cricket, averaging 95.14 an innings, it is so stupendous that it must be accepted.

'I believe that Trumper could have made more runs than he did, for I know what his attitude to run-getting was, and indeed, what was the attitude of the times, but the fact is inescapable, Bradman DID score the runs, he did it consistently; he so often did it brilliantly. Trumper was the most fascinating of them all. He was a genius. Bradman never lacked the fascinating touch, as is proved by the crowds he drew and held. He was also a genius.'

It must have been difficult for a man such as Johnnie Moyes to attempt a comparison. He played on the same field as Trumper and truly admired him as batsman and man. Moyes, too, had great admiration for Bradman, as both batsman and man. He describes them both in the genius class.

In Sir Leonard Hutton's recent book *Fifty Years In Cricket*, he describes his early years at Yorkshire, where the former great England and Yorkshire all-rounder George Hirst gave young Len some priceless advice: 'Whatever tha does, don't get like Victor Trumper.'

'As any batsman, young or old, would have given anything to be another Trumper, I asked why.'

'He was so superstitious that he made his life a misery,' the old man replied.

Hutton was then 15. He was told that Trumper was extremely superstitious about his cricket gear and that Trumper had worn the same pair of batting trousers throughout his career. They became threadbare. George Hirst, who enjoyed many a Test battle against Trumper, wanted the young Hutton to buy a new bat, just after having watched him try out at the Headingly nets.

'All things are comparative,' wrote Hutton. 'I am convinced that between 1930 and 1940 Bradman saw the ball earlier and moved his feet quicker than any other batsman in the world, and probably before or since. In 1934 he still produced huge scores although he was fighting ill health and by 1938 he had, by his own standards, sobered down fractionally.

'Once discussing batsmen with Wilfred Rhodes (the great Yorkshire and England left-arm spinner and opening batsman), the grand old man said emphatically: 'I bowled against them all from 1900 to 1930...Hobbs, W G Grace, Trumper, Ranji and many more, but Don Bradman was the greatest.'

One of the great cricket writers, F S Ashley-Cooper thought Trumper could play the orthodox game was well as anyone. 'But,' he writes, 'Trumper's ability to make big scores when customary methods were unavailing placed Victor above his fellows.

'His timing has never been excelled and in the art of placing the ball he was unsurpassed. He always seemed to divine far quicker than most men the best way in which a ball should be played and then brain, wrist and bat acted in perfect unison. At times he would apparently change his mind at the last moment — he was always very quick on his feet —

but, even then, the resulting hit was, more often than not, pre-eminently a master-stroke.'

Certainly such a description could be made of Bradman. The Don was lightning on his feet, seemingly always in the perfect position. I recall a colleague in my newspaper office telling me that when Bradman jumped out to get to the pitch of a spinner, he pounced as would a cat on a mouse.

I shall never forget The Don coming into the South Australian dressingroom to have a friendly chat and lend some advice to Greg Chappell. The year, 1967. It was my first season of first-class cricket and Greg's second. In those dim, dark years of yore Greg Chappell was predominantly an on-side player. He often hit deliveries pitched on the off stump past mid-on and had a penchant for whipping balls off the middle and leg stumps high over square leg. Yet, at that stage of his career, Chappell struggled to dominate bowlers who concentrated their attack on or just outside the off stump, especially those who could swing or cut the ball away from the right-hander. The Don spoke with young Greg about his grip. Then the great man picked up a bat and played a shadow cover drive. Marvellous. I was spellbound. The front foot forward and the flashing blade. The Don performed that shadow drive a couple of times. It could have been Victor Trumper going through the motions, but it was The Don, in the flesh, the greatest bat of all time. Nothing could erase that moment from my mind. I envisaged Bradman in a new and exciting light. After all, I had only seen glimpses of him as a player and only on film clips.

Would now Victor Trumper appear and unleash shadow drives, pulls, cuts and show just how he managed to tuck fastish yorkers on the stumps sweetly away past the square leg umpire as bowler and fieldsmen alike stood and gaped in awe? Would not Charlie Macartney, the man who succeeded Trumper in audacity, the man who before The Don took every bowler — indeed every Test attack against Australia — by the scruff of the neck and shook the living daylights out of it, suddenly appear and show his mettle? No, that was too much to ask. But The Don's appearance that day was a godsend for me. It gave me some insight into the man's ability. Just a few shadow cover drives. It was enough to whet this writer's appetite. I wanted more.

To glean more about Bradman, I read the nearest thing next to Shakespeare among the cricket writing fraternity: I read Cardus. As a youngster it was purely and simply hero-worship. I make no apology for that, but after having met him, having sought and gained his advice on matters not always to do with cricket, I found Sir Donald Bradman to be a most generous man. He does not live in the past and admires today's top cricketers. He is the epitome of logic and has always had a commonsense approach to all of his endeavours. In the backyard games I played with my brother, Nicholas, my side aways contained Victor Trumper opening the batting with The Don batting at number 3.

But it was Neville Cardus who brought Trumper home to me. 'You can never speak to an Australian about Victor Trumper without seeing his eyes glisten with pride and affection; Trumper will always remain for your true Australian the greatest batsman that ever lived.' Cardus wrote this in *The Summer Game* (Rupert Hart-Davies, second edition, 1937) in 1929. So there would have been thousands of people who fondly recalled Trumper's triumphs, as the great batsman had been dead just 14 years. It was published 12 months before The Don's first magnificent assault on English soil, when he hit 334 at Leeds and 974 runs for the five Test series.

Cardus continued: 'But it was in England that Trumper achieved his most wonderful play; every lover of the game will pause for a space in the hurly-burly of the present period's Test matches to spare a moment in which to do homage to Trumper.

> The shadow stayed not, but the splendour stays
> Our brother, till the last of English days

'Was it not genius that made Trumper a master batsman in conditions not common to Australian batsmen? Trumper in 1902 took our finest spin bowlers by the scruff of the neck, usually from the first ball sent to him, drove them, thrust, glanced and carted them, right and left, for all the world as though they had been schoolboys. Amongst those same bowlers happened to be Rhodes, Haigh, Lockwood, J T Hearne, Hirst, Barnes, Trott, Wass and Braund. No shibboleth about an outer and inner ring of fieldsmen ever trouble Victor Trumper. He was master of all strokes and he could use almost any one of them at his pleasure, no matter the manner of ball bowled at him.'

Cardus first saw Trumper's magic at Manchester in 1902, when Victor had the crowd enthralled by hitting the first Test century before lunch. The young Cardus can thank Victor Trumper for having fired his imagination — if indeed such a thing was needed — that day in July, 1902.

'Trumper's winged batsmanship was seen in the Golden Age of cricket; he was, at his finest, master of some of the greatest bowlers the game has known. When he played for Australia, Clem Hill, Monty Noble, Joe Darling, Syd Gregory and Warwick Armstrong were batsmen with him. Splendid as the cricket of these men might be, day after day, whenever Trumper got out the light seemed to go for a while from an Australian innings. The eagle is gone and now — crows and daws. We make an artist's immortality by thinking upon and loving his work, Trumper was an artist-cricketer; let him live again in the mouths of men whenever Test matches are in action. Since he accomplished some of his greatest innings in this land, English cricket owes much to his ghost.'

Victor Trumper, Charlie Macartney and Don Bradman are links in the chain of golden greats.

Bradman's record is so stupendous that no-one from any age of cricket could deny him the crown as King of all Batsmen. But Trumper was a great player. There is little doubt the attitude of the era, to score a century then hit out, prevented him from going on to hit many double and triple centuries on the Test stage.

Macartney also had a cockiness about him; a seemingly inherent air of ascendancy at the crease. He toured England with Trumper in 1909, and after the Kaiser War he thrilled the Sydney Hill with a brilliant 170 not out against Johnny Douglas's England team. That day Don Bradman's imagination was fired. He told his father that he would one day play on the SCG.

Perhaps the link between Trumper and Bradman was forged that day when Macartney hit that glorious century. Don Bradman was then aged 12. Victor Trumper's ghost? Australian cricket was also soon to become eternally thankful.

BIBLIOGRAPHY

Batchelor, Denzil. *The Book of Cricket*. Collins, 1952.

Brown, Lionel. *Victor Trumper and the 1902 Australians*. Secker & Warburg.

Cashman, Richard. *'Ave a Go, Yer Mug*. Collins, Sydney, 1984.

'Country Vicar, A'. *Cricket Memories*. Methuen, London, 1930.

Ferguson, Bill. *Mr Cricket*. Nicholson Kaye, London, 1957.

Frindall, Bill. *The Wisden Book of Test Cricket 1876–7 to 1977–8*. MacDonald & Jane's, London.

C B Fry. *Great Batsmen, their Methods at a Glance*. Macmillan, 1905.

C B Fry. *The Book of Cricket*. George Newnes, London.

Hill, Les. *Australian Cricketers on Tour 1868–1974*. Lynton Publications.

Hill, Les. *The Bill Whitty Story*. Published privately.

Hutton, Sir Leonard. *Fifty Years in Cricket*. Stanley Paul, London, 1984.

Iredale, Frank. *Thirty-three Years in Cricket*. Beatty Richardson, Sydney, 1920.

Knight, A E. *The Complete Cricketer*. Methuen, 1906.

Laver, Frank. *An Australian Cricketer on Tour*. Bell & Sons, London, 1907.

Macartney, Charles. *My Cricketing Days*. Heinemann, 1930.

Mailey, Arthur. *10 for 66 and all that*. Phoenix, 1958.

Martin-Jenkins, Christopher. *Who's Who of Test Cricketers*. Rigby, 1982.

Moyes, A G 'Johnnie'. *A Century of Cricketers*. Angus & Robertson, Sydney, 1950.

Moyes, A G. *Australian Bowlers*. Angus & Robertson, Sydney, 1953.

Moyes, A G. *Australian Cricket: A History*. Angus & Robertson, Sydney, 1963.

Noble, Monty. *The Game's the Thing*. Cassell & Co, 1926.

Page, Michael. *Bradman: The Illustrated Biography*. Macmillan Co. of Australia, Melbourne, 1983.

Pollard, Jack. *Six and Out*. Pollard Publishing, Sydney, 1964.

Pollard, Jack. *Australian Cricket: The Game and the Players*. Hodder & Stoughton, 1982.

Raiji, Vasant. *Victor Trumper, The Beau Ideal of a Cricketer*. Vivek Publications, Bombay, India, 1964.

Reese, T W. *History of New Zealand Cricket, Vol 1*. 1914.

Robinson, Ray. *On Top Down Under*. Cassell, Australia, 1975.

Thompson, A A. *Pavilioned in Splendour*. Museum Press, London, 1956.

Times, The. *MCC 1887-1937*. The *Times*, London.

Trumble, Robert. *The Golden Age of Cricket*. Published privately, 1968.

Warner, P F. *How We Recovered the Ashes*. Chapman & Hall, London, 1904.

Warner, P F. *The Book of Cricket*. J M Dent & Sons, London, 1911.

Webber, Roy. *The Phoenix History of Cricket*. Phoenix, 1960.

Whitington, R S. *An Illustrated History of Australian Cricket*. Lansdowne Press, 1972.

Wisden Almanacks, especially 1903 and 1916 editions.

ACKNOWLEDGEMENTS

My thanks to all those people who so generously helped out with information and/or photographs for this project. I particularly thank S S 'Ram' Ramamurthy, of Whyalla, who lent me the 1902 Trumper diary. Ram procured the diary from Victor Trumper's nephew Charles, who is a kind and generous man and lives in Artarmon, not far from where his famous uncle lived and played cricket for the Gordon Club. Ram also supplied a number of photographs from his extensive collection. Many of these photographs adorn Ram's Whyalla home. The 1902 diary was the inspiration I needed to write the life and times of Victor Trumper. I spoke to many people about Trumper the man; Trumper the cricketer. Some, such as Sir William McKell, spoke of Trumper with a faraway look in their glistening eyes. Sadly, Sir William, an ex-NSW Premier and Governor-General of Australia, died before he could read this book.

Special thanks must also go to the following: Australian Cricket Board, especially David Richards, Ray Steele, Ron Steiner; former Board secretary Alan 'Justa' Barnes; Sir Donald Bradman, for his comments on style; Lionel Brown, Woodford Green, Essex; Jack Bailey, secretary of the Marylebone Cricket Club, Lord's; Mark Camplin, Lord's; Ronald Cardwell, Australian Cricket Society, Sydney; Richard Cashman, University of NSW, Sydney; Colin Clark, relieving principal at Crown Street School, Sydney; Frank Collins, Mollymook, NSW; Des Corcoran, Ex-SA Premier, of Adelaide; Peter Cornwall, The News, Adelaide; Phil Derriman and Kevin Berry, Sydney Morning Herald, Sydney; Ed Devereaux, London; Gavin Easom, Adelaide; Jack Egan, Sydney; Essex County Cricket Club; Ric Finlay, Hobart; David Frith, Guildford, Surrey, London; Glamorgan County Cricket Club, Wales; Vic Grimmett (Clarrie Grimmett's son), a photographer in Adelaide; Stephen Green, curator at the Lord's Museum; Radcliffe Grace, Melbourne, whose research of the Board and, in particular, the 1912 controversy was of great value; Chris Harte, author, cricket historian and editor of the Adelaide branch of the Australian Cricket Society's magazine, Cathedral End; Rex Harcourt, Melbourne Cricket Club Museum; Hunter 'Stork' Hendry, Rose Bay, NSW; Les Hill, Mt Gambier; Drs Rita and Maxwell Howell of the Department of Human Studies; University of Queensland; Murray Hedgecock, News Bureau chief, London; Sir Leonard Hutton, London; Jack Iredale, Sydney; Ginty Lush, Sydney; John Fairfax and Sons, Sydney; Dr John Lill, Melbourne Cricket Club secretary; Gordon Mallett, Beacon Hill, NSW; Alan McGilvray, Sydney; Pat Mullins, Brisbane; Bill Murray, Sunday Mail, Adelaide; NSW Baseball League; NSW Rugby League; Tom Nicholas (Trumper's nephew) and the Nicholas family of Middlesex, England, for numerous photographs of Trumper's mother and father and Victor's relatives; NSWCA honorary librarian Cliff Winning; Nottinghamshire County Cricket Club; Horace Perrin, Bucks County Cricket Club; Jack Pollard, author, Sydney; Punch (magazine) London; Jack Quigley, Sydney; Bob Radford, NSWCA secretary, Sydney; Irving Rosenwater, world-famous statistician of Sydney; the late Ray Robinson, Sydney; Bob 'Swan' Richards, Melbourne; Jerry Skene, WD & HO Wills, Adelaide; Sir Victor Alfred Trumper Smith, Canberra, ACT; SACA general manager Richard Watson and staff with special mention to Ray Sutton, Adelaide, Peter Simon, Adelaide, SA; Reg Simpson, Nottingham, England; State Library of Adelaide, NSW (especially the Mitchell Library) and the staff at those libraries' archives; Dale Smith, of funeral director Walter Carter Pty Ltd, Sydney; Ray Titus, Adelaide Charlie Trumper (Vic's nephew); Gladys Trumper (Vic's sister-in-law); Lorraine Trumper; Barrie Trumper; Tom Trumble (son of Hugh Trumble whose last tour of 1902 was Victor Trumper's most brilliant) of Melbourne; the Victorian Cricket Association; Alan Turner WD & HO Wills, Sydney: Mary Whitty, of Tantanoola, South Australia.

Kevin Berry of Sydney Vic Grimett, and Jan Dalman of Adelaide photographed the various items of Trumper memorabilia lent to me for this book.

And thanks to my brother Nick for allowing me to always have the name of Victor Trumper in 'my side' in our many backyard games back in those days of yore in Chatswood and Perth.

My eternal thanks to my wife, Christine, who gave marvellous help in reading the manuscript and offering commonsense assistance, and to her and my son, Benjamin, for having to endure the thumping of my typewriter in the dead of night.

The other day I asked Benjamin who was the best batsman in the world. He said, without hesitation: 'Don Bradman.' I then asked him who was the greatest batsman before Bradman. He replied, 'Victor Trumper.' Yes, this work has been worthwhile.

INDEX